THE FACTS ABOUT NIXON

The Facts About
NIXON

An Unauthorized Biography

by

WILLIAM COSTELLO

THE VIKING PRESS

NEW YORK • 1960

To my wife
Helen Murchie Costello
in appreciation

"I have consistently maintained that where the record of an individual, his record of voting, his public remarks on issues, indicate how he might approach an international or a national problem, that record should be brought to the attention of the people. I expect *mine* to be brought forth."

—Vice-President Richard Nixon
in an interview with Henry Brandon,
The Sunday Times, London,
January 4, 1959

Contents

ix

Foreword

At one stage this volume might have emerged as little more than a fact sheet; at another as a long profile. Somewhere along the way, as the documentation grew, the skeleton took on flesh, but there is still room for a word of caution concerning the author's presumption in calling his work, for want of a more satisfactory term, a biography.

My undertaking was simply to assemble the facts and let the record speak for itself. I specifically rejected what the Marchesa Iris Origo has called the three insidious temptations of biography: to suppress, to invent, and to sit in judgment. I took for gospel Dr. Johnson's truism—the last refuge of the biographer in any age—that "we cannot see into the hearts of men, but their actions are open to observation."

What this platitude does not suggest but what became apparent during months of research was that the most exhaustive and painstaking exploration of "the record" would still fail to present Richard Nixon as a fairly rounded, three-dimensional man so long as access to his private papers was foreclosed.

I mention this because politics makes for posturing, for playacting, for the studied gesture, the calculated word, all of which are part of the record but not necessarily the essential part of the man. The main facts may lie outside the public view, in his intimate letters, his hasty memoranda and telegrams, the minutes of conferences, his diaries and journals, or his correspondence with a trusted friend. In the human equation, what is observable is not the whole truth nor even the bigger part of it. Nowhere is this more true than in the case of a public figure who is still in midcareer.

For this reason, a work based on an assembly of facts making up Nixon's public personality becomes a political profile of sorts, but not precisely, in a generic sense, a biography. The inner man, the lusty, gusty creature of impulse and passion, shines through too infrequently. His motives are elusive. His peccadillos, his private resentments are hidden. In this age, when behavioral patterns are catalogued and cross-indexed with a cynical eye toward effects, it would be naïve to suppose that any such outer presentment could be a substantive measure of the man.

Falling back, then, on Dr. Johnson's formula was not a matter of choice; there was no alternative. Earl Mazo, for his vivid, authoritative portrait of the Vice-President, had interviews and access to private papers to supplement his exhaustive exploration of sources, but no such cooperation was vouchsafed to me; perhaps since Nixon's greatest ambition is unfulfilled it would be unrealistic to expect it. A chance to test that surmise came inadvertently from a letter written to him February 5, 1959, explaining the project and saying:

"Naturally, in the interests of accuracy, it would also be extremely helpful if in the next month or so you could carve out an hour or two to talk to me . . . but I won't press the matter if you find your schedule too crowded."

Subsequently there developed a series of cordial telephone conversations with his appointments secretary but no written acknowledgment of my request, and when the last word of the manuscript was set down seven months later it had still not been possible to arrange an interview.

In these circumstances, as his personality unfolded from a study of the record, it seemed that I should write the book, not as a bare chronology, and not as a conglomeration of overdramatized episodes, but with a conspicuous orientation toward Nixon's distinctive talents as a campaigner. The plan of the book therefore places special emphasis on Part Two and permits the remainder of his career to fall into perspective around it.

The public record on which the book relies falls generally into three categories: the *Congressional Record,* the texts of Nixon's speeches, and the news chronicles of the day; relatively little of it is based on the memories and biases of his contemporaries. Particular acknowledgment should of course be made to that great institution of record, *The New York Times,* its brilliant

Washington bureau chief, James Reston, and the political writers of his staff who keep current history in focus.

The list of others whose reports have been helpful is long and distinguished, and in addition to those otherwise acknowledged in the text, I am particularly indebted to John T. Alexander, Russell Baker, James Bassett, William M. Blair, William E. Bohn, John F. Bridge, Albert Clark, Leslie Claypool, Charles B. Cleveland, William R. Conklin, Lawrence E. Davies, Willard Edwards, Laurence C. Eklund, Sidney Fields, Philip Geyelin, Clay Gowran, Dan Green, Robert T. Hartmann, Martin S. Hayden, Gladwin Hill, Garnett D. Horner, Carroll Kilpatrick, William Knighton, Clayton Knowles, William H. Lawrence, Paul R. Leach, Joseph A. Loftus, Murrey Marder, James Y. Newton, Crosby Noyes, Vernon O'Reilly, Philip Potter, Herbert Philbrick, Adela Rogers St. John, Jack Steel, Lester Tanzer, Herbert Trask, James Warner, Charles Whipple, Helen Waterhouse; and to columnists Joseph and Stewart Alsop, Marquis Childs, Peter Edson, Doris Fleeson, David Lawrence, George E. Sokolsky, William S. White, the late Tom Stokes, and of course the dean of them all, Walter Lippmann.

Mention should also be made of earlier volumes on the Vice-President by Ralph de Toledano and James Keogh, and especially that by Earl Mazo; and of the valuable contributions of Robert J. Donovan, William Flynn, William V. Shannon, and Richard Rovere to the literature.

I must express my appreciation to Gilbert A. Harrison, editor and publisher of *The New Republic,* and to Charles Bolte and others at The Viking Press, who conceived and nurtured the project; to my wife, who found time from her academic duties to assist in the revision of the manuscript; to Loie Gaunt, of Vice-President Nixon's staff, who was most gracious and helpful in providing texts and other source material; and to Edna Evans and Ann Doyle, my research assistants, whose loyal and painstaking work in the files made the documentation both accurate and copious.

If there is a point of view, if there are oversights, errors, or faulty inferences, these are entirely my own.

Washington, D. C., September 15, 1959

PART ONE

CANDIDATE

CHAPTER I

———◆———

1960 and After

I

"A SUBDUED, almost self-effacing Vice-President Nixon stood in St. Paul's." So said the *London News Chronicle,* describing the scene November 26, 1958, as the President's representative stood solemnly beside Queen Elizabeth in ceremonies dedicating the great cathedral's American Memorial Chapel.

"Beneath the Vice-President's firm, composed exterior," the *News Chronicle* added, "one could detect the awe of the village boy who had come such a long way in such a short time."

It was a gratuitous touch, and perhaps not in the best taste, but for Richard Milhous Nixon it was the echo and the counterfeit of familiar usage.

From the very beginning, Nixon's had been a stormy progress. As a public personality, he has identified himself with the hybrid, revolutionary patterns of the twentieth century's mass man. As a spokesman for his times, he has projected a wonderland in which images move simultaneously to left and right. As a salesman with a high coefficient of belligerency, he has been a man of many issues.

His sole purpose and preoccupation has been politics. Not for a moment has he relaxed or deviated. In fourteen years he has made himself a worldwide symbol of conflict.

3

Whether he goes on to a more exalted place in American life will depend, in his view, not primarily on anything he can do to change the patterns of the age but on his own adaptability. In revolt like so many of his generation against the aristocratic principle of leadership, he professes no sense of personal destiny. He has called himself a "fatalist about politics." In his philosophy, men do not make the times; it is rather the reverse.

"Political positions have always come to me because I was there," he said, "and it was the right time and the right place. . . . It all depends on what the times call for."

This passive determinism is overlooked more often than not. Yet it is basic to his character. It infuses the whole with a temperamental air of detachment or impassiveness that sometimes seems almost unfeeling. It exists side by side with a welter of contradictory images which have proliferated with each new accession of power and public stature.

On the one hand he is the earnest, high-minded junior executive. He is incorruptible, he is "sincere," he is eager to please. He leads a blameless personal life. His favorite posture is ingratiating. Before statesmen he is grave and attentive. In college auditoriums he is studious and probing. On social occasions he is a master of small talk.

He is the "young fogy," solemnly presiding over the agenda of the National Security Council; he is the activist, now up, now down, but anxiously on the alert for a bill or a compromise. He is the friend of progress with just the right vision of hope, the enemy of communism with just the right moral tone of indignation. He has a folksy touch and a stock in trade of homely, colloquial illustrations. When he smiles, he does so to put the listener at ease and not necessarily to reflect his own feelings.

President Eisenhower has called him the "most valuable member of my team."

Obversely, Nixon is called on to stand muster as the suave and ruthless partisan. Whatever his motives or methods, he is suspect. To his enemies he is unprincipled, he is faithless, he is tricky. His humor is thin and brittle, his temperament moody and insecure. However violent his opinions, however harsh his attack, he preserves a hard, offish, passionless composure. Mixing innuendo and invocation, he deplores sin without hating it and promises salvation for all who vote Republican. To some he is a hatchet man pure and simple, and to others a "cardboard man," often with two sides but without depth as a person. Like salesman Willy Loman, he is traveling on a shoeshine and a smile.

A prominent Republican who supported him in 1952 says, "It is a question whether he has convictions, or conclusions."

His is the new-style popularism, a polished mastery of the shadowplay, "creating the illusion of magnificent drama" by the subtleties of an oversimplified appeal and the skillful exploitation of the mass media. As a pitchman he makes it clear that the problem at issue is basically simple and that once it is explained in easily understandable terms, as he is capable of explaining it, every right-thinking person will see the obvious solution—his solution. Complexities are quickly reduced to old-fashioned, one-syllable terms of right and wrong.

He has a talent for exploiting the inevitable, for seizing the initiative, for keeping in with the outs, and for never getting between the dog and the lamp post. He has been called a political freak, for almost every other politician in his age bracket with any foreseeable future is a Democrat.

To judge from Nixon's own words, his inner self remains an enigma. What he reveals publicly is a spare, spruce, expurgated version of the whole. In his self-portraiture he lets it be thought that his emotional makeup differs fundamentally from that of his fellows, that he can bottle up his gustier impulses by a massive effort of will, and that only as occasion requires does he uncork the bottles for political effect.

Ralph de Toledano was the first to reveal Nixon's rule of thumb that ". . . the only time to lose your temper in politics is when it's deliberate. The greatest error you can make in politics is to get mad." Similarly, in discussing the riots at Lima and Caracas where he so nearly lost his life, Nixon told Robert T. Hartmann that he was not angry—"because he never allows anger to predominate, and his chemistry is such that when a situation is tough he gets analytical and cold."

"I did not lose my temper," Nixon explained after the San Marco incident. "I intentionally don't lose my temper when other people are angry."

The Vice-President dwelt on the same theme when he tried to recapture for Stewart Alsop his feelings during those trying moments in Latin America.

"My reaction to stress," he said, ". . . is sort of chemically de-layed. While it is going on, I feel cold, matter-of-fact, analytical. At Lima . . . when I saw the soft answer would not work, that they wouldn't let me speak, I allowed myself the luxury of show-ing my temper and called them cowards. It was deliberate, letting my temper show. . . . Then after a crisis like that is over, I feel this tremendous letdown . . . as though I'd been in a battle."

If those around him sometimes find him cool, distant, per-functory, his eyes not always in step with the expression on his face, it is because of his habit of withdrawal, a habit he has justi-fied as a tactical necessity in some situations.

". . . Your mind must always go," he said, "even while you're shaking hands and going through all the maneuvers. I developed the ability long ago to do one thing while thinking of another."

One of the best-authenticated accounts of Nixon's ability to turn his feelings on and off comes from his undergraduate days at Whittier College when he was taking an eager part in amateur dramatics. In one production, playing a bereaved old innkeeper, Richard had the stage entirely to himself at a climactic moment, and during rehearsal he was having trouble projecting the old man's tragic grief. It was the drama coach, Dr. Albert Upton, who saved the scene.

"Dick," he said, "concentrate real hard on getting a big lump in your throat, and I think you can cry real tears."

Dick practiced until he had the trick pat, and at the final per-formance tears flowed like magic. What recalled the incident for Dr. Upton was the sight of a news picture, in 1952, of Nixon crying on Senator Knowland's shoulder in the denouement of the expense-fund crisis. "But mind you," Upton added hastily, "Dick is never spurious. He really felt it."

In campaigns Nixon has prided himself on his skill with audi-ences. Once, in California, however, under severe provocation, his control splintered. When a particularly noisy, obnoxious heckler threatened to break up a meeting, Nixon finally turned on him, and casting aside his practiced urbanity gave the man a savage tongue-lashing. Then in a fiery flash of candor he shouted, "When we're elected, we'll take care of people like you! Okay, boys, throw him out!"

Such lapses have been rare. What fires of rage or rebellion may smolder in Nixon's innermost self can only be surmised.

William S. White inferred that the Vice-President's self-control involves an immense and sustained effort.

Nixon has earned a reputation as a tough political in-fighter and backroom fixer. As a partisan he has been compared to Harry Truman. Like the former President, in matters of party welfare, "he doesn't know where to stop—he goes the limit."

Some of his excesses have been excused by friends on the plea that he is ambitious. Senator Robert A. Taft, a public servant whose conscience yielded nothing to his political ambitions, was one who rejected that defense. After the 1952 convention, in conversation with Joseph Polowsky, a friend and supporter, Taft spoke of Nixon regretfully as "a little man in a big hurry," noted that he had a "mean and vindictive streak" when frustrated, and summed up his personality as one tending to "radiate tension and conflict." The senator expressed a fervent hope that circumstances would never permit Nixon to accede to the presidency.

Another eminent American who refused to accept the portrait of Nixon as an inoffensive eager beaver was Speaker Sam Rayburn. During forty-seven years in the House, Rayburn's one inflexible rule had been never to speak ill of fellow members, but he broke the rule for Nixon. After the Vice-President's brush with the treason issue in 1954, Rayburn rumbled, "So far as we are concerned, his name is mud." In a rare moment of bitterness he told intimates that Nixon had the "cruelest face" of all the thousands of congressmen with whom he had served.

Nixon's partisan nearsightedness was never better exemplified than in his 1956 Lincoln Day speech in New York. In what was to become a *cause célèbre,* he boasted of Republican party advances in the field of civil rights and capped the recital by declaring proudly, "And speaking for a unanimous Supreme Court, a great Republican Chief Justice, Earl Warren, has ordered an end to racial segregation in the nation's schools."

Politicians and editors were aghast. A clamor of voices protested that the court had no partisan identity. *The New York Times* called the juxtaposition of the GOP and the high court "an immense disservice to the Chief Justice." The Scripps-Howard Washington *Daily News* rebuked Nixon with the charge that he had "dragged the Supreme court into sidewalk politics by the outlandish claim. . . . It was inaccurate, unnecessary and unpardonable," the paper said. Others asserted that the Vice-President had overstepped "all bounds of propriety," that he had blundered, that he demeaned "the entire caliber of justice by seeking to imbue it with a partisan flavor."

The harshest stricture came from columnist Walter Lippmann, who told readers, in discussing Eisenhower's health and Nixon's putative qualifications to serve with him as a possible successor: "A man who will exploit for partisan purposes such a decision of the Supreme Court does not have within his conscience those scruples which the country has the right to expect in the President of the United States."

In the face of such disapproval, Nixon has more than once shown stoic durability. When he could not surmount blunders with an exhibition of cool, raw, uninhibited courage as in the "Checkers" speech, climaxing the 1952 expense-fund affair, he has taken refuge in silence. What he has lacked in brilliance he has made up in tenacity.

II

Approaching the climactic struggle of his career, the Vice-President at forty-seven must reckon with a set of major imponderables, some inherited and some of his own authorship. There are such questions as: What is the electoral arithmetic of 1960 and how can it be related to the issues? What can be done to neutralize an undercurrent of defeatism threatening his nomination? How can he guard against erosion of his standing with the party hierarchy and simultaneously mobilize mass support? Where do he and the Republican party stand philosophically in relation to each other and to the issues of the day?

During his years as Vice-President, Nixon has earned an unrivaled place in the higher councils of the party, not merely at the formal, institutional level, but no less so among the grand sachems off stage. He began as a have-not persuading other have-nots to equate their interests with his. He showed a talent for plain talk and abrasive hyperbole. Success provided him with a power base in the electorate and automatically with a place in the ranks of the haves, and it became a matter of course that in time his new status would be acknowledged by the true haves of the power elite. The very fact of his advancement, however, has been the means of placing him in a perilous ideological cross fire.

Between the right and left wings of the GOP there has been a basic conflict over the strategy for electing a national ticket. The Taft formula was that, to win, it was necessary only to bring out the full conservative vote, long repelled by Republican candidates of a New Dealish hue. The doctrine of the party's avant-garde, on the other hand, has been that only by attracting liberal votes from Democrats and independents can the GOP hope to attain a national majority. Eisenhower went to the White House as a spokesman for modern Republicans of the latter persuasion, but halfway through his second term he had allowed the party's conservative leadership in Congress to bring him around to their basic position.

The choice for Nixon is fundamental. It starts with two assumptions: that the presidency in 1960 will be settled without reference to the South, and that an important segment of the Democratic party in the North can be transferred bodily to the GOP. The question then is: which segment?

Liberals in the Republican party want to claim their spiritual fellows. They prefer the successful formula of 1952 and 1956—an attractive candidate running on a liberal civil-rights, social-security, and labor program. The conservative view favors retrenchment and a fiscal program tailored to appeal to the industrial middle class and the well-to-do workers who would stand to lose most by inflation. Proponents of the latter formula would hope to sharpen ideological differences, would make the GOP a majority party by consolidating the conservative vote. The liberals argue that in the era of Communist agitation, the mass man, and a worldwide population explosion, such hopes are illusory.

Nixon's position has been elastic. Searching for a workable formula, he straddled the issue in a speech June 20, 1949, while still in the House.

"The Republican party has gotten itself in the position of being classed as the tool of big business and vested interests," he said. "This charge is false, and we should make a resounding declaration of independence from Wall Street, from labor bosses and other vested interests."

This free-wheeling attempt to find a middle way by crying a plague on both houses was risky. The element of risk was historical, an effort to obliterate a line of demarcation that has vindicated the American two-party system for over a century. The classic distinction between the parties traces straight to the early days of the Republic. The Federalist party, progenitor of the Republican, began with Alexander Hamilton's conviction that only the "rich and well-born" had the wisdom to govern because the "mass of the people . . . seldom judge or determine right." Hamilton's aim therefore was to channel property and power into the hands of those whom Providence had ordained as the elite, thus at one stroke creating an aristocracy of wealth and an aristocracy of status.

It was not until 1828 that the aristocratic concept of the state was challenged and rejected. In that year Andrew Jackson gave the Federalists their first real defeat and in doing so not only gave life to the doctrine of popular sovereignty but also oriented the Democratic party permanently as the popularist party.

Since that day neither party has been able to disown its heritage. For the Republicans, Theodore Roosevelt tried in his time and Robert La Follette in his, but the image of Republicanism as the party of the rich and well-born persists.

Moreover, the class that can be called "propertied"—that is sufficiently wealthy to leave its children a substantial legacy—grows smaller, and a great deal of wealth is invested in liquid properties like stocks and bonds, which create no emotional overtones that can be rallied in a political campaign. Thus, Taft's thesis was more widely challenged than endorsed, and the avant-garde in the GOP ranks saw no choice but to run on a popularist base and outpromise the Democrats in the field of social welfare. Since there is really nothing socialistic about the Democratic party (it advocates neither public ownership nor nationalization of production), the contest between Democrats and Republicans becomes one of timing, of degree, of personalities.

As late as January 20, 1958, at a New York Republican rally, Nixon had not chosen his ground; he was still temporizing with negative generalities, still whipping the New Deal and the ADA, still letting his own philosophy be inferred rather than affirmed.

". . . If we have nothing to offer," he said, "other than a pale carbon copy of the New Deal, if our only purpose is to gain and retain power, the Republican party no longer has any reason to exist and it ought to go out of business." Then, as on many other occasions, his determinist philosophy persuaded him to accept the party for whatever it appeared to be at the moment, and he set forth no crusading policy requirements to inspire Republicans.

In the ensuing election, Nixon looked to the far right for votes and failed to find them, and the question afterward was whether he did not see that "the Republican future must be cast in a new mold," or whether he still hoped to blend and blur left and right into a single image.

Nixon's dilemma is twofold. His instinct for political pragmatism tells him it is the masses, not the elite, who have the votes. He cannot serve the interests of the few without the support of the many; yet he cannot win the support of the many without taking something away from the few.

In the long run he cannot go on serving two masters. It is at least a fair presumption that Wall Street has noted privately his scruples about Wall Street. If he is for racial equality, then *ipso facto* he alienates those in the South and elsewhere who are not. If he blames inflation on the wage-push, labor will not vote for him; if he blames it on the price-push, industry may not finance him. If he hands farm-price control back to the commodity speculator (the market place!), farmers burdened with devalued surpluses will not vote for him; and if he is for perennial subsidies, he cannot hold firm for fiscal integrity. As time goes on the choices grow more difficult, and more rather than less numerous.

III

Offsetting Nixon's success at the organizational level has been the growth of the most frustrating and frightening suspicion that can plague a candidate—the whisper that he is not electable.

Henry Clay was the first to be tormented by this phantom of defeatism. As early as 1816, when he was only thirty-nine, his name was mentioned in the presidential sweepstakes. In 1824 he was low man in a field of four candidates, polling 37 electoral votes out of 261. He won the nomination of the National Republican party in 1832, when Jackson was an easy victor in his bid for a second term; was passed over in 1836 and 1840 in favor of William Henry Harrison; and in 1844, running as a Whig against Polk, he failed for a third time to win the presidency.

Six disappointments might have crushed another man, but in 1848 Clay let his name be advanced for a seventh time; by then even his warm friends and admirers were without hope; John Crittenden wrote: "My conviction, my involuntary conviction, is that he cannot be elected."

A century later, it was the same refrain that beat Taft at four successive Republican conventions. In the age of popularism, when to be shopworn is to be unprepossessing, even the suspicion that a candidate cannot win is enough to deefat him.

The Clay-Taft tradition of defeatism has dogged Nixon's tracks since 1954, when his all-out effort was not enough to keep the control of Congress in Republican hands, and after 1956 references to it cropped up with increasing frequency. In publications covering a broad political spectrum, assessment of Nixon's presidential chances in 1960 has hinged on whether he is electable. A random sampling among dozens of articles shows the character of this speculation.

October 21, 1958, news conference question, Philip Potter, Baltimore *Sun*:

> Some political observers feel . . . that you are in solid with state organizations . . . but that you are so controversial, at least among Democrats, that you just can't win. Would you care to assess your chances?

November 29, 1958, W. H. Lawrence, *The New York Times*:

> As the front-runner, with every indication of strong support within the party organization, his greatest danger is that he will be tagged —as the late Senator Robert A. Taft was tagged—as a "man who can't win."

January 21, 1959, Joseph Alsop, *New York Herald Tribune*:

> Nixon himself has never concealed his opinion that "the polls beat Bob Taft" by making it appear that "Taft was a sure loser."

July 24, 1959, John F. Bridge, *Wall Street Journal*:

> Rightly or wrongly, even many staunch Nixon supporters are often quick to say, "He can't be elected."

August 4, 1959, George E. Sokolsky, King Features Syndicate:

The propaganda device used against Richard Nixon is the same old gambit used against Robert A. Taft, namely, that Nixon cannot be elected. This is being repeated over and over again every day: "He can't win."

Defeatism on such a scale has posed an obvious challenge. No one doubted the Vice-President's standing among professional politicians, but in the face of a "can't win" psychology it was a question whether or how soon the Nixon position might be fatally eroded even among professed dedicated supporters.

Another and no less basic question was raised by the can't-win talk: how could Nixon have acquired so dubious a standing with the mass of the electorate? If he has not been deliberately maligned, what suggests itself is that his skill in the art of communication has been exaggerated. Has he been talking about issues too remote or too unreal to evoke a response? Or has he, as alleged, talked about them irresponsibly? In either case, he would not be the shrewd master politician pictured in the Sunday supplements.

The record of his campaigns is pertinent. The launching pad in his race for office was the issue of Communist subversion. He seized on it cannily in 1946 to beat Jerry Voorhis; he used it even more effectively against Helen Douglas in 1950. Success crowned his effort a third time in 1952 with the slogan "K-1, C-3" (Korea, Communism—Corruption—Controls). It was on his fourth try in 1954 that he ran into the law of diminishing returns; plain subversion had been worn threadbare in the numbers game, and subversion embroidered with innuendoes of treason proved too much for the credulity of the voters. After that failure Nixon turned his attention to other topics. In his last two campaigns he tried moderation, but the milder his slogans the fewer his votes. He had been type-cast as a man who cried wolf, and when he became a wolf-crier in a wilderness empty of wolves, the public was bored and went back to electing Democrats.

In attempts to measure Nixon's popularity, the polls have reflected one significant ambivalence. Among Republican voters he has led the field since 1954, first as the 1956 favorite if Eisenhower had not been a candidate for re-election, and since 1956 as a contender for the 1960 nomination. The Gallup poll at random intervals showed these readings:

	Percentage of GOP Voters Favoring Nixon
September 1954	35
January 1955	30
September 1955	25
January 1956	55
February 1957	63
August 1957	48
January 1958	51
March 1958	64
November 1958	51
January 1959	56
May 1959	58
July 1959	61
August 1959	65
October 1959	68

After Nelson Rockefeller's impressive 1958 victory for the New York governorship, the polls for a time showed a dramatic loss of support for Nixon, and although his ratings recovered in succeeding months, especially after his trip to Russia and Poland, the fluctuation was enough to suggest that his position with rank-and-file Republicans was not impregnable.

At the same time, Nixon has not run impressively when paired off against leading Democrats. In these hypothetical races, he made such showings as these:

	Stevenson	Nixon
February 1955	61	39
October 1955	53	47
February 1956	59	41
July 1956	54	46
February 1958	52	48
August 1958	46	54
January 1959	51	49
August 1959	51	49

	Kennedy	Nixon
August 1957	53	47
March 1958	58	42
June 1958	51	49
December 1958	59	41
July 1959	61	39
August 1959	52	48

	Stevenson–Kennedy	Nixon–Rockefeller
March 1959	50	50
July 1959	56	44

In Nixon's calculations, the arithmetic of 1960 is governed by two bench marks.

First, in total registrations, the Democrats hold a clear national majority, even outside the old Confederacy, and would seem likely to retain control of Congress as they have twelve times out of the last fourteen.

Second, it would be statistically possible, on the basis of precedent and the 1958 returns, for a strong Republican to win the presidency in the face of a Democratic sweep. To do that, according to a *Congressional Quarterly* analysis, he would have to run from 1 to 5 per cent ahead of the GOP congressional ticket in twenty-three northern states with 272 electoral votes. On the other hand, a relatively weaker Democrat could win the presidency, without a single Southern electoral vote, merely by riding on the coattails of successful Democratic congressional candidates.

In 1956 Eisenhower turned the trick handsomely for the Republicans, and the riddle facing GOP strategists is to find a candidate with his "plus values" to repeat that success. The only relevant statistics for comparative purposes are these: Nixon in 1950 ran 7 per cent ahead of the California congressional slate in his party; Eisenhower ran 3 per cent ahead in 1952 and 6.8 per cent ahead in 1956. Nelson Rockefeller's 1958 lead over the GOP congressional ticket in New York was 5.8 per cent.

If the electoral arithmetic does not encourage Nixon's hopes, and if he is too controversial to win as a personality, what remains is to capitalize on his experience, especially his travels abroad. This conclusion has fathered a new success formula in Republican circles. The electorate, it is argued, does not in this generation apply the same judgments to state and to national tickets. While voters may remain loyal to Democrats on local pocketbook issues, they will vote for a Republican ticket nationally if they feel greater confidence in its ability to deal with problems affecting peace and foreign affairs.

This attempt to pre-empt the peace issue is tailor-made for Nixon's use, if indeed it did not originate with him. From 1947 on, he voted consistently to support the Cold War, and as an administration spokesman he has taken substantial risks to defend the concept of a free-world coalition and the Eisenhower foreign policy and foreign-aid budgets. As a result of nine trips overseas during his vice-presidency, Nixon is armed against parochialism. He has made himself knowledgeable in international affairs, and has a ready-made platform from which to sell himself, as he sold Eisenhower in 1956, as "the man who can keep the peace."

In its treatment of the issues, the GOP as a whole does not transcend the dilemma posed by the 1960 electoral arithmetic. A major inhibiting factor so far as Nixon is concerned is that he has important alliances in the nationalistic wing of the party which has yet to acknowledge rights and duties going beyond the narrow orthodoxy of statism, and his career does not encourage a belief that he can preserve those alliances without impairing his hopes in the internationalist wing.

Thoughtful examination makes it appear that, if Nixon has faltered, it has not been in the character of his global ideals, which have been admirable, but in trying too often to translate them in narrowly partisan terms. His horizons have broadened with the years, his intelligence is quick and perceptive, but his independent policy judgments have not shown themselves infallible, and he is most notable as a tactician and debater, not as a policy maker or innovator. His is in many ways the American success story, not far removed from the log-cabin tradition of an earlier day, but with atypical overtones. In particular, the fellowship of reconciliation in which he spent his Quaker boyhood grows more remote in spirit as it does in time.

CHAPTER II

———◆———

1946 and Before

I

RICHARD MILHOUS NIXON is an authentic product of the American pioneer tradition. On both sides of his family he traces his ancestors back to Colonial times. In the main they were farmers, artisans, tradesmen.

Like his forebears who fought the austerities of the wilderness to live, Nixon has driven himself with ascetic singleness of purpose; he is what he has made himself because no effort was impossible, no goal unattainable. In the words of his wife, Pat, "We come from typical everyday American families that have had to work for what they got out of life but always knew there was unlimited opportunity. . . ."

Like most Americans, Nixon is barely a generation removed from the soil. He has no ties with what passes today for an aristocracy—the first families of banking and corporate wealth. His place in society is his own—the place of a parvenu who by native shrewdness, energy, and aggressiveness has been able to make his way into the realm of power manipulation.

II

Nixon's family name is a mutation of the Gaelic words meaning "he faileth not," which with the fey disrespect of the Irish for

17

the rules of spelling has been variously rendered as Nicholl, Nicholson, MacNicholl, Nicholas, Nickson, and Nickerson. The first Nixon in the New World of whom there is record was a James Nixon who settled in the colonies in 1753 and who was buried at Brandywine Hundred, Delaware, in 1775.

In his will James gave each of his two sons, George and James junior, a hundred-acre farm; in addition James junior got two Negro slaves, Ned and Nance; each boy received livestock and portions of a cash estate amounting to £235. James junior remained in Delaware, but after the war his older brother George joined the westward tide of migration, settling first near Washington, Pennsylvania, and eventually in Clinton County, Ohio.

In an 1833 pension application, this same George related that in the crucial early months of the Revolutionary War his company "joined the Army of Washington, recrossed the Delaware River with him and were stationed with him at Trenton on the memorable second of January 1777 when the British marched to attack the Americans. . . . The American troops . . . were marched towards Princeton. . . . They met the rear of the British troops where a battle was fought and the latter defeated, in which this deponent bore his share to the best of his skill and understanding as Ensign in said Company and has now in his possession the very Sword and Spontoon (half-pike) by him carried on that occasion."

George married Sarah Seeds, the daughter of an old Delaware family, in Holy Trinity Church, Wilmington, August 17, 1775, and died in Ohio in 1842 at the age of ninety. His eldest son, George (II), was born at Brandywine Hundred in 1784; at the age of twenty-two he married Hannah Wilson, sixteen-year-old daughter of a blacksmith and wagon-maker of Washington, Pennsylvania. Hannah's mother was a descendant of a Quaker, Robert Scothorn, who came from Nottinghamshire to Philadelphia in 1682. However, George and Hannah were members of the Methodist Church, and the records show that the Nixons for four generations were Methodists.

Nixon's great-grandfather, George Nixon (III), was born in 1821 in a log house at Washington, Pennsylvania; on January 10, 1843, he married Margaret Ann Trimmer, seventeen-year-old daughter of Anthony Trimmer, the only line of German or

Dutch blood in Nixon's ancestry. In 1853 George (III) moved to Ohio, where he settled on a farm in Elk Township. In 1861 he enlisted in Company B, 73rd Ohio Voluntary Infantry Regiment, and fell July 3, 1863, on the bloodstained fields of Gettysburg. Twenty months later his wife died, leaving eight orphan children.

Nixon's grandfather was Samuel, born October 9, 1847, the second son of George Nixon (III). Ten years after his father's death, April 10, 1873, he married Sarah Ann Wadsworth, twenty-one-year-old daughter of Thomas Wadsworth, a storekeeper whose family originally came from Maryland. Besides operating his farm, Samuel found time to teach school and carry mail. Sarah Ann, the mother of five children, died of tuberculosis at McArthur, Ohio, seven years after giving birth, on December 3, 1878, to Francis Anthony Nixon, the Vice-President's father, who went to live at the farm home of his uncle, Lyle Nixon.

It was the Milhous branch of Richard Nixon's family that first put down roots in California. Genealogists have traced its origin in the Western Hemisphere to Thomas and Sarah Milhous, Irish Quakers born in County Kildare toward the end of the seventeenth century, who left Ireland seeking religious freedom and settled with their three children in Chester County, Pennsylvania, in 1729. Their descendants followed the frontier as it pushed southward, but in the troubled years before the Civil War they moved north again to Indiana when their Quaker philosophy rejected slavery as a social institution. One of these abolitionist Milhous ancestors on the north bank of the Ohio carried his convictions to the point of running a station on the Underground Railway that spirited fugitive slaves north. Hannah Milhous Nixon, daughter of Franklin and Almira Milhous and mother of the Vice-President, was born in a towering square frame farmhouse near Butlerville, Indiana, one of a family of seven girls and two boys.

In 1897, ten years after the founding of Whittier, California, as an ideal Quaker colony, Hannah's father, an orchardist, piled furniture, nursery stock, and lumber for a new home onto a freight car and crossed the continent to join the new community of Friends in the West. It was not until ten years later that Frank Nixon made his way to California. After the death of his mother when he was seven, Frank had grown restless, and in the fourth grade he quit school to go to work as a farmhand and make his own way.

In the years that followed, the years when a good farmhand earned 75 cents a day and his keep, Frank joined the westward tide of migration as a rolling stone and jack-of-all-trades: streetcar motorman, glassworker, potter, painter, potato farmer, sheep rancher in Colorado, telephone linesman, carpenter, and roustabout in the oil fields. Reaching southern California in 1907, he became a motorman on the old red trolleys linking Los Angeles and Whittier. Although himself a Methodist he settled in the vicinity of Whittier, attracted by the placid, well-ordered bearing of the Quaker community. There at a party on February 15, 1908, Frank Nixon met Hannah Milhous; four months and ten days later they were married.

After his marriage Frank worked briefly as a foreman on his father-in-law's ranch, then tried his hand at an orange grove in the San Joaquin Valley near Lindsay. Moving back to the southland in 1912, Frank bought a barren hillside 25 miles south of metropolitan Los Angeles at the settlement of Yorba Linda and planted a lemon orchard that was a failure from the start. On the summit of the hill he built a two-story frame house where the future Vice-President of the United States was born January 9, 1913.

Despite the failure of the lemon grove, the Nixons remained at Yorba Linda for ten years. Details of that period are meager. Frank worked at carpentering and various other jobs. Richard was reared in the strict Quaker tradition, for Frank had adopted his wife's profession of faith. All attended church three times on Sunday and every Wednesday evening, and when Richard grew old enough, he played the organ at meeting house and taught Sunday school. Card-playing and dancing were forbidden. Richard was remembered as sober, serious, and disciplined, even as a child. He walked half a mile to school each day; before and after school he performed the normal chores of a farmer's son; he seldom played. He had a record of perfect attendance as a second-grader, skipped the third grade, and missed but a single day in the fourth grade.

Years later, when oil was discovered under his orchard, Frank Nixon was to learn that Yorba Linda could have made him a millionaire, but in 1922 he gave up trying to make a living from his lemon grove and sold out.

III

Back in Whittier the rolling stone came to rest. Frank and Hannah bought a filling station, three miles outside town, one of the first gasoline pumps in the area, a stroke of enterprise that helped greatly to stabilize the family fortunes.

"The house was a simple one," Nixon recalled many years later. But "in the living room was a mahogany upright piano that Mother insisted on having although I was the only one in the family who played it. Next door was the garage with connecting stairs that led to three bedrooms and a bath above the garage. The downstairs bedroom off the living room was where two of my brothers died."

Nixon spent a frugal, hard-working boyhood in Whittier, but it was by no means the poverty-stricken household that some have reported.

"My father was fairly successful," Nixon has said. "The filling station was going two or three years when the old Quaker church nearby was put up for sale. My Dad bought it, moved it close to our filling station, and made it into Nixon's Market, a country store. If it hadn't been for the expense of my brothers' sickness we would have been fairly well off, with the store.

"I remember that my Dad sold half of the acre on which our house was located in order to pay medical bills. My Dad was an individual—he'd go to his grave before he took government help. This attitude of his gave us pride. Maybe it was false pride, but we had it."

Richard was the second of five sons. A younger boy, Arthur, died of tubercular meningitis at seven when Richard was in his first year of high school. Soon after that the oldest brother, Harold, suffered a second attack of tuberculosis, which resulted in his death five years later. Those five years were a tragic time for the Nixons. Hannah first took her son to the mountains a hundred miles from Whittier and then, in a desperate effort to find a more beneficent climate, moved him to Prescott, Arizona. There, to help meet the added expense, she ran a nursing home for Harold and three other tubercular bed patients.

During the years of Mrs. Nixon's absence, father and sons

sold groceries and gasoline and cared for themselves. Meals and housekeeping amenities were sketchy except on Sundays, when there was time for a roast. The store stayed open until nine or ten o'clock at night, and the boys were expected to carry their share of work. After hours, Richard would sit in the kitchen, beside the gas oven, studying until two or three in the morning.

After Whittier grammar school, Richard entered Fullerton High School, transferring to Whittier High for his last two years. In Richard's junior year, to give him the pocket money he needed and at the same time keep faith with the Quaker philosophy of individual self-sufficiency and personal dignity, his father gave him complete charge of the vegetable counter in the family store. Richard did the buying, driving to the Los Angeles public market before sunrise to bargain with the local produce growers and hurrying back to arrange his displays before leaving for school. All the profit he could make was his, and all he could save went into a college bank account, for he had already become interested in studying law.

Neighbors recall him during those years as a shy, serious boy who applied himself as avidly to his school books as he did to his household duties. The adjectives applied to him were always complimentary: determined, methodical, diligent, resourceful, conscientious; but no one ever called him a prodigy.

It was perhaps partly through the Nixon store that young Richard acquired his first interest in public affairs. His father (who died in 1956), was an extroverted personality who suffered from ulcers; a hard-driving, fiery-tempered man with outspoken views on political issues and a taste for vigorous argument. His store, an anachronistic hangover of the vanishing cracker-barrel era, became a neighborhood rendezvous; and although Richard and his brothers learned not to challenge their father in debate, they had the stimulus of the provocative environment he provided.

Richard's shyness in boyhood gave way to a new self-confidence when he acquired what was to be a lifelong interest in debating. From the first he was outstanding. As a Fullerton High sophomore he won the Constitutional Oratorical Contest, and the school yearbook in 1928 praised him as the sophomore representative of West Coast high schools in the National Oratorical Contest. At Whittier High he won the same contest in both his junior and senior years, and as a testimonial to his classroom efforts his diploma bore the gold seal awarded for scholarship by the California Interscholastic Federation.

His high-school debating coach, Mrs. Clifford Vincent, remembers she used to feel "disturbed" at his superiority over his teammates. "He had this ability," she said, "to kind of slide round an argument instead of meeting it head on, and he could take any side of a debate."

In his final year at high school Nixon also ran for and won his first political office—general manager of student-body affairs. One of his biographers refers to him even then as a "controversial" member of the student body, one who had definite opinions and expressed them. His Whittier high-school principal, O. C. Albertson, recalls, "Dick was a marked man when he transferred to us. He was a leader in scholastic and student activities—a self-starter—very popular. I think of Dick as a 'fighting Quaker.' "

One other incident that year had special meaning for Nixon's future, at least in an allegorical sense. After graduation he joined his mother and ailing brother in Arizona, and there with characteristic energy he proceeded to get a job. At Prescott's Slippery Gulch Rodeo he put his platform experience to work as barker for the Wheel of Fortune. *Time* magazine, years later, when Nixon was running for the vice-presidency, was authority for the statement that when Nixon first assumed the role of a spieler his booth "became the most popular in the show," a dubious compliment since it was a come-on for a gambling concession in the back room.

The years 1930-1934 saw Nixon as an undergraduate at Whittier College, a local Quaker institution, majoring in history, covering himself with distinction as a debater, still helping to pay his way by running the fresh-vegetable counter at the family store.

The pattern of diligence, seriousness, and aggressive sociability that had been established in high school repeated itself. Nixon seldom went to parties; no one remembers his telling a joke or squandering time on frivolities. He had work and books to occupy him. But he understood his classmates and their drives and motivations perfectly.

During all four college years he went out doggedly for football and never made the team except as a freshman when only eleven men turned out. Besides lacking weight and speed, he had two left feet. Nevertheless, he refused to give up. He said later, "I got a good seat on the fifty-yard-line." His coach, Wallace Newman, recalling the weeks that would go by without Richard's ever playing a minute, said, however, "He was wonderful for morale, because he'd sit there and cheer the rest of the guys, and tell them how well they'd played. To sit on the bench for the better part of four seasons isn't easy. I always figure, especially in the case of Dick, who excelled in everything else, that kids like that have more guts than the first-string heroes."

His frustrated football ambition did, however, give birth to a legend that was to be applauded subsequently by his political enemies. Once in a long while Richard would be permitted to play in the last few minutes, and one of his classmates, who was a linesman, recalled later: "When Dick went in, I always got out the five-yard penalty marker. Dick was so eager I knew he'd be offside just about every play."

One of the fields in which Nixon excelled was campus politics. He started by being elected president of the freshman class, and by the time he was a senior he was president of the entire student body.

He had a talent for picking an issue. One such, in his senior year, was the student appeal for permission to hold school dances on the campus. The strict Quaker authorities had always forbidden dancing, "were horrified at the idea" of sanctioning such self-indulgence on school property. Personally Nixon had little interest. He himself had not learned to dance until he was a sophomore and then not well and never with pleasure. Many years later, when he represented the United States at the 1957 Ghana independence ceremonies, he carried his early Quaker aversion to the point of avoiding dancing with the Duchess of Kent at a state ball in Accra. But, at Whittier, as student president, he used all the arts of debate and argumentation to carry the day, and eventually won over the board of directors by pointing out that college dances were being held anyway "in Los Angeles dens of iniquity."

He was graduated second in Whittier College's class of 1934. Harvard might have been his goal—he had been eligible to apply for a Harvard scholarship four years earlier—but Duke University was starting its law school that year and to establish high academic standards it offered nineteen scholarships for its first class of thirty-six students. Nixon was awarded one of these—a two-hundred-dollar tuition grant; to keep it he had to maintain a B average.

He was a slim, boyish twenty-one, with dark, heavy eyebrows and sparkling eyes, innocent of eccentricities in manner or appearance, when he arrived at Durham, North Carolina, in September 1934. Those were the middle years of the Great Depression, and Nixon's allowance from his family was only thirty-five dollars a month. That income he supplemented, under a grant from the New Deal's National Youth Administration, by doing research in the law library, at thirty-five cents an hour, for Dean H. Claude Horack.

"I couldn't afford the dormitory," Nixon recalled later, "so at first I stayed at a downtown boardinghouse with fourteen preachers. But I had to move because of the noise."

There is a legend, traced to a university maintenance employee, that Nixon then took squatter's rights in a small abandoned toolshed in a heavily wooded area near the Duke campus. The odds are that this story is apocryphal, and the confusion may have arisen because, early in his first year, Nixon with three other students rented a room in a white ramshackle farmhouse set in the tall pines a mile from the campus. The four shared two double beds in a big bare room without lights or water and with only an old pot-bellied sheet-iron stove for heat.

Their landlady was a Mrs. Henderson who lived with her small son in a separate part of the house. Nixon's roommates were William R. Perdue, who eventually became vice-president of the Ethyl Corporation, Fred S. Albrink, who rose to a Navy captaincy, and Lyman Brownfield, who settled down to a prosperous law practice in Columbus, Ohio.

The virtue of "Whippoorwill Manor," as they called their lodgings, was that the rent was nominal—Nixon's recollection later was that they paid $5.00 a month apiece, but Brownfield set the figure much lower at $50 a year, or $12.50 apiece. Yet for all its primitiveness the place had its own pastoral attractions. Its remoteness bespoke a sense of physical and psychological elbowroom. In spring and fall the weather was mild and the walk through the woods was lovely. On winter nights they stoked the stove with papers and fired it red hot to break the chill while they undressed.

Part of the time they took their meals at Mrs. Pierce's boarding-house—25 cents for a meal of "strictly home style cooking, serving and eating," with fifteen or more crowded cheerfully around the table, all dedicated to the boardinghouse reach. To save money, the four bought secondhand textbooks, sometimes cooperatively. For lack of heat and lights at the rooming house, they did their studying at the law library and took their showers at the gym. For three years, Nixon used his trunk for a closet.

Now and then Nixon had a half-hour to listen to one of the campus bands or to play handball, now and then an afternoon to go to a football game, or even more rarely an evening and the price of a date with a girl. He wrote for the law review, and during the summer between his second and third years he stayed on at Duke to do research on a long article. The one luxury he allowed himself was politics; as a senior he ran for the presidency of the Duke Bar Association and won.

At their graduation in 1937, Perdue, Brownfield, and Nixon headed the class in that order and automatically won election to the Order of the Coif, the national honorary law fraternity. In his choice of a career Nixon had first turned hopefully toward New York; there during the 1936 Christmas holidays, with two classmates, he applied for admission to some of the biggest and best-known law firms in the country. When this feeler drew only one provisional reply, he turned a speculative eye on the FBI.

One of Richard's lasting friendships at Duke was with Dean Horack, who wrote in a letter of recommendation to J. Edgar Hoover of the FBI: "Mr. Richard Nixon is one of the finest young men . . . that I have ever had in my classes. He is a very superior student, alert, aggressive, a fine speaker and one who can do an exceptionally good piece of research when called on to do so."

Hoover in reply promised Nixon an interview and an examination and careful consideration for an appointment, but in a quick shift of plans Nixon decided against the FBI and chose instead to practice law in his home state. To qualify he took a summer cram course for the California bar examinations. He was one of the 46 per cent that passed, and on November 9, 1937, he was sworn in as a member of the bar at San Francisco. Immediately afterward he joined the law offices of Wingert and Bewley, at the Bank of America Building, in Whittier.

IV

As a whole, Nixon in his school years had no greater impact on those around him than might have been expected of any boy of distinctly better than average intelligence. True, there was the Sunday-school teacher who once prophesied in a burst of enthusiasm that he would some day be president; there was the school editor who described him as the boy with the intellectual look above the eyebrows; and there was the classic yearbook quip that he had "left a trail blazed with fluttering feminine hearts." But these are prophecies that have long been an indigenous part of the American idiom; and even those who gave Nixon credit for a degree of precocity never seem to have let themselves be persuaded that he had any of the qualities of a true prodigy, political or otherwise. His entire school career was of one piece: intelligent without brilliance, humorless, industrious, perceptive, socially responsible.

If there was little in his school years to cast the shadow of future great events, there was even less in the first eight years that followed his graduation from law school at Duke. For four years he practiced law; for a few months he tried the wartime bureaucracy in Washington; he served three and a half years as a naval officer. Again he was dutiful, alert, competent, but undistinguished.

Tom Bewley, head of his law firm, besides running his private practice was city attorney; and his aim was to groom his new associate as a trial lawyer and assistant city attorney.

"We had a few drunks, some parking problems, traffic stuff," Bewley recalled. "That was the type of case Dick handled. He also worked with members of the council, drafting ordinances and the like. . . . He was thorough. He bored right into the heart of a question. And he had courtroom psychology. He could talk so that butter wouldn't melt in his mouth, or he could take hold of a cantankerous witness and shake him like a dog."

In Bewley's recollection his junior partner never relaxed except now and then to go to a football game. Nixon never went to lunch "just for fun." He used to work early and late; at mealtimes he was "always making a speech or conferring with a client." His law-office secretary said, "He was always sending me out for pineapple malts and hamburgers. He just about lived on them, although Mexican food was his favorite."

In the practice of law Nixon was successful enough to set up a makeshift branch—a desk in a real-estate office—in the neighboring community of La Habra; and the advent of new food-processing techniques encouraged him to try a business venture. With a group of associates who raised $10,000 in capital, Nixon became president and attorney for the Citra-Frost Company, whose object was to market surplus oranges in the form of frozen juice. For lack of a suitable container—and research facilities for its development—that attempt at meeting a payroll collapsed after eighteen months.

In his spare time Nixon served as a trustee of Whittier College and president of the college alumni association; became an active member of the Twenty-Thirty Club (a kind of junior chamber of commerce), a Sunday-school teacher, and an actor in a Little Theater group.

In the winter of 1938, when he was twenty-five, he met Thelma Catherine ("Pat") Ryan, a pretty, red-headed, temperamental teacher of commercial subjects at the local high school. The origin of their romance has already been tinged with apocrypha. According to one version, the director of the Little Theatre group needed an amateur actor to play district attorney in a murder mystery, *The Dark Tower,* and called Nixon in for the role. Pat Nixon's story has somewhat more sentimental overtones. In this version, Nixon learned that Pat was playing the second romantic lead in the play, hurried to the first rehearsal, tried out for the part opposite her, and got it.

"On our first date he told me he was going to marry me," said Pat, thus lending verisimilitude to her account, "but I wasn't ready to settle down."

It was not, in truth, a whirlwind courtship, for they went together more than two years before they were married, June 21, 1940, in a Quaker ceremony at the Mission Inn. Pat's reluctance to "settle down" too quickly was not implausible.

She was born in the bleak copper-mining town of Ely, Nevada, March 16, 1912; her Irish father, a hard-rock miner, had worked his way westward from Connecticut, and finally settled during her childhood on a small farm near Artesia, a town some eighteen miles from Los Angeles. From that time on, her life was one of hardship. Both parents had died by the time she was seventeen, and after finishing high school she went to work in a bank in Artesia to earn money for further education. In 1930 she left the bank to drive some elderly family friends back to Connecticut, and once in the East found work in the X-ray laboratory of a hospital near New York. She took a summer course in radiology at Columbia University in 1932, and the following year took her savings westward to enter the University of Southern California.

At USC, from 1933 to 1937, she graded papers and worked part time at a department store; even played walk-on parts in two movies, *Becky Sharp* and *Small-Town Girl*. She studied merchandising and qualified for a teacher's certificate, and when she met her future husband she was teaching shorthand and typing in Whittier. Except for the innocent escapism of the play-acting world in which she met Richard Nixon, there had been little but drudgery in her life; no less of the hard realities for her than for him; yet for all the spring-steel resoluteness of her character, she remained friendly and unassuming.

Their marriage was less than six months old and she was still working, when the Japanese struck at Pearl Harbor and they were caught up in the turbulence of a world at war.

The first break in the quiet pattern of their lives came when Nixon left Whittier for Washington to offer his services to the government. That was a moment when the Office of Price Administration was overwhelmed with the problem of creating a rationing system; hundreds of lawyers were needed to draft regulations and handle rulings. Nixon applied to the office of the associate general counsel of the Office of Price Administration, Professor Thomas I. Emerson of Yale University law school, and was hired on the spot.

One of his supervisors, Professor Jacob Buescher, said that Nixon in taking the job insisted on receiving the lowest possible salary, on the ground "that the boys who were then being trained to hit the beaches were paid a lot less."

Nixon began government work on his twenty-ninth birthday. He was assigned to the section handling coordination of rubber-rationing regulations, won a raise from $3200 to $4600 a year, but spent an unhappy seven months in the bureaucracy. He found people in the department "more liberal and left-wing than his thinking," according to J. Paull Marshall, who occupied the next desk and shared his Republican sympathies. Nixon himself has been quoted as saying about his OPA experience: "I learned respect for the thousands of hard-working government employees and an equal contempt for most of the political appointees at the top. I saw government overlapping and government empire-building at first hand."

In the spring of 1942, after only a few weeks at OPA, Nixon applied for a Navy commission, disregarding the fact that as a Quaker he could easily have claimed exemption from active service. His commission came through in late summer, and on September 2, as a lieutenant, j.g., he was sent to Quonset, Rhode Island, for training. Although he put in for sea duty, his first post was at an unfinished naval air base at Ottumwa, Iowa, where he served as aide to the executive officer. It was a long way from the front, but Nixon the politician took it in stride, welcoming the opportunity to add a new geographical area to his previous knowledge of the West and South.

On his next application for sea duty, six months later, Nixon was more successful, and in May 1943, leaving his wife working for OPA as a price analyst, first in Washington and later in San Francisco, he shipped out to the South Pacific as operations officer with the South Pacific Combat Air Transport Command. In the next fifteen months with SCAT, setting up temporary bases for getting airborne cargo into combat zones, he moved with the advancing, leapfrogging front along the chain of islands whose names formed the litany of the Pacific fighting man—Guadalcanal, Bougainville, Vella Lavella, Green Island.

Except for one period on Bougainville, when the area was under bombardment for twenty-eight nights out of thirty, Nixon's unit was stationed for the most part on the outer fringes of the combat zone. His outfit consisted of a dozen or more enlisted men, besides radio operators and base service personnel. Their job was to land on a beach, equipped principally with hand tools, and hack out of the jungle a landing strip suitable for DC-3s. That meant scrounging what he could in the way of building materials to house the men and the radio shack, besides clearing the strip itself and providing primitive facilities for supplies in transit and for litter cases being shipped out to hospitals in the rear.

One of his wartime buddies, Edward J. McCaffrey of Concord, Massachusetts, recalls him as a self-reliant young commanding officer (by that time he was a full lieutenant), and a tireless worker. "He made an awful lot of sense. He had no more rank than most of us . . . but he commanded a lot of respect from the guys with whom he came in contact. When things got a bit hectic, he never lost his head. No matter how badly things got fouled up Nick got his part of the operation straightened out and he did it without a lot of hullabaloo."

On Green Island he insured his popularity not only with his own unit but also with transient flight crews by opening "Nixon's Snack Shack," the only hamburger stand in the South Pacific. Mysteriously, in the middle of the jungle, tired pilots found free coffee, fruit juice, and sandwiches materializing alongside the strip. For his own men Nixon at one point also set up an informal school where he gave talks on business law.

On his own behalf, to fill the long empty hours, Nixon turned from the mores of his Quaker background and addressed him-self to the art of poker. Lester Wroble, a Chicago businessman who served with him, said Nixon would play poker for hours, his face like a rock, and "a hundred Navy officers will tell you that Nix never lost a cent at poker." The money he won at the poker table was to prove instrumental later in launching him on his political career.

As the beachheads moved away from the South Pacific and as the early logistical shortages were overcome, Nixon's unit was dismantled and reassigned. Toward the end of 1944 he found himself back at Fleet Air Wing 8, Alameda, California, and subsequently on special orders at the Navy Bureau of Aero-nautics at Washington. There, the war's end found him a lieuten-ant commander on the Navy's legal staff, attached to one of the teams renegotiating and terminating contracts in New York and Baltimore with such aircraft firms as Bell and Glenn L. Martin.

V

One unresolved and pertinent question relating to Nixon's formative years is the part that the Quaker faith ultimately assumed in conditioning his moral posture. During his boyhood Quaker-ism exerted a powerful influence. His great-grandmother and his great-great-grandmother on his mother's side were well-known itinerant Quaker preachers. His mother, Hannah, a strongly religious woman, hoped at one time that Richard too might become a preacher.

While he lived at Whittier, he attended services with his parents regularly four times a week; and Captain Albrink remembers that even at Duke law school Nixon, on Sundays, went regularly to Quaker meetings in nearby Raleigh or attended chapel at the university. At his graduation from Duke, Nixon's grandmother, then in her eighties, crossed the continent with his mother and brother to attend the exercises. The nature of the grandmother's influence bespeaks itself in Albrink's recollection that she still used the Quaker plain speech, "thee" and "thou," and there is on record a tender, respectful Christmas letter that Richard addressed to her only a few months earlier, alluding to her as an "illustrious" and "remarkable" person.

"My grandmother set the standards for the whole family," he recalled. "She was always taking care of every tramp that came along the road, just like my own mother. She had strong feelings about pacifism and very strong feelings on civil liberties. She probably affected me in that respect. At her house no servant ever ate at a separate table. They always ate with the family. There were Negroes, Indians, and people from Mexico—she always was taking somebody in. . . . She had a big house on the boulevard and every year at Christmas and usually once during the summer we had a family reunion. She kept the family together through the years."

Nixon himself has had little to say about his religious views; he believes "in keeping my own counsel about personal matters." At Denver in 1952 he told John T. Alexander of the *Kansas City Star* that one thing he did not believe in was "wearing my religion on my sleeve." Still it is relevant that, although Quakerism may remain the wellspring of his beliefs, his personal code of behavior no longer reflects the orthodoxy of his forebears. At college he pleaded the case for dancing; in war he took up arms; in the service he took up cards.

In the 1950 senatorial campaign, in an allusion to the Korean war and the need for strong, continuing defenses, Nixon argued for his brand of "fighting Quakerism," saying: "It is not easy for me to take this position. It happens that I am a Quaker; all my training has been against displays of strength and recourse to arms. But I have learned through hard experience that, where you are confronted with a ruthless, dictatorial force that will stop at nothing to destroy you, it is necessary to defend yourself by building your own strength."

His political career and the innuendo-laden style of his campaigning have raised further questions about his ethical dedication to Quakerism. Although his English teacher at Whittier College described him as a "typical American Quaker," one of his schoolmates, lawyer Merton G. Wray, confessed an inability to reconcile "his massive retaliation policy in politics and as a public official with what I understand of the Quaker philosophy and of their fellowship of reconciliation."

Richard Rovere, weighing the moral values implicit in the 1952 Checkers speech, found it fantastic that one of the Quaker faith should have made a claim to virtue on his own behalf on the ground that his wife wore, not mink, but a "respectable Republican cloth coat." Rovere concluded: "He may aspire to the grace and nobility of Quakerism, but if so he has yet to comprehend the core of the faith."

Although he took an active church role in Whittier before the war, teaching Sunday school while he practiced law there, Nixon has not attended meeting or been recorded as a member of the Friends Meeting House in the capital since moving to Washington. When he made public his income-tax returns in 1952, he showed church deductions of $55 in 1949, of $40 in 1950, and of $50 in 1951, all to the East Whittier Friends Church.

No one could presume to infer from so quick a catalogue of changes whether it reflects a gradual evolution of religious thought or merely a plastic adaptation to the behavioral pattern of his generation.

PART TWO

CAMPAIGNER

CHAPTER III

The Way It Began

IT WAS August 1945. World War II was ending and for the first time in six years Republicans dared turn their attention from the immediate peril of fascism toward the object of their first hatred, the New Deal. The death of Roosevelt had not allayed the contagion of discontent in Republican ranks: Harry Truman's economic philosophy was not yet clearly discernible but there was reason to fear the worst.

In California's Twelfth Congressional District, sprawling across the brown foothills from the southern border of Los Angeles to the San Gabriel mountains, Republicans for ten years had been trying to unseat Representative Jerry Voorhis. The son of a millionaire father, Voorhis was an idealist who had once in his youth registered as a Socialist, a political evangelist who drifted into politics in the wake of Upton Sinclair's EPIC (End Poverty in California) movement, and wound up in the Democratic party. His record had caused Washington correspondents to vote him the "best congressman west of the Mississippi," and California bankers and oil men to call him the worst.

Voorhis had voted for Federal control of tidelands oil, and had initiated legislation that curtailed the profits of banks dealing in government bonds. He had worked for cheap credit, cooperatives, and public power. He was unassailably anti-Communist;

37

had in fact introduced the measure which eventually became the Voorhis Act, Public Law 870; this measure required that any organization controlled by a foreign government must register with the Department of Justice. He had fought communism and Communist penetration of the CIO-PAC as a member of the Un-American Activities Committee, until he felt compelled to resign as a protest against the committee's investigatory methods. The West Coast Communist paper, *People's Daily World,* complained bitterly that "Voorhis is against unity with Communists on any issue under any circumstances."

At the moment that MacArthur was preparing for his triumphant entry into Tokyo, a group of GOP businessmen, bankers, and party workers of the Twelfth District met in the San Marino area to explore the 1946 election outlook. Voorhis still looked unbeatable. They had no likely candidate of their own in sight. Still, the election was fifteen months away, and they voted to try again. The decision was to form a candidate-finding "Committee of One Hundred," and to launch the drive they circulated a publicity handout that got feature display in twenty-six newspapers in the district:

> WANTED: Congressman candidate with no previous experience to defeat a man who has represented the district in the House for ten years. Any young man, resident of the district, preferably a veteran, fair education, no political strings or obligations and possessed of a few ideas for betterment of country at large, may apply for the job. Applicants will be reviewed by 100 interested citizens who will guar-antee support but will not obligate the candidate in any way.

Roy Day, Republican district chairman, was made head of the committee, which included all GOP officials in the district, officers of GOP clubs, and a smattering of representative party workers running the gamut of the area's economic interests. Day was instructed to schedule four open meetings for interviewing and selecting candidates. The first of these public sessions produced only two applicants, both highly unprepossessing; at a second meeting six others followed; after which there was another private huddle of the leadership. At this meeting in September 1945 Richard Nixon's political career had its inception.

It was Herman L. Perry, head of the Bank of America in the prosperous citrus and avocado district of Whittier, who first proposed Nixon's name. Uncle Herman, as he was called, was a conservative in every fiber. He looked on the New Deal as a charnel house of iniquity and on Jerry Voorhis as a socialist or worse. As Perry explained it later, he and Nixon's Grandfather Milhous were Quakers together and had served on the Whittier College board of trustees. Before the war Nixon's law offices were in the Bank of America building. Perry had observed Richard Nixon and found in him ". . . the personal appeal, the legal qualifications. He had been in Washington and around the world. In my mind he was a natural."

Nixon's first intimation that political lightning had struck came in the form of a telegram asking him to telephone Perry. At that moment, still in the uniform of a lieutenant commander, Nixon was handling contract terminations for the Navy in Baltimore. For him, as for millions of other civilian soldiers, it was an anxious moment. His wife was expecting a child, and his separation from the service would be in a matter of weeks. To friends in Washington he confided that he must soon begin looking for a job, and he found it hard to choose between Washington and a return to the drudgery of a small-town law office in Whittier.

Over the phone, Perry asked two questions: was Nixon a Republican and was he available? On the second point, there was never an instant's doubt: he was very much available! On the other point, legend has tried to suggest a doubt, for Nixon is said to have replied, "I guess I'm a Republican. I voted for Dewey in 1944."

Attempts have been made to infer from this casual response that there actually might be reason to question Nixon's original dedication to Republicanism. The facts hardly warrant such a suspicion. When he settled in Whittier before the war, Nixon had registered as a Republican, June 15, 1938. His Whittier law partner, Thomas Bewley, was GOP city attorney. In 1940 Nixon campaigned for Willkie. To be able to vote for Dewey in 1944, he had to take the trouble to cast an absentee ballot from the South Pacific.

A close friend of his OPA days, J. Paull Marshall, testified also to Nixon's basic Republicanism. "We were the only Republicans in OPA," Marshall said. ". . . I think he got his idea to run for Congress when he was working in OPA. . . . He just felt we needed sounder thinking than we had in government in those days. We used to talk about that."

Nixon's parents were lifelong Republicans. At times Frank Nixon's Republicanism strayed as far leftward as Theodore Roosevelt and Robert La Follette but never so far away from orthodox conservatism as to embrace the Democratic party. His wife Hannah once recalled the time in 1916 when her sympathies turned to Woodrow Wilson and "when I told Mr. Nixon he just went pale and white."

There is no reason to believe that the idea of entering politics came as a novelty to Nixon. As early as 1937 Dean H. Claude Horack at Duke had discussed with him the subject of politics as a career. Horack's advice was straightforward.

"Dick, if you're really interested in politics," he said, "go back to your home town and establish yourself in a law firm."

And that was exactly what he did.

After his telephone conversation with Perry, Nixon waited only long enough to receive the committee's $300 expense check before flying to California. In the interval, however, Perry had been busy, having written a personal letter to each of the hundred committee members, plugging his candidate. When Nixon arrived back in California the stage had been set; there was no opposition. The *Whittier News* of October 3, 1945, reporting on Nixon's appearance before the selection committee September 29 at the William Penn Hotel, said the whole affair consumed only ten minutes. Nixon told the committee that he recognized two schools of thought about the nature of the American system.

"One advocated by the New Deal is government control in regulating our lives," he said. "The other calls for individual freedoms and all that initiative can produce. I hold with the latter viewpoint. I believe the returning veterans—and I have talked to many of them in the foxholes—will not be satisfied with a dole or a government handout. They want a respectable job in private industry where they will be recognized for what they produce, or they want an opportunity to start their own business. If the choice of this committee comes to me, I will be prepared to put on an aggressive and vigorous campaign on a platform of progressive liberalism designed to return our district to the Republican Party."

The committee's first vote, with 77 members present, was 55 to 22, or 63 to 14, depending on whose memory seems most trustworthy. The second ballot made it unanimous.

What the Committee of One Hundred had hired was an appealing symbol. Nixon was young, a war veteran, had an attractive wife, was a capable lawyer. From the point of view of the publicity media over which he was to be merchandised, he was a symbol with which the voter could identify. He had the synthetic quality of acceptability and all the marketable aptitudes. He was of average appearance, neat, sincere, youthful, vigorous, socially gracious, good-tempered, polite to his elders, and a veteran; was, in short, endowed with the best graces of housebroken political exurbanism or a Hollywood casting bureau. His personality was devoid of sharp corners or notable eccentricities about religion or economics or education, and he had all the self-possession and adaptability necessary for the skillful use of the mass media.

The accent on personal attractiveness gave him a pliable, plastic quality on which to superimpose the image of the earnest, forthright, high-minded young go-getter—a patchwork of personal mannerisms which not only set him off from his rivals but gave him just the right blend of inspiration and tact.

CHAPTER IV

Schooling, Chotiner Style

Nixon had the good fortune to learn in his first campaign that there was a trick to winning elections—indeed a whole bagful of tricks—and he proved himself an apt pupil. His teacher was his campaign adviser, Murray Chotiner, a Los Angeles lawyer who was to remain one of Nixon's political intimates until he ran afoul of a Senate investigating subcommittee in 1956.

Chotiner was one of the fathers of the new synthetic Madison-Avenue-style politics in America. For years Hollywood had shown what could be done with movie stars and crooners by conditioning and manipulating public attitudes. The early crudities of press agentry had over the years been refined. Big business had added respectability by pioneering market research, opinion polling, mass advertising, and the niceties of product identification.

Chotiner's discovery was that, by choosing an acceptable stereotype, a political personality could also be packaged and merchandised without reference to any of the serious issues of life and politics.

California was an ideal field for experimentation in new social technologies of this kind because the state's political structure was a partisan wonderland. Hiram Johnson's 1911 revolt against corruption and bossism in the parties had crystallized in statute form; it wiped out patronage, installed nonpartisan city governments, outlawed nominating conventions, and threw primaries open to everyone. Indeed, by legitimatizing "cross-filing," it turned the primaries into a weird partisan Donnybrook. In that environment, party machines and conventional bosses withered and died. The result was an electorate free to follow its own disorganized whimsies.

California politics became even more unpredictable as a result of the massive migration that tripled the state's population in a single generation between 1930 and 1955. These were years of restless change—of depression and drouth and war and new industrial growth. More than a fair share of those who came were the flotsam and jetsam of an economy in transition. Their social philosophy was largely at odds with the settled order of things. Before 1930, California had been rock-ribbed Republican: in that year, among 120 legislators at Sacramento, only 13 were Democrats. By the time Nixon was old enough to run for office, Republicans were outnumbered on the registration lists by a million votes.

This was the political climate in which Murray Chotiner learned to excel. With an uninformed and disorganized electorate to start with, winning elections became an exercise in the arts of communication. Chotiner had tested his skill on Earl Warren and William Knowland, and when it came Nixon's turn, Chotiner knew what to do and how to do it, complete with scripts, speeches, itineraries, issues, strategy, surveys, billboards, campaign clubs, and off-stage whispers.

Nixon brought into the partnership his training in debate and public speaking, a technique which in time gave him a commanding platform presence, capable of manipulating an audience like a musical instrument. Grafted onto these skills was Chotiner's mastery of modern communications and public relations.

Chotiner, of course, was not alone in his application of merchandising methods to politics. Techniques followed a statewide pattern generally, but in one detail the conservative north, which for generations had been the political makeweight of the state, differed from the burgeoning southland. Northern strategy was to regard Democratic registration as a temporary aberration, the caprice of a wayward friend who could and ought to be coaxed back into the true fold. But in the south, under the leadership of the Chandler family and the *Los Angeles Times,* whose crusading Republicanism neither asked nor gave quarter, the Democratic party was regarded as the hiding place of devious and pernicious enemies of the republic, who could be routed only by frightening their more timid cohorts into embracing Republican orthodoxy.

It was Nixon's ill fortune to fall into the hands of the hobgoblin, fear-and-scare school of persuasion and to learn the gospel that, as Theodore White put it, the "minority party can win only by supercharging enough zealots to ignite thousands of apathetic neutrals."

There was nothing haphazard about Chotiner's methods, a fact which might not have been generally recognized had it not been that the Republican National Committee in 1955 prevailed on him to tour the country giving secret lectures at GOP "political schools." A transcript of one of these lectures was circulated after it fell into the hands of an enterprising reporter, and it thus became possible to study in some detail the techniques by which Nixon's career was advanced. The Democrats called this treatise "probably one of the most cynical political documents published since Machiavelli's *The Prince* or Hitler's *Mein Kampf* . . . a textbook on how to hook suckers."

The lecture, of nearly 14,000 words, is a truly knowledgeable document. With professorial thoroughness Chotiner developed his subject topically, discussing in turn such practical problems as timing, starting the campaign, cataloguing volunteer workers and contributors, how to pick a candidate, how to select a campaign theme, how to deflate the opposition, how to limit the issues, campaign ethics, smears, attacks and counterattacks, and the details of organization. Nothing is omitted: a sophisticated catalogue of political mayhem.

Chotiner started from a thoroughly logical premise that "in this great medium of politics, where millions of dollars are spent, where huge manpower is used in the conduct of a campaign . . . it is important that we realize that we have to use more professionals." In order to realize on an investment of this kind running into the millions, Chotiner advocated leaving nothing to chance. In the case of Knowland and Nixon, he said, the campaign "began one full year ahead." And why start so early?

"Because," the professor explained, "you need that time to deflate your opposition. . . . There are many people who say we don't want that kind of campaign in our state. They say we want to conduct a constructive campaign and point out the merits of our own candidate. I say to you in all sincerity that, if you do not deflate the opposition candidate before your own candidate gets started, the odds are that you are going to be doomed to defeat."

For a campaign to be successful, Nixon's mentor explained, there is also a trick in the selection of your candidate. You cannot just foist him on the voters willy-nilly. "People want to feel *they* are selecting the candidate," he said, "rather than having the candidate tell them 'I am going to run, hell or high water.' . . . It is really simple to let the people select their candidate. All you have to do is to get a number of people talking: 'Now if we can only get so-and-so to run for this office.' " And to emphasize that this was no mere academic theorizing, he revealed that Knowland in 1941 had used that device to get Earl Warren elected governor of California.

With a deft, passionless, surgical touch, Chotiner went on to dissect the anatomy of campaigning.

"What is the difference between legitimate attack and smear?" he inquired. ". . . It is not a smear, if you please, if you point out the record of your opponent. . . . Of course, it is always a smear, naturally, when it is directed to our own candidate."

To illustrate the nice ethical considerations involved in such judgments, Chotiner cited an unrecorded episode from the 1946 Senate race in which Knowland beat Will Rogers, Jr. Knowland had given "explicit instructions that under no circumstances were we ever to say a word against the opposition candidate." The staff, however, was in no wise deterred by this order.

"A search was made of the record of Will Rogers, Jr.," Chotiner confided. "Among his many activities was a contribution to the *People's Daily World* in Los Angeles, a paper, let us say, to be charitable, that has espoused a left-wing philosophy in a very extreme nature. A member of the Democratic State Central Committee made up a 'white paper' in which was listed the record of Will Rogers, Jr., and it was sent out broadside throughout the state of California, obviously not from our headquarters."

Chotiner's political maxims were heavily tinged with pragmatism. In setting up a campaign organization, he advised, "make sure that you have a separate organization that is set up of Democrats or independents or whatever you may want to call them."

In order to insure favorable newspaper publicity, write to every newspaper at the beginning of the campaign, asking for their advertising rates. "It tells them we are thinking of putting an ad in the newspaper. It may help on some of our stories. . . .

"We come to the question of ethics in the campaign. I cannot overemphasize the fact that truth is the best weapon we can use." (This is his only reference to ethics in politics.)

"We never put out the complete voting record for our candidate, vote by vote, in spite of the demands from people within our organization. The reason is—even if your candidate has voted 99 per cent right according to the person who reads the record, the 1 per cent will often turn the prospect against you."

When your candidate is under attack, Nixon's manager counseled, don't answer until the opposition has exhausted its ammunition; you may find the public is uninterested. "But if you find the attack has reached such proportion that it can no longer be avoided in any way, when you answer it, do so with an attack of your own against the opposition for having launched it in the first place.

"May I suggest to you," said Chotiner, alluding to the Checkers speech, "that I think the classic that will live in all political history came on September 23, 1952, from Los Angeles, California, when the candidate for the Vice-Presidency answered, if you please, with an attack against those who made one on him!"

Richard Nixon, of course, played the leading role in that Los Angeles political classic, and he played it well, as one can infer from a careful study of Chotiner's analysis, because he had the benefit of expert coaching in the art of winning elections. In 1955 Nixon himself testified to his interest in these techniques when he spoke before the Radio and Television Executives Society. In an effort to be helpful to the broadcasters, he offered some clinical suggestions. In particular he stressed the importance of "sincerity" in a TV address and explained how sincerity could best be achieved. Do away with a written text, he advised, and use instead "your fireside chat, a straightforward, sincere type of presentation."

This approach, Nixon emphasized, does not mean the speech

is unprepared. It should *seem* unprepared, but to create this impression requires more, not less, work.

"A good off-the-cuff informal speech takes more preparation than a speech you read, and the candidate must realize that he can't just get up there and talk off the cuff without having spent hours in preparation," Nixon said. His advice on this occasion offered a new insight into the speech he delivered March 13, 1954, when Stevenson had criticized the Administration as "half-Eisenhower and half-McCarthy." "I don't have a prepared written text," Nixon said on that occasion, in opening his rebuttal. "I find that when I feel very strongly on a subject I speak a little more effectively when I just refer to the notes that I've made myself."

As another insight into the tricks of the trade, Nixon advised candidates not to make fifteen- and thirty-minute speeches but to concentrate instead on one-minute and five-minute spots.

"People will say a spot announcement does not give an audience a chance to know the candidate," he observed. "Sometimes that is a good thing for the candidate!"

"Spot announcements at least get your name and face in the minds of the average people," he said, "and you will find in analyzing election contests that a great number of voters vote only names. When they vote they don't know what the candidate stands for. They don't know much about him, and they vote the name, and consequently using the television medium as a billboard for spot announcements is very effective."

And then in another touch of dry humor, he added, "It is very hard to get up and tune the television station off before the one-minute spot anouncement goes off."

In later campaigns, Nixon wore his cynicism less obtrusively, but his primary interest still centered on the how of battle rather than the why. In picking candidates, he told Earl Mazo, he had laid down the general proposition that ". . . the ideal age should be thirty to forty years in the House, thirty-five to fifty years in the Senate . . . not ultra-liberal or ultra-conservative . . . a broad-gauged understanding of the world conflict and international affairs . . . a constructive program of civil rights . . . economic conservatives, but conservatives with a heart. . . .

"I don't go along with the idea of selecting candidates just because they are pretty-boys who look and sound good on television. . . . I am convinced that being a smooth actor and a fast talker on television may appeal to people in the short run but not in the long run. Sincerity counts above everything else on television."

Out of his experience over a dozen years he has distilled a set of precepts which, however valid as an explanation of his private motivation, still reflect the basic tactics of Chotinerism. Axioms such as:

"There is no public relations gimmick that will take the place of hard work."

"In a political campaign you've got to dramatize your case."

"You should fight the battle on the ground on which you are strongest; avoid the tactical error of fighting on your opponent's strongest ground."

"Whenever anybody attacks, the way to answer is not simply to defend but to take the offensive."

An examination of Nixon's campaign methods does not necessarily call for a moral judgment, for to be expert in techniques is not to be immoral, in politics any more than in engineering. Expertise is properly a means to an end. What made Nixon's preoccupation with techniques suspect, however, was that they became an end in themselves, a calculated part of the synthetic image that he with the help of his financial backers contrived.

CHAPTER V

Voorhis and 1946

I

Nixon's 1946 debut in politics set the pattern for all that was to follow, a circumstance that explains why contemporary history knows him pre-eminently as a campaigner. He started in the best Chotiner style, promising a "fighting, rocking, socking campaign," a promise he has never retracted.

For most politicians, elections are a tedious interlude, to be fought and forgotten. Not so for Nixon. What he has done on the stump sets him apart from others in his generation. Since his first appearance on the stage in 1946, he has waged six campaigns, each distinctive as a vignette in tactics and all alike in their fiercely partisan undercurrents.

What he did between elections was never quite so clear as what he did on the hustings. When he became a target of mistrust, when he was attacked or defended, it was not because of his views on substantive policy or his part in the implementation of policy, but rather because of his stance as a talkative onlooker. He has talked unceasingly—during campaigns, and about campaigns, and about strategic considerations for future campaigns. He has been quick to take positions on public issues whenever they seemed to touch on the conduct of campaigns. He has remolded and rationalized issues adroitly whenever they needed tailoring to fit the exigencies of a campaign.

If there is such a thing as Nixonism, it is to be found, not in the substance of his politics, not in any clear ideological commitment, but in the character of his polemic and his public personality, in a manner and a mode of public behavior unrelated to any vital issue. He is the embodiment of what Eric Sevareid once described as a "publicity saint"—a personage whose life is spent in headlines and before the camera, perennially armed with a comment or commitment, less well known for anything he does than for his prescience in being johnny-on-the-spot to talk about it. In the ebb and flow of political battle, he has never been identified with any major cause; no one knew whose side he would be on in the recurring wars over tariffs, hard money, easy credit, preventive war, or economic federalism, for even when he has come forward boldly to cast a vote or take a stand there has been no discernible pattern to his commitments.

The political atmosphere in 1946 was ideally suited to the Chotiner-Nixon style of in-fighting. It was the year of "Had enough? Vote Republican!"—the year that returned the Republican Eightieth Congress, later castigated by Harry Truman as the "do nothing" Congress.

Chotiner did not actually serve as Nixon's campaign manager in his first bid for public office. At that time his energies were chiefly engaged in masterminding William Knowland's Senate campaign, but by agreement with Roy Day, for a $500 fee, he undertook to serve also as part-time publicity man and consultant for Nixon, a considerable favor to be granted a political neophyte whose chances at best were less than sanguine.

Because the Committee of One Hundred had been farsighted enough to pick Nixon thirteen months before the election, and because his Navy discharge came shortly afterward, he had almost the full year recommended by Chotiner to prepare his first campaign. It was in January 1946 that he returned to California. At that time Dick and Pat Nixon were both thirty-three years old, and the birth of their first child was barely a month away. During the war Pat had worked and saved and Nixon had played poker with better than average success; their savings together amounted to $10,000, a nest egg which they had guarded as a down payment on a home. Now, as a gesture of faith in his political future, they agreed to gamble half their savings on the election and invested the other half as the down payment on a house.

In later years a good many details of that campaign have been obscured by legend. Nixon had assurances of support from the Committee of One Hundred, besides his own $5000, but there was nothing luxurious about his campaign setup. As Mrs. Nixon described it later in a magazine article, they rented a small office in downtown Whittier, then borrowed desks, chairs, tables, a throw rug for the floor, an old leather sofa, and a typewriter. Pat ran the office with the help of a former schoolmate, Marian Budlong.

Voorhis intimated later in his book that the Nixon campaign headquarters may not have been quite so impoverished as this story would suggest. The congressman said the representative of a large New York financial house made a trip to California in October 1945, about the time the Committee of One Hundred was picking Nixon, and called on a number of influential people in southern California. The emissary "bawled them out" for permitting Voorhis, whom he described as "one of the most dangerous men in Washington," to continue to represent a part of California in the House. As a consequence, Voorhis said, "many of the advertisements which ran in the district newspapers advocating my defeat came to the papers from a large advertising agency in Los Angeles, rather than from any source within the Twelfth District. And payment was made by check from that same agency."

Just how much or whether outside interests actually contributed to Nixon's campaign has never been made clear.

II

Filing date for the primaries was March 19, and Nixon, like Voorhis, cross-filed on both the Democratic and Republican tickets, a strategem which in California sometimes resulted in the capture of both nominations and election in the primary. Nixon tackled the drudgery of canvassing the district, speaking when and where he could. One factor worked in his favor: he had full time for campaigning while his opponent was tied down with congressional duties in Washington. It is a sidelight on his political adaptability that he campaigned in his lieutenant com-

mander's uniform until he became aware that gold stripes were
almost an affront to hostile and rank-conscious ex-GI's; after that
he hastened to get back into mufti.

The primary campaign was innocuous, but the vote when it
came in June was not reassuring for the young war veteran.
Voorhis walked off with the Democratic nomination, and he
polled well enough in the Republican primary to give him a lead
of 7000 votes over Nixon's total. It looked as though Nixon could
be written off as another loser.

The young lawyer was well aware of the odds against him. Discussing it years later he said, "Voorhis looked impossible to defeat. He was intelligent, experienced, he had a national reputation
and came from a well-known California family. Why did I take
it? I am a pessimist, but, if I figure I've got a chance, I'll fight
for it. And I thought *this was as good a time as any to get into
politics.*"

Nixon, as his campaign leaflets billed him, was the "clean, forthright young American who fought in defense of his country in
the stinking mud and jungles of the Solomons" while Voorhis
had "stayed safely behind the front in Washington." The campaign began on that wholesome note, but it took a sinister turn
at the Republicans' kickoff rally in Whittier, August 29.

"I want you to know," said Nixon, "that I am your candidate
primarily because there are no special strings attached to me. I
have no support from any special interest or pressure group. I
welcome the opposition of the PAC, with its Communist principles and its huge slush fund."

This was the first reference to a line of attack which was not
only to dominate the rest of the campaign but which was to become the hallmark of the Nixon campaign technique. It was what
Patrick O'Donovan later described in the *London Observer* as
the "then developing technique of lightly smearing an opponent
with communism."

Until that time, there had been no allusion to communism and
no reason to believe that the CIO or its Political Action Committee (the PAC) was even tangentially involved in the Twelfth
District contest. It was a fact that at that period certain CIO
unions in California, notably those of the oil, steel, automobile,
and rubber workers, had been penetrated by Communists, and
that some county and state organizations had not been cleansed

of the Red taint. It was also a fact, then as later, that labor support had generally been thrown on the side of Democratic rather than Republican candidates.

No hint of the Communist issue had appeared in Nixon's primary campaign; and there was no lack of evidence that Voorhis had long and consistently opposed both communism and the left-wing excesses of labor. Nevertheless, following the August 29 kickoff speech, communism became the principal issue. Ten years later Nixon was quoted by one of his biographers as saying that "communism was not the issue at any time in the '46 campaign. Few people knew about communism then, and even fewer cared."

In view of the record it is difficult to see how Nixon could have made that statement. In one of his campaign leaflets, headed "America needs new leadership now," the text asserts: "A vote for Nixon is a vote against . . . socialization of free American institutions; against . . . the PAC (Political Action Committee), its Communist principles and its gigantic slush fund." The same leaflet goes on to say: "Basically the issue to be settled in this election is conflict between political philosophies. The present congressman from this district has consistently supported the socialization of free American institutions."

Nixon and other campaigners on his behalf repeatedly referred to Voorhis as "the PAC candidate and his Communist friends." In an attempt to put a stop to these charges Voorhis ran an advertisement in the *Whittier News* September 11, saying: "It is a matter of record published in newspapers throughout the state that the CIO Political Action Committee does not endorse my re-election."

Later when Voorhis' denials began to catch up with the GOP charge, Nixon quoted from a report by a committee of the Los Angeles chapter of the national PAC organization recommending that the national group endorse Voorhis. As it turned out, the national group did *not* endorse him. Yet by waving this committee proposal before Voorhis at one campaign meeting, Nixon established in the minds of many voters a suspicion that Voorhis had allied himself with the Communists.

What emerged little by little as the campaign progressed was the technique later known as "guilt by association," a distinct innovation in American political mores, an imputation not of partisan unfitness but of treason itself. Who introduced it? Since Nixon had not resorted to this device in the primary, the weight of evidence pointed toward some influence outside his own Twelfth District. It pointed in the general direction of national GOP headquarters. There, party-liners had been given access to a study made at the instance of the United States Chamber of Commerce, whose object, using the new sociological techniques of motivational research, was to find a popular issue capable of beating the Democrats.

What the study showed, in summary, was: (1) the public feared communism and would vote against it; (2) Communists had infiltrated some labor organizations, notably the CIO; (3) organized labor had favored and was in some areas deeply involved in Democratic party politics. The report charged "a real and dangerous penetration of government," speculated that "a half-dozen Communists may have gotten into our national legislature," pointed out that "practically all CIO unions readily support the PAC," and asserted that two top advisers in the CIO got direct orders on PAC policy from the Communist party. It suggested that Democratic politicians, fearful of the PAC's power, kowtowed to the organization (and therefore to the Communists) in picking candidates.

The survey therefore recommended to Republican candidates that by linking communism to labor, and labor in turn to the Democratic party, the very weakness of the Republican party could be used as a means of shifting the political center of gravity from left to right, and could be transformed into an instrument for the undoing of the Democrats. The stratagem, in essence, was to convince voters that Democrats could be equated with Communists.

The Twelfth District was plastered with posters telling the voters "A Vote for Nixon is a Vote for a Change." Ads blanketed the thirty-two district newspapers, of which only one was for Voorhis, and one other neutral. Typical of these ads was one on October 18, in the *Covina Argus-Citizen,* a half-page display which told voters among other things:

> Don't Be Fooled Again!
> Five times Jerry Voorhis has had the support of the radical groups because he was at one time a registered Socialist and always supports the radical viewpoint

Voorhis has the indorsement of the National Political Action Committee because he voted their viewpoint 43 times out of 46 opportunities during the past four years.

On all issues involving Russia, the CIO Political Action Committee looks after the interests of Russia, against the interests of America; and whenever a bill is introduced in Congress that would interfere with the Russian, or Communist (subversive) program in this country, the CIO Political Action Committee gets busy and uses its millions to defeat the measure.

While he has been carrying the Democratic colors in recent years for his political purposes, REMEMBER, Voorhis is a former registered Socialist and his voting record in Congress is more Socialistic and Communistic than Democratic.

Voorhis later said that not all the campaign was fought in the open. A variety of tricky stories were circulated for the edification of the gullible. One, for example, insisted that Voorhis had voted to increase the ceiling price on Florida oranges but not on California oranges—a palpable invention, since no such proposition was ever presented. There was pressure on merchants not to sign newspaper statements supporting Voorhis, on pain of forfeiting their bank credit. An editor who wrote a friendly editorial was evicted by his landlord. Reports were circulated, falsely, that Voorhis was trying to stop the production of beer and liquor.

An insidious telephone campaign was carried on by Nixon supporters, but whether with the candidate's knowledge has never been clear. "This is a friend of yours," an anonymous caller would say. "I just want you to know that Jerry Voorhis is a Communist." Then the phone would click dead. One biographer has called this whispering campaign an "invention of typewriter pundits." Such denials are unconvincing, for the story has been amply corroborated.

As a minor coup, Nixon had sought and obtained the endorsement of Harold Stassen, then a rising star among GOP presidential possibilities. One fruit of this maneuver was the editorial blessing of the *Los Angeles Times,* which pointed out that Nixon, as a friend of Stassen, shared the political philosophy of the former Minnesota governor. "He is no reactionary in his thinking," said the *Times,* "but he is distinctly not a leftist or a parlor pink."

III

Meanwhile, Nixon, canvassing the 200,000 voters of the district, introduced himself as a "liberal Republican." He refrained from attacking the New Deal in all its aspects, but he pulled no punches in attacking Voorhis.

The congressman later called it "the bitterest campaign I have ever experienced." What caused his cup of bitterness to run over was a series of five debates that climaxed the contest. They had their origin in a sentimental gesture. After the birth of Patricia, Congressman Voorhis had sent the Nixons, as he did all new parents in his district, a government pamphlet on *Baby Care*. To it he attached a note saying "Congratulations. I look forward to meeting you soon in public."

Voorhis got his wish in a painful contretemps. To liven up the campaign, the Independent Voters of South Pasadena, a nonpartisan organization, approached both House candidates with a proposal for a public debate, offering to pay the costs, which eventually amounted to $35. The first response from the Nixon forces was suspicious, but they were under pressure to take a calculated risk. Nixon, as a newcomer in politics, had not been getting the crowds, and his campaign was bogging down despite unflagging effort. Voorhis, who had himself won his first election victory after such an encounter and who had found no opponent in four subsequent campaigns willing to meet him in debate, rose confidently to the challenge.

Some of Nixon's advisers were apprehensive, but with Chotiner's support he argued, "If I don't carry the fight to Voorhis, this campaign will never get off the ground." Nixon was not only right in his political estimate, but he also had the advantage of his own skills and training as a debater. Voorhis was a poor match for him; the congressman had built himself up as a public figure with a kind of saintly fervor, a half-evangelical, half-mystical appeal that relied more on sincerity than on logic. Nixon's strength lay in the fact that he had made himself adept in every platform device in the litany of argumentation, and he had the clearly defined Republican party line as an ideological guide.

The first debate was held at a South Pasadena junior high school, and the challenger at once seized the initiative. He quoted out of context from one of Voorhis' books on monetary policy and demanded an explanation; the Democrat consumed his time in a rambling, irrelevant, and unconvincing justification. Nixon, waving a paper in a manner later made famous by McCarthy, charged that it contained evidence that Voorhis had received the endorsement of the National Citizens PAC, and Voorhis labored vainly with denials. Again, Nixon accused the congressman of voting for gas rationing, for meat rationing, for grain rationing. From first to last the incumbent was on the defensive, floundering awkwardly, putting out imaginary brush fires.

After it was over, Voorhis turned to his long-time campaign manager, Chet Holifield, and asked hopefully, "How did it go?"

"Jerry," said Holifield, "he cut you to pieces. He had you on the defensive all the way. He picked the battle ground and you let him fight on his own terms."

Voorhis sighed. "What do you suggest?"

"You have two choices," Holifield said. "You can either get in there and make a slugging match of it, no holds barred. Or you can cancel the other four debates—refuse to appear with him on the ground that he is using dirty tactics."

Voorhis shook his head slowly and said, "You know I can't do that. I have given my word to meet him in five debates, and I can only keep my word."

Those debates finished Voorhis and made Nixon. As the crowds grew, the thirty-three-year-old challenger accelerated his attack. In the best Chotiner style, he told them it was a fighting campaign; he deflated the opposition; he limited the issues; he never made the mistake of attacking the strength of the opposition. The crowds caught the smell of blood—the drama of the Old Champ who was in for a beating at the hands of an appealing youngster. Nixon never relaxed the pace of the first encounter; he maintained a slashing, hit-run offensive that shifted ground constantly and never gave Voorhis a chance to get set. The congressman only got more hurt and confused and more ineffective.

"There are those walking in high official places in our country," Nixon declaimed, "who would destroy our constitutional principles through socialization of American free institutions. There are the people who front for un-American elements, wittingly or otherwise, by advocating increasing federal controls over the lives of the people. . . . Today the American people are faced with a choice between two philosophies of government; one of these, supported by the radical PAC and its adherents, would deprive the people of liberty through regimentation. The other would return the government to the people under constitutional guarantee, and, needless to say, that is the philosophy for which I will fight with all my power in Congress. . . ."

By the time the last debate was held, at the San Gabriel Mission, the campaign had come to life, and the campaigning technique that was to be Nixon's badge of identification had reached full flower. By a careful blend of innuendo, the sleight-of-hand juggling of words, meaningful non sequiturs, and controlled displays of indignation, he could impugn his opponent's integrity without ever making a direct accusation. Projecting his debating skills into a new dimension, he learned how to employ the various devices of the half-truth, the misleading quotation, the loose-jointed logic, that were indispensable in the creation of the Big Doubt.

When the votes were counted, Nixon had been elected by a margin of 64,784 to 49,431.

IV

The sequel was anticlimactic. It came in the form of a letter from the defeated congressman. Back in Washington, packing his files and musing over his experiences in a decade of hard service, Voorhis told his successor in a long, generous letter:

> I remember most poignantly the time . . . when I first came to Washington. Little did I realize then all that the job entailed. . . . During the ten years of my service I came to have a profound respect for the Congress of the United States and to realize the critical importance of its work. . . .
> This letter is simply to say, as I said in my newspaper release after the election at home, that I sincerely wish you well as you undertake the tremendous responsibilities which will soon be yours. . . . I want you to know that I will be glad to be of any help that you believe I can render.

There was another paragraph, not often quoted by Nixon's friends, but a source of comfort to his enemies. "I have refrained," said Voorhis, "for reasons which I am sure you will understand, from making any references in this letter to the circumstances of the campaign recently conducted in our District. It would only have spoiled the letter."

A couple of weeks later, Voorhis related in his book, he returned from lunch to find Nixon standing in his outer office. In the interval there had been no letter of acknowledgment and the meeting did little more than preserve the amenities. They smiled and shook hands. They talked in the inner office for more than an hour and parted, Voorhis said, "I hope and believe as personal friends."

This forbearance was admired or envied among those who looked upon Voorhis as something of a saint, but seldom shared. A dozen years after the 1946 campaign, politicians who had respected Voorhis still spoke bitterly of his defeat, still refused to condone the methods by which he was destroyed. In the pragmatic school where "nice guys finish last," the results spoke for themselves, but events proved that Nixon's victory was not without its price.

CHAPTER VI

The Lady Named Douglas, 1950

I

By 1949 Nixon was armed for bigger game. He had the Hiss case behind him.[1] He had demonstrated the viability of communism as an issue. In 1948 he had won re-election in the primary, running unopposed on the Republican ticket and winning by 3000 votes over Stephen Zetterberg in the contest for the Democratic nomination.

Nixon's opportunity to make the 1950 race for the Senate came as the result of a sudden realignment in the Democratic party. Senator Sheridan Downey, who had served the California oil interests loyally, had intended to run for re-election despite poor health; but he backed away precipitately from the effort when Congresswoman Helen Gahagan Douglas announced she would oppose him for the nomination. With Downey out of the race, the Republican nomination took on new value; moreover, the California oil interests needed a friendly candidate, since Mrs. Douglas, a liberal New Dealer, was openly hostile on the tidelands and other oil issues.

The choice fell easily on Nixon. For one of his special campaign talents, 1950 was a providential year. It was the year in which Senator McCarthy launched his shrill crusade against "Communists in government." It was the year of the Korean

---

[1] See Chapter XV.

war. It was the year in which the Communist issue took a sinister turn in the Smathers-Pepper contest in Florida, in the Monroney-Alexander contest in Oklahoma, in the Tydings-Butler race in Maryland, the Thomas-Bennett battle in Utah, and the Graham-Smith runoff in North Carolina.

It was the year in which a young congressman like Nixon need have no hesitation in pointing a finger of partisan scorn at the White House itself. After President Truman had asserted that under his administration the position of the United States had improved on the world front, Nixon on May 2 during the primary campaign told a reporter for the *San Diego Journal* that he considered Truman's claim "the most dishonest remark in America's political history."

"There is no question that we have been losing the Cold War," he went on. "You seriously wonder if a man is qualified to lead this nation after such a statement as Truman made."

The 1950 contest was in all respects a Chotiner-Nixon tour de force, testing and refining their virtuosity and resourcefulness.

The conspicuous feature of Nixon's primary campaign was a handbill sent to all registered Democrats and captioned "As one Democrat to Another . . ." Inside were photographs of his family and of the candidate as a war hero, and the story of his part in the Hiss case. Since it was not always easy for busy and uninstructed voters to tell a Democrat from a Republican in cross-filing California, this handbill, which never identified Nixon as a Republican, probably went a long way toward confusing the electorate.

The leaflet drew a scornful protest from Leslie E. Claypool, political editor of the *Los Angeles Daily News,* who wrote:

"Actually the impression is given that Nixon is a Democrat—and some of his critics are wondering if his antipathy to perjury would go far enough to prevent him from using this sort of advertising if he were under oath as Alger Hiss was when Nixon nicked him. It is surprising that a man who poses as the soul of truth and honor would permit such a deceitful device to be used to fool thousands of Democrats new to this county."

Nixon's efforts in the primary received a valuable assist in the snide campaign waged by Manchester Boddy, publisher of the *Los Angeles Daily News,* who opposed Mrs. Douglas for the Democratic nomination. It was Boddy who first referred to Mrs.

Douglas and her supporters as "red-hots," at a time when the word "red" meant only one thing in California. In a desperate effort to keep party control in the hands of the conservative Downey faction, Boddy charged that he found evidence of a "statewide conspiracy on the part of a small subversive clique of red-hots to capture, through stealth and cunning, the nerve centers of our Democratic Party." Boddy's defense was that he was "trying to steer a middle course between the liberal-left wing of the Democratic Party and the ultraconservativism of the Republican Party."

What Boddy actually did was to give the Nixon headquarters a campaign windfall for the general election, and Murray Chotiner lost no time in capitalizing on it. In the manual sent to every worker Nixon's campaign manager said: "We must appeal to Democrats to help win the election. Therefore, do not make a blanket attack on Democrats. Refer to the opposition as a supporter of the socialistic program running on the Democratic ticket."

Later, when the going got rough, Chotiner sent campaign chairmen a memorandum headlined "Important Strategy," which warned: "Helen Douglas is trying to portray a new role as a foe of Communism. Do not let her get away with it! It is a phony act."

Nixon himself had warned immediately after the June 6 primary that he would force Mrs. Douglas to "tell where she stands."

"If she doesn't, I'll do it for her," the congressman said.

The outcome of the primary seemed to indicate the contest would be close. Nixon polled 1,000,000 votes, Mrs. Douglas 890,000. In addition, there were approximately 725,000 "swing" votes, of which 535,000 had been cast for Manchester Boddy. If party loyalties prevailed, it looked like a photo-finish.

II

Three weeks after the primary Korea was afire and history had joined Nixon's campaign apparatus. Months earlier the congressman had intended to concentrate on the New Deal and the Fair Deal; at a dinner announcing his candidacy, November 3, 1949, he told a Los Angeles audience:

"Believe me, I am well aware of the Communist threat and I do not discount it. But I am convinced that an even greater threat to our free institutions is presented by that group of hypocritical and cynical men who, under the guise of providing political panaceas for certain social and economic problems in our society, are selling the American birthright for a mess of pottage."

In his Lincoln Day address, he hammered again at the theme of socialism: "Today the issue is still slavery—the type of slavery in which an all-powerful state seeks complete domination and control over the lives and liberties of the people. The Soviet Union is an example of the slave state in its ultimate development; Great Britain is halfway down the same road; powerful interests are striving to impose the British socialist system upon the people of the United States."

After the outbreak of fighting in Korea, the priorities changed but he lost neither an issue nor momentum. Communism became the paramount enemy, and Nixon's reputation as a young Red-hunter and as a conservative Republican made it easy for him to shift gears from socialism to communism and back again until the two terms became almost interchangeable.

Some effort has been made to suggest that Nixon's staff rather than the candidate himself was responsible for his running on the Communist issue, but Murray Chotiner has testified otherwise. Analyzing Nixon's skill in exploiting the mood of 1950, Chotiner recalled: "Practically everybody in the organization told Dick, 'You must not talk about communism. It has been overworked.' . . . And I remember in case after case, Dick Nixon told audiences, 'I have been advised not to talk about communism; but I am going to tell the people of California the truth, and this is one thing we cannot stop talking about as long as the menace of international communism faces us here in the United States.' "

Nixon fired his first broadside August 30 in a radio address originating in Washington; as headline catchers, he demanded on the one hand the resignation of Secretary of State Dean Acheson (a popular GOP gambit at that stage), and urged on the other hand a program of all-out mobilization, controls, and higher taxes for victory in Korea. He said Truman's decision to fight in Korea "should have the wholehearted support of the Congress and the American people." This did not prevent him from charging that Mrs. Douglas "during the six years she has been in Congress, has consistently supported the State Department's policy of appeasing communism in Asia, which finally resulted in the Korean war."

Mrs. Douglas, opening her campaign in a statewide broadcast

September 6, described Nixon as a reactionary "beside whom Bob Taft is a flaming liberal." Her strategy was to run on the Democratic record, and to debate the mounting rural and urban problems of California, but instead she found herself at the very outset defending her own record in the fields of foreign policy, defense, and opposition to Communist aggression. She had fought hard for the Marshall Plan, for reciprocal trade, for the mutual-aid program and for measures to aid Korea, but her explanations and the fact that she had disregarded the political impact of a half-dozen key votes kept her on the defensive throughout the campaign.

In the official campaign material on both sides, heavy emphasis was laid on voting records. Comparison was easy, since both candidates had served in the House through the Eightieth and Eighty-first Congresses. Once they took to the stump, however, scant attention was paid to these voluminous analyses. Instead the spotlight was focused on a few key votes—those dealing with Korea, defense, internal security, Communist control, and the Cold War.

In this struggle the Nixon headquarters went all out to exploit a device that had first cropped up in the Democratic primary, that of linking Mrs. Douglas's voting record with that of the ultra-left-wing Congressman Vito Marcantonio of New York, an outspoken fellow traveler.

Even before the fall campaign was officially under way, Nixon's manager for southern California, Bernard Brennan, issued a statement August 30 charging that Mrs. Douglas's "record as a member of Congress discloses the truth about her soft attitude toward communism. During five years in Congress Helen Douglas has voted 353 times exactly as has Vito Marcantonio, the notorious Communist party-line congressman from New York. . . . How can Helen Douglas, capable actress that she is, take up so strange a role as a foe of communism? And why does she when she has so deservedly earned the title of 'the pink lady'?"

Mrs. Douglas's anti-Communist credentials, like those of Jerry Voorhis in 1946, were unassailable; the Reds had denounced her repeatedly as a "capitalist warmonger," and she had earned distinction in the House Foreign Affairs Committee for her active support of anti-Communist measures. Nevertheless, in the 1950 campaign, she was the target of a calculated campaign to pin the Red label on her. Chief weapon in the Nixon arsenal was the "Pink Sheet," a leaflet containing a tangle of innuendo, half-truths, and distortions, which was to become a classic exhibit in the art of imputing guilt by association.

Headlined "Douglas-Marcantonio Voting Record," it began with these words:

"Many persons have requested a comparison of the voting records of Congresswoman Helen Douglas and the notorious Communist party-liner, Congressman Vito Marcantonio of New York."

This arbitrary pairing of their names contained a damning but fraudulent insinuation that there existed also an ideological alliance between Marcantonio and Mrs. Douglas; this false impression was reinforced when the Pink Sheet went on to assert:

"Mrs. Douglas and Marcantonio have been members of Congress together since January 1, 1945. During that period, Mrs. Douglas voted the same as Marcantonio 354 times. While it should not be expected that a member of the House of Representatives should always vote in opposition to Marcantonio, it is significant to note, not only the *great number of times* which Mrs. Douglas voted in agreement with him, but also the issues on which almost without exception they always saw eye to eye, to wit: Un-American Activities and Internal Security."

To clinch the polemic, after alluding briefly to 24 of these votes and assuming the case to have been proved, the handbill concluded shamelessly that Nixon had voted "exactly opposite to the Douglas-Marcantonio Axis!"—as if an axis had been demonstrated.

The cold hindsight of history offers a less emotional insight into the record than that of the Pink Sheet. To begin with, Nixon himself, even though a Republican, voted with Marcantonio 112 times during the four years they were in the House together. Moreover, the 354 votes alluded to in the Pink Sheet included many noncontroversial matters of relatively minor importance, matters on which Marcantonio usually voted as a Democrat, even though he was a member of the American Labor party, who had originally run for office on the Republican ticket.

One highly respected reference service, Editorial Research Reports, determined that during the five-year period covered by the 354 votes, there were actually 76 "outstanding" roll-call votes in the House. On 66 of these Mrs. Douglas and Marcantonio voted the same way, and in 53 cases they were voting either with a majority of the House itself or with a majority of the Democratic party. Hence it would have been more meaningful to have accused Mrs. Douglas of having voted with a majority of the House or a majority of her party 85 per cent of the time than it was to torture statistics to invent an imaginary "axis."

As for the thirteen occasions on which Mrs. Douglas and Marcantonio were not aligned with such majorities, eleven dealt with such issues as housing, rent control, price controls, and the like. Only two were concerned with matters of "internal security" —the Mundt-Nixon Communist control bill of 1948, which the Senate also refused to pass; and the McCarran internal security bill of 1950, when she voted to sustain President Truman's veto.

On issues of foreign policy, Mrs. Douglas voted with the majority, adhering to the bipartisan containment program on all occasions but one; that exception was the Greek-Turkish aid bill, the cornerstone of the Truman Doctrine. Holding that Turkey's defense was first of all the responsibility of the United Nations, and that Greek aid following Britain's bankrupt blueprint would avail nothing, in the showdown vote, May 9, 1947, she voted "No" after the House had turned down the amendments she proposed. Moreover, what the Pink Sheet did not point out was that the Greek-Turkish bill passed by a vote of 287 to 107; and among the 107 in opposition there were, besides Mrs. Douglas and Marcantonio, 94 Republicans. Again, in censuring Mrs. Douglas for voting against extension of the Selective Service Act in 1948, the Pink Sheet failed to point out that she had voted for the bill on two other occasions, in 1946 and 1950. In 1949 she voted for a seventy-group Air Force and for expansion of Army and Air Force man power.

On 10 out of the 76 key votes, Mrs. Douglas and Marcantonio did not vote alike. Two of these bills were noncontroversial. Eight dealt in one way or another with communism, and it is significant—at least so far as the Pink Sheet is concerned—that on these eight roll calls Mrs. Douglas's vote was cast to strengthen the American position overseas vis-à-vis communism, not to weaken it, as Nixon charged.

Part of the Pink Sheet attack on Mrs. Douglas hinged on the fact that on various occasions, five in particular, she had opposed the majority when the House voted contempt citations against recalcitrant witnesses, most of whom took refuge in the Fifth Amendment rather than answer questions about communism. There can be no doubt that many witnesses were Communists or fellow travelers, but that was not always the only point at issue. Mrs. Douglas did vote for many contempt motions, including those citing Gerhard Eisler, Leon Josephson, Julius Emspack, William L. Patterson, and two right-wingers, Edward A. Rumely and Joseph P. Kamp.

In the prevailing climate of opinion it was easier for congressmen to go along with the majority—and Nixon's appeal was aimed at the popular mood—but there is at least this much to be said about the legal niceties of Nixon's 1950 polemic: statistics vindicate Mrs. Douglas. In a staff study by the House Un-American Activities Committee, covering the period of March 1947 to November 1957, it was found that Congress voted a total of 83 contempt citations, of which 31 were on behalf of the Un-American Activities Committee. Indictments were returned by grand juries in 73 cases. Of the 73 cases that went to trial, juries convicted 30 witnesses of contempt, while juries in 43 cases voted for acquittal.

In other words, 30 persons were convicted out of 83—approximately 38 per cent. If such a quantitative breakdown means anything, it suggests Congress showed questionable judgment in 62 per cent of the contempt citations—and any member voting in the negative, far from being pro-Communist, had better than a fifty-fifty chance of being right.

Another set of controversial votes related to defense and Korea. Late in 1949, Nixon joined House Republicans in voting to cut foreign military assistance in half, but then voted for a House-Senate conference report restoring most of the cut after it had been amended to include Formosa. Mrs. Douglas tried to make an issue of the fact that on January 19, 1950, Nixon joined in a 192 to 191 vote that killed a bill providing $60,000,000 in economic aid for Korea; the defense of Nixon and other followers of the China Lobby was that the bill contained nothing for Formosa, and he did in fact vote for Korean aid in another bill February 9 when it was coupled with an authorization to spend previously appropriated China-aid funds in Formosa.

III

Before the senatorial campaign was forty-eight hours old, both sides had yelled "foul." By the end of September an editorial in the *Independent Review* charged there was a conspiracy to defame Mrs. Douglas "by falsely accusing her through infamous insinuations and whispered innuendo of being a Communist."

In this same editorial, September 29, there appeared for the first time an appellation that was to plague Nixon throughout his political career. "Representatives of her senatorial opponent, Tricky Dick Nixon," the editorial asserted, "are the chief mouthpieces for this partisan effort to crucify Mrs. Douglas. . . ."

From that time on, to his enemies, Nixon became "Tricky Dick," and his bemused friends never ceased wondering what "indefinable" quality in his personality persuaded others to accept the nickname.

It may or may not be relevant that Governor Earl Warren let it be known that his organization would not lend active support to Nixon's campaign.

Meanwhile Nixon roared up and down the state in a commodious station wagon equipped with a record player and loudspeaker system. With a crusading intensity of manner and purpose he spoke from morning to night, sometimes as many as fourteen times a day. He made a thousand speeches in sixteen weeks.

Accompanied by his wife, an assistant, and a driver, he started his days with a breakfast meeting at 8 o'clock. From then on, in a grass-roots appeal that crossed and crisscrossed the state, his itinerary called for stops at less than hourly intervals. At a typical "station stop" his sound truck was parked at a convenient place selected by his advance man. The driver played a record or two to attract an audience. Nixon then made a five- or ten-minute talk and allowed another quarter-hour for questions.

In these appearances Nixon adhered generally to the "basic speech" that he had prepared at the outset of the campaign and used as his keynote address September 18 in a whirlwind series of appearances at San Diego, Los Angeles, Fresno, and San Francisco. In its major outlines this speech followed the tenor of the Pink Sheet—a skillfully tailored version of his opponent's voting record, which concluded: "My opponent did not vote as a Democrat. She did not vote as a Republican. . . . It just so happens that my opponent is a member of a small clique which joins the notorious party-liner, Vito Marcantonio of New York, in voting time after time against measures that are for the security of this country."

In her counterattack Mrs. Douglas denounced "such pip-squeaks as Nixon and McCarthy who are trying to get us so frightened of communism that we'll be afraid to turn out the lights at night." And in answer to Nixon's charge that she had voted repeatedly against authorizations and funds for the Un-American Activities Committee, her defense was that "the committee had become a court, with the power to smear innocent names across the nation's headlines, without even enough charity to invite its victims to appear before it in self-defense. . . . I do not believe in trial by headline. Congress is subject to all kinds of political pressures. I do not believe we can make a committee of Congress into a court and maintain justice."

Nixon apologists have blamed the press for the unflattering portrait of him that grew out of his earlier campaigns. This contention does not hold water. It does not explain why the press should have chosen to victimize an isolated Republican candidate, especially when newspaper ownership was predominantly Republican. Nor does it accord with other known facts. In 1946 Nixon had the support of thirty out of thirty-two newspapers in his district. In the 1950 primary a *New York Post* article reported that Mrs. Douglas had "been the subject of a virtual newspaper blackout." Publishers denied the charge and tried printing tabulations to disprove it, but the fact was that Mrs. Douglas felt herself obliged to buy radio time and newspaper advertising space in an effort to reach the voting public.

An independent survey of the 1950 campaign by the Institute for Journalistic Studies at Stanford University developed statistically the fact that the press leaned heavily toward Nixon. Taking twelve papers—nine supporting Nixon, two supporting Douglas, and one neutral, with total circulation roughly six to one in Nixon's favor—an actual count of news stories showed that friendly references to Nixon exceeded unfriendly references by 31.6 per cent, while the margin of friendly over unfriendly references to Mrs. Douglas was only 2.4 per cent. Using an index figure derived from these percentages, Nixon's net advantage over Mrs. Douglas was 29.2 per cent. The disparity may not have been attributable entirely to newspaper bias, since Nixon kept Mrs. Douglas on the defensive most of the time and his publicity setup was more aggressive. Nevertheless, although Mrs. Douglas, like her opponent, toured the state in a sound truck and handled herself well before audiences, it was a fact that she had difficulty in reaching mass audiences through the mass media, and if there was press bias, it tended to favor Nixon rather than his opponent.

Only once did the 1950 senatorial campaign touch the depths that were to be most fully explored in the 1954 election struggle. That was when Senator Joseph McCarthy spoke on Nixon's behalf October 10 over a regional network from Los Angeles. In a sneering, hate-filled attack on the Truman administration, McCarthy cried treason and joined Nixon in declaring that Dean Acheson must resign as Secretary of State.

"He must go," said the Wisconsin Republican. "We cannot fight international atheistic communism with men who are either traitors or who are hip-deep in their own failures. . . .

"Ask the basket-cases if they agree that Acheson is an 'outstanding American.' I am sure the mothers of America will notify the administration this fall that there is nothing 'outstanding' about washing away with blood the blunders and traitorous acts of the crowd whom the Democrat candidates have pledged to protect if they are elected. . . .

"The chips are down . . . between the American people and the administration Commicrat Party of Betrayal."

At a still lower level, an even less prepossessing aspect of the campaign was fought out on Nixon's behalf in the back alleys of politics. An undercover campaign of anti-Semitic bigotry was directed by Gerald L. K. Smith, based on the fact that Helen Gahagan, herself of Irish descent, was married to Melvyn Douglas, who was half Jewish.

Gerald Smith and his Christian Nationalist crusade were joined by Wesley Swift and his Anglo-Saxon Christian Meeting in all-out support of Nixon. As early as February 27, 1950, Smith told a meeting of his "crusade" that the man who uncovered Alger Hiss "is in California to do the same housecleaning here. Help Richard Nixon get rid of the Jew-Communists."

After the primary Smith hammered on the theme: "Helen Douglas is the wife of a Jew. You Californians can do one thing very soon to further the ideals of Christian Nationalism, and that is not to send to the Senate the wife of a Jew."

Nixon finally said in Washington that he had not asked for the support of these men but both Smith and Swift continued to campaign for him aggressively. No one suggested that Nixon was personally anti-Semitic; in fact, the B'nai B'rith Anti-Defamation League issued a statement exonerating him completely from any taint of anti-Semitism; but the record indicates that on that occasion he looked the other way while the hate-mongers were tub-thumping on his behalf.

Subsequently, in a speech on October 19, 1952, alluding to Gerald Smith, Joseph P. Kamp, and Gerald Winrod as "those who threaten civil rights from the right," Nixon boasted of having opposed State Senator Jack Tenney for the GOP nomination to Congress because Tenney had refused to repudiate the support of Smith.

Nixon was also made a temporary pawn in an international power play by the China Lobby. After the Communist conquest of the China mainland in 1949, Chiang Kai-shek's agents in the United States hired a New York public-relations firm, Allied Syndicates, Inc., headed by David Charnay, to represent the Bank of China. The China Lobby had two objectives: to force the removal of Dean Acheson as Secretary of State, on the theory that his exodus would open new avenues for renewing the struggle against Mao Tse-tung; and to prevent the recognition of Red China and the freezing of the Bank of China funds.

After Nixon's speech in August demanding Acheson's resignation, Charnay made a trip to California, where he was opening a branch office, and made it a point to meet Nixon October 8 at a Beverly Hills party. That same night, Charnay telephoned the New York apartment of Leo Casey, a member of his publicity staff, and ordered Casey to take a midnight plane for Los Angeles. There Casey organized the "Independent Voters Committee for Nixon," a paper organization whose publicity handouts found a ready welcome in the pro-Nixon press. Specifically, Casey said he worked hard to convince Negro voters that Nixon was their man because of his "liberal" views, although at the time Nixon himself had said, "I have been asked why I have not appealed to minorities. Because in my opinion there are no minorities."

Not until the campaign was over did Leo Casey learn that he had been in California not to "open doors," as he was first told, but as an agent of the Bank of China. On a number of occasions he had seen, entering and leaving Charnay's office, and later conferring with Nixon, a dapper Chinese who was referred to as the "Major." Eventually, this Major proved to be Louis Kung, son of H. H. Kung, Chiang Kai-shek's brother-in-law. What shocked Mr. Casey (and what later impelled him to tell the story in Washington) was the order from a representative of Charnay's firm that he go to Washington when the new Congress met and "deliver Nixon to the Major." Mr. Casey replied he wouldn't think of "delivering" an American senator to a foreign agent. Later, when he told the story in Nixon's office, the senator thanked him noncommittally.

IV

In a tactic that he was to exploit later on a national scale, Nixon exerted his best efforts to widen the breach in opposition ranks. First paying fulsome tribute to Democrats of an earlier generation, he proceeded to shed crocodile tears over the present standing of the party and pleaded with true Democrats to seek refuge in Republicanism.

"Today, nationally and in our own state of California," he said, "it [the Democratic party] has been captured and is completely controlled by a group of ruthless, cynical seekers after power, committed to policies and principles completely foreign to those of its founders. . . . Call it planned economy, the Fair Deal, or social welfare—but it is still the same old Socialist baloney, any way you slice it."

As the campaign gained momentum, Nixon profited by a wide-open split in Democratic ranks. George Creel, known as President Woodrow Wilson's propaganda director in World War I, together with sixty-three other prominent Democrats, joined in a statement repudiating Helen Douglas and endorsing Nixon. Chotiner capitalized on this defection by publishing another handbill that pictured a smiling Nixon with smiling wife and babies, and saluted readers: "Fellow Democrats!" Inside, after quoting President Truman and Senator Downey, it went on to declare: "Is Helen Douglas a Democrat? THE RECORD SAYS NO!"

President Truman at a news conference went out of his way

to speak approvingly of Mrs. Douglas and sent Averell Harriman, Attorney-General McGrath, and others into California to help, but it was by no means an all-out effort and certainly far weaker than the Republican party's effort on Nixon's behalf.

In the end Mrs. Douglas joined the hue and cry against communism, and when she did that she was lost. As Chotiner testified later, she couldn't beat Nixon at his own game. He said: "Dick Nixon was talking about communism at home . . . and Helen Douglas was talking about handouts. . . . We could not outbid the administration. . . . We kept talking about a strong America . . . and what happened? Mrs. Douglas, in desperation . . . started to debate with Dick Nixon's issues. . . . She made the fatal mistake of attacking our strength instead of sticking to attacking our weaknesses."

As the campaign drew to a close, the influential *Los Angeles Times,* pillar of Republican party strength in southern California, conceded editorially that California was "the only State where communism becomes a main issue." And the paper, after calling Nixon "the most conspicuous opponent of communism in Congress," went on to dismiss Mrs. Douglas as a "glamorous actress who, though not a Communist, voted the Communist party line in Congress innumerable times . . . the darling of the Hollywood parlor pinks and Reds."

In the closing hours of the campaign, the Nixon forces launched a telephone drive, promising that for anyone who answered his telephone saying, "Vote for Nixon," there would be:

PRIZES GALORE!!! Electric Clocks, Silex coffeemakers with heating units—General Electric automatic toasters—silver salt and pepper shakers, sugar and creamer sets, candy and butter dishes, etc., etc. WIN WITH NIXON!

The vote was 2,183,454 for Nixon; 1,502,507 for Mrs. Douglas—a plurality of 680,947. Nixon ran 7 per cent ahead of the GOP congressional slate, but 5.6 per cent behind Governor Warren.

Organizations supporting Nixon reported campaign expenditures of $62,899, compared with Mrs. Douglas's $156,172 and Governor Warren's $324,000. Outside analysts concluded that the Nixon campaign must have cost between $1,100,000 and $1,750,000.

The epilogue to this chapter in Nixon's career was written obliquely in January 1957, when British publisher David Astor had a long off-the-record interview with the Vice-President. As reported by a *New Republic* columnist (May 5, 1958), Astor was much impressed by Nixon's grasp of world problems, but finally managed to ask how, in the light of his present attitudes, he explained his campaign against Helen Douglas. Nixon looked up from his desk with dignified sadness and said, "I'm sorry about that episode. I was a very young man."

CHAPTER VII

Preconvention Campaign

I

No EPISODE in Nixon's career has left a more enigmatic trail than the steps leading to his nomination for the vice-presidency. The record contains only glimpses, and these so few that the story may always remain obscure unless he chooses to tell it himself. Tradition holds that candidates for the office of Vice-President need only be available at the right moment to "balance the ticket," and whatever Nixon did as a discreet and wary traditionalist was merely enough to give him a high degree of visibility when the list of availables was being canvassed.

As a minority member of the Senate in 1951, he could not fail to be acutely aware of the festering discontent in Republican ranks. The need for a national victory, so nearly won and so dramatically lost in 1948, had assumed psychotic dimensions. Senator Taft of Ohio became the symbol of a brooding, dedicated will to win, but no Republican exempted himself from the compulsive, fatalistic togetherness of the hour. Each in his own way set himself to find the touchstone of victory.

Nixon had been a senator barely four months when the fortunes of politics gave him a providential leg up. The *Congressional Record* for May 14 reveals that on that day the junior senator from California was excused from attendance at Senate sessions for one week, to enable him to serve as a member of the

United States delegation to the World Health Organization meetings in Geneva.

Nixon answered roll call again on May 21, and there would have been no hint that his trip to Europe had been anything but official had he not himself revealed otherwise on the floor of the Senate June 5. The upper house was debating the need for a Central Arizona irrigation project, and in the course of a very brief expression of opposition, Nixon alluded to an otherwise unsuspected aspect of his trip to Europe.

". . . I had a very interesting experience two weeks ago," he said, "when I sat in the office of General Eisenhower in Paris. I was impressed, let me say parenthetically, with the excellent job he is doing against monumental odds, in the position he holds. He pointed out to me that one of the greatest tasks which he has at the present time is to convince our allies abroad of the necessity of putting first things first. . . ."

More than a year later, the Scripps-Howard *Daily News* in Washington contained a brief allusion to the visit and an assurance that Nixon had "stopped at Eisenhower's headquarters, not to talk politics, but to learn about NATO and SHAPE." Nixon recalled, in an interview published in a news magazine August 29, 1952, that that was the first time he had ever met Eisenhower. "I stopped in Paris and talked with him for an hour. His main interest was in the Hiss case and subversive activities in general." Other reports indicate the general complimented the young senator on his anti-Communist activities and was favorably impressed at this first encounter.

The *Congressional Record* contains no other reference to Paris or the meeting between the general and his future running mate. But it is not irrelevant that May 1951 marked the beginning of the great Republican pilgrimage by which the general was persuaded to declare himself; in the procession that commuted between the United States and Paris that year, Nixon was one of a long list of party leaders that included Paul Hoffman, John J. McCloy, Senator Frank Carlson of Kansas, Harold Stassen, Lucius Clay, Henry Cabot Lodge, and others, and Nixon's name was one of the first on the roll.

Later that month, to attest the senator's growing stature in party circles and his presumptive alliance with Stassen, he was one of forty-five men invited to a New Jersey private estate for a

Stassen strategy conference. For Nixon this meeting had one significant aftermath. Some months afterward, in a desperate search for votes, Stassen testified to Nixon's national political coloration by offering to trade him the vice-presidential nomination in return for the support of the California delegation. It was an empty gesture but a straw in the wind for the senator.

II

It was only a matter of days after the New Jersey gathering that Nixon took to the hustings. A keynote address June 28 for the Young Republican National Federation convention at Boston (telephoned over a bad public-address system) became in a very real sense the keynote of his own campaign to make friends and influence delegates. The speech laid out an elaborate set of formulas, propositions, and issues.

To begin with, Nixon recognized that nationally, as in California, the Republican party was not in a position to win by itself.

> I say we Republicans have been talking to please ourselves for the past twenty years, and we have found out that there aren't enough of us to win.

In a mood reminiscent of Chotinerism, he prescribed tactics:

> I believe there is only one sure-fire formula for victory. We have to work, we have to fight, we have to stand for something. . . . Let's see that the Republican Party in 1952 puts on the kind of a fighting, rocking, socking campaign that will bring home to the people the merits of our candidate and our program.

He laid out a program:

> . . . cut all non-defense expenditures right down to the bone. . . . Attack inflation at its source . . . in the final analysis a balanced budget and high production are the only effective answers to inflation. . . . We shall not allow this emergency to be used to socialize any basic American institution.

On the subject of internal security he reviewed the Hiss case and its implications:

> The tragedy is that our top administration officials have refused time and time again to recognize the existence of the fifth column in this country and to take effective action to clean subversives out of the administrative branch of the government.

And, using the same arithmetic that had proved successful in arousing California audiences in 1950, he indicted the Truman administration's foreign policy:

> Six years ago the United States was the most powerful nation on the face of the globe. We had the strongest Army, the strongest Navy, and the strongest Air Force in the world. We had a monopoly on the atomic bomb. As far as people in the world were concerned, there were approximately 1,760,000,000 on our side and only 180,000,000 on the Communist side.
>
> Six years have passed—six years of conferences, of little wars like the one in Korea, of lack of leadership in Washington. And what is the situation today? Today we are no longer stronger on the ground, we are stronger in strategic air but weaker in tactical air. We're stronger on the sea but weaker beneath the sea. We no longer have a monopoly on the atomic bomb, though we believe that we have more than has our potential enemy. And when we analyze the breakdown in peoples in the world, what do we find? Today there are only 540,000,000 people that can be counted on the side of the free nations—our side. There are 800,000,000 people on the Communist side, and there are 600,000,000 that will have to be classified as neutral—countries like India and Pakistan. In other words, six years ago the odds in people in the world were 9 to 1 in our favor, and today they are 5 to 3 against us.
>
> . . . We have lost 600,000,000 people to the Communists in six years—100,000,000 a year.

The essence of Nixon's case, however, aside from communism and corruption, was contained in a passage near the beginning of the speech in which he posed this rhetorical question:

> How can we win in 1952? That is the $64,000,000,000 question. I say the $64,000,000,000 question because that's the annual cost of keeping the present administration in Washington.

Perhaps it is never wholly fair to confront a politician with the cold hindsight of statistics, but Nixon's choice of the 64-billion-dollar idiom shows up in such a comparison as something less than prophetic and more than campaign oratory. Here are the figures for Truman's last six fiscal years in the White House, as tabulated by the Bureau of the Budget and published by the U. S. Government Printing Office:

	Expenditures	Surplus or Deficit
1947	$ 39,032,000,000	$ 754,000,000 surplus
1948	33,069,000,000	8,419,000,000 surplus
1949	39,507,000,000	1,811,000,000 deficit
1950	39,617,000,000	3,122,000,000 deficit
1951	44,058,000,000	3,510,000,000 surplus
1952	65,408,000,000	4,017,000,000 deficit
Total	$260,691,000,000	$3,733,000,000 surplus

It thus appears that in June 1951 the federal government was spending 44 billion dollars, not 64 billion, and it was not until the next fiscal year, when the heaviest burdens of the Korean war were being paid for that the Truman administration's budget reached 65 billion. A comparison with the first six fiscal years of the Eisenhower administration (excluding 1953, since that budget was shaped by both administrations) shows the following:

	Expenditures	*Surplus or Deficit*
1954	$ 67,772,000,000	$ 3,117,000,000 deficit
1955	64,570,000,000	4,180,000,000 deficit
1956	66,540,000,000	1,626,000,000 surplus
1957	69,433,000,000	1,596,000,000 surplus
1958	71,936,000,000	2,819,000,000 deficit
1959	80,871,000,000	12,871,000,000 deficit
Total	$421,122,000,000	$19,765,000,000 net deficit

So much for Nixon's prescience. In the Eisenhower administration, expenditures never once got below the idiomatic 64 billion dollars a year; in a comparable length of time Eisenhower spent a total of 421 billion as against 260 billion for Truman; Eisenhower piled up a net deficit of nearly 20 billion compared with a net surplus of 3.7 billion for the Truman era.

III

Nixon's midsummer speech in Boston was not only a keynoter for the Young Republicans but the formula that he carried the length and breadth of the country that year. In Philadelphia February 26, 1952, at the forty-third annual meeting of the Pennsylvania Manufacturers Association he was still blaming the Truman administration for the loss of 100 million people a year, still charging that foreign policy had failed because of "the seeds of the error which curses our present policy." He told the gathering, "It is immaterial whether these losses have been sustained because of the questionable loyalty of some of those who made our policy or because of their stupidity or honest mistakes of judgment."

"Over the past eight months," he said in his peroration, "I have had the privilege of traveling through and speaking in twenty-five states, and no one can travel through America . . . without realizing . . . we have the resources and . . . we are on the side of freedom, of truth, of justice against godless totalitarianism, slavery and oppression. All we need is leadership—

courageous, strong, decent, firm American leadership. . . ."

When he spoke May 8 before New York Republicans, two months before the convention, he had a blue-ribbon audience that included Governor Thomas Dewey. It was his usual fighting speech, delivered without notes, since by that time he could give it backward or forward from memory; and when he finished, two such disparate party faithful as Representative John Taber and Senator Irving Ives turned simultaneously toward Dewey to endorse it as a great speech, a coincidence whose meaning was hardly lost upon the governor.

In a sense there was something ritualistic about that performance. Dewey had virtually made up his mind in favor of Nixon for the vice-presidency, on the strength of the latter's growing reputation, and had arranged the New York appearance as a final test run. After dinner he invited the senator to his hotel suite for a long talk culminating in a blunt discussion of the vice-presidential nomination. It was at least a tacit commitment. The fact that Nixon was thus sounded out in advance by so potent a kingmaker as Dewey did not become generally known until long afterward, but the revelation that the deal was made in May shed a comic light on some of the gyrations at Chicago in July.

If Nixon's crystal ball was cloudy on the subject of the budget, it was no less so in his diagnosis, from his place on the substitutes' bench, of the Korean war strategy. Throughout the period leading up to the 1952 convention, he hammered hard at the Democrats on the Korean issue. In a typical statement of his position he told a convention in Chicago that the administration's Far Eastern policy had resulted in the loss of China, and for lack of a policy to end the Korean war threatened to bring on World War III. In conformity with GOP tactics that year, the senator strongly endorsed General MacArthur's program, although nothing had occurred in the months since the general's dismissal as supreme commander to support his analysis.

"They fail to recognize that there are only two alternatives to MacArthur's policy," he asserted, "continuing the Korean war without any real hope of winning it, or ending it with a political settlement. . . .

"The only political settlement possible would amount to appeasement, because the price of settlement which the Communists insist upon is a seat in the United Nations and control of Formosa—laying the foundation for eventual Communist domination of all Asia and in the end an inevitable world war. . . .

"Eventually we'll have to adopt some of MacArthur's recommendations."

This was the line of attack that audiences at party rallies enjoyed, and Nixon was, as always, eager to please.

In the income-tax returns which he published after becoming Vice-President, 1951 revealed itself as the year in which his outside earnings reached their peak. He received $6,611.45 in fees for speeches, some delivered on a lecture tour and sixteen booked independently. His paid appearances were made before civic groups, bar associations, trade associations, and a labor group; in addition, he spoke without payment at numerous Republican party rallies and fund-raising dinners, was in fact one of the party's most-sought-after speakers.

His popularity that year was symptomatic. Widespread popular frustration found expression and was embodied in his drumfire assault on the party in power. Alger Hiss had gone to prison for perjury in March, and audiences identified Nixon as the nemesis who had put him there. McCarthyism had given impetus to Nixon's charge that the administration had been lax in cleaning Communists out of government. The Korean war had brought American arms face to face with Communist arms, and a profound mood of war weariness together with a fear that the limited struggle might erupt on a global scale made the public all the more ready to listen to charges that errors in foreign policy were responsible. Nixon, by focusing the symptoms of discontent, by standing forth as an articulate foe of the status quo and standpattism, made himself into a recognizable oracle of change—and, as 1952 was to show, the voters were ripe for change.

At that time a cloud no bigger than a politician's hand cast a fleeting shadow. In a congressional investigation of influence-peddling, Nixon's name came up March 20, 1952, in testimony before a House ways and means subcommittee. The witness was Senator Owen Brewster of Maine, who had been chairman of the Republican senatorial campaign committee in 1950. He revealed that Nixon of California and Young of North Dakota had appealed to him—in fact had "besieged" him—for help that year in their respective primaries. The rules of the committee, however, flatly prohibited such assistance.

Brewster testified that, since it was customary for the committee to provide $5000 to each Republican senatorial candidate in the general election and since both Nixon and Young had assured him that their principal battles would be in the primary, he devised a stratagem to assist them. In May of 1950 Brewster and his wife borrowed $10,000 from a Washington bank; they turned it over to a noted political "fixer," Henry "the Dutchman" Grunewald; Grunewald in turn sent checks for $5000 each to the campaign managers for Nixon and Young. Later that summer when the senatorial campaign committee forwarded its usual contribution to the two candidates, ostensibly for the fall campaign, their managers repaid Grunewald, who repaid Brewster, who in turn paid off his note at the bank.

In this remarkable transaction no law was violated, but Brewster testified that he used Grunewald as a "conduit" because he wanted a man "who had a capacity to keep his mouth shut." He admitted frankly that the effect of his action was to circumvent the rules of the committee over which he presided. Nothing came of these revelations, except Brewster's subsequent defeat at the polls, but Nixon's critics argued that the latter had participated in the deception with his eyes open.

IV

As for speculation about the 1952 convention and the Republican nominee, Nixon's public utterances were a model of discretion. Although he was a convention delegate, committed by law to Governor Earl Warren, he pleaded for the selection of "the man who can best sell our program to the most people," and then tactfully sidestepped this latter's identity by adding, "I challenge you to name any one of the prominently mentioned Republican candidates who wouldn't be a tremendous improvement over what we have in the White House now. . . ."

His tact need not have been mistaken, however, for indecision In his interview later with Stewart Alsop he revealed: "I remember in 1952, when Bob Taft came to my office and said he would like my support for the nomination. I explained why I was for Eisenhower, and Taft, who was a big man, didn't resent it."

CHAPTER VIII

———◄►———

The Convention Pays Off

I

ALTHOUGH Nixon was able to give short shrift to Senator Taft, he found it impossible during the weeks of preconvention jockeying to declare himself publicly for General Eisenhower. What inhibited him was the fact that he had been elected a member of the California delegation, whose seventy votes were pledged by law to Governor Warren until he released them.

Toward the end of winter Nixon had considered an alternative strategy. He had been approached by Representative Thomas Werdel of Bakersfield and other leaders of an anti-Warren cabal who considered the governor "too liberal." These right-wing Republicans, with a half-million-dollar campaign fund, had proposed that Nixon place himself at the head of a rival ticket of convention delegates in the June primary. Nixon wisely recognized the folly of bucking, with such a phantom slate, the organization headed by Warren, Knowland, and the *Los Angeles Times,* but he made a deal to join the Warren slate on condition that he be allowed to select twenty-three of its members. At the 1948 convention in Philadelphia, as a very junior congressman, he had watched the convention from the galleries, but in 1952 he could not only lay claim to a place on the state delegation but make certain that loyal supporters like Pat Hillings and Joe Holt were also there to protect his interests.

Warren's hopes at this time lay in a possible deadlock between the Eisenhower and Taft supporters. It was essential to his plan that the big California delegation show no preference for either of the leading candidates; otherwise, word that it was ready to shift might tip the balance in advance. Nixon, however, felt that Warren's chances were remote. And it is one of the facts of California's political history that he did not consider himself indebted to Warren. In the 1946 campaign the governor had refused to endorse Nixon and actually had written several friendly letters to Voorhis. Again, in the 1950 race, Warren had refused to help him against Mrs. Douglas, except for an oblique and belated endorsement.

In the horse trading leading up to the convention, Paul Hoffman, as one of Eisenhower's chief lieutenants, conferred twice with Nixon, once in the spring and again shortly before the convention when Nixon and Chotiner were together. Hoffman's objective was to win the votes of the California delegation on the second ballot if it appeared that Eisenhower needed only a few votes to win and that Warren's cause was hopeless. Since California came early in the roll call, a break there might be psychologically crucial. The Eisenhower forces knew that, if Warren released the delegation, they would have 52 votes to Taft's 18.

During this same period Herbert Brownell also had let it be known at a Gridiron dinner that vice-presidential lightning could strike Nixon in return for the latter's support within the California delegation. Chotiner made no secret of his preference for Eisenhower, but the senator, maintaining the same noncommittal pose that had served him from the beginning of the intrigue, was content to let it be inferred that he stood ready to switch at the first opportunity.

At that time Hoffman also conferred with Senator Knowland, Warren's right-hand man, but wholly without success. It was known that Knowland had been offered second place on a Taft ticket if he would throw his support to the Ohio senator on the second ballot. It was likewise known that Knowland disagreed with Governor Warren on some points and at some junctures. Nevertheless, despite the pressures on him, Knowland remained loyal to Warren and refused to be seduced by either Taft or Eisenhower forces.

Nixon, on the other hand, was careful to leave himself room to maneuver. In a San Francisco broadcast just before the June primary at which the delegation was chosen, Nixon declared:

"I have constantly stated that the Republican convention should select the very strongest possible nominee at Chicago. . . . It appears that Senator Taft and General Eisenhower will both go to Chicago with slightly over 500 delegates committed to them. It takes 604 to nominate. A much stronger candidate is Governor Warren. The California delegation with its 70 votes therefore holds the key to the situation. If the convention does not turn to Governor Warren, our delegation will be in a position to throw our vote to the candidate who will be selected."

To follow up this masterly piece of equivocation, Nixon conducted a private poll of California sentiment. On June 11 he mailed 23,000 letters to his 1950 precinct workers, asking them to name not their second choice but "the strongest candidate the Republicans could nominate for president." Whether the Eisenhower Citizens Committee paid, as charged, for printing and addressing this straw vote, evidence exists that Nixon did use his Senate franking privilege to cover mailing costs. Later when Murray Chotiner was questioned about Nixon's use of free government postage for political purposes, he refused to say the story was untrue, but only insisted that "the whole situation someone is trying to create is ridiculous."

When the Warren forces learned of the Nixon canvass, they interpreted it as a stab in the back, a deliberate attempt to undercut the governor's position. Even if Warren came out ahead, it would do nothing to strengthen his position as a favorite son; on the other hand, if he failed to win, it would be a crushing psychological blow. Warren's fears were confirmed when news began to "leak" from Washington that Eisenhower was running far in front. At that stage, Bernard Brennan, a veteran Republican trouble shooter who was a close political associate of Warren and who had headed Nixon's 1950 campaign organization in southern California, was rushed to Washington by plane; there he was able to persuade Nixon not to publish the results of the plebiscite. It was a question, of course, whether the damage had not already been done.

II

As a member of the resolutions committee, Nixon went to Chicago July 1, a week before the convention was to meet. This gave him a chance to watch preconvention maneuvers and take soundings with state leaders, many of whom were indebted to him for his appearances at party pep rallies in 1951. What he saw convinced him there would be no Eisenhower-Taft deadlock, and therefore no hope for the Warren strategy.

What happened after that has been a subject of bitter controversy. The California delegation had left Sacramento July 3 for the train ride halfway across the continent. The atmosphere was one of gaiety, with the governor's daughters dancing in the lounge car to the pounding of a piano, and with patriots in a light-hearted mood celebrating the Glorious Fourth with firecrackers and cap pistols.

At 9:30 on the evening of July 4, the mood changed. When the train paused at Denver, it took on another passenger, Richard Nixon, who had flown in from Chicago, full of convention gossip. In a matter of minutes, the train seethed with rumors that California's strategy must be changed or it would be "left at the post." The Eisenhower bandwagon could not be stopped, so the argument ran, and if California moved quickly so as not to waste its votes, it would be in a position to suggest as a quid pro quo the choice of Nixon as vice-president.

Ill feeling ran high; there was even talk of denying the state's junior senator a berth on the train. By the time the special reached Chicago, the delegation was split wide open. In the eyes of loyal Warrenites, Nixon's tactics constituted deliberate sabotage. From first to last the contention of pro-Nixonites was that the senator thought Warren should know exactly how the convention was shaping up, since his only chance to gain major recognition for California in party affairs was to release the delegation at the tactically correct moment. Nixon carefully avoided newsmen's questions about his part in the affair by dropping off at a suburban station fifteen minutes before the train pulled into the Chicago loop.

Whatever the truth about the campaign-train intrigue, relations between Nixon and the governor's forces deteriorated rapidly.

The pro-Nixon version was that the senator, unable to get any information from Warren headquarters, struck out for himself "to do the best he could." The pro-Warren view was that Nixon double-crossed the governor and devoted his energies solely to the advancement of his own fortunes.

The senator consolidated his chances for the vice-presidential nomination under circumstances that deepened latent antagonisms in the hierarchy. The cleavage showed clearly for the first time in the fight over the Langlie "fair play" resolution, a move to outflank the Taft forces by denying sixty-eight Southern delegates whose seats were contested the right to vote on which delegations should be seated. The effect of the Langlie proposal would be to unseat Taft delegations from Texas, Georgia, and Louisiana on the plea that Taft's forces had gained control of these delegations by corrupt means, and to seat three pro-Eisenhower delegations instead.

The California delegation caucused to get a consensus. It was recognized that, if the Langlie resolution was adopted, the Taft forces would suffer a serious and perhaps even fatal setback. In that case Warren's last hope of a convention deadlock would vanish. Leaders of the California delegation were well aware of the implications of the vote, and Knowland, stubbornly loyal to his Warren pledge, felt that California should split its vote so as to keep Warren's chances alive.

It was at this crucial juncture that Nixon showed his hand publicly for the first time. Dashing to the microphone and summoning his talents as an orator, he pleaded the moral issue. Practical politicians, including Taft himself, were aware that there was no moral issue at all; the question was one of political power and expediency, of a choice between a lesser and a greater evil. Nevertheless, Nixon took the position that, if Knowland refused to yield, both he and Warren would be guilty of cynically splitting the difference on a matter of ethics.

"I feel that any candidate who is nominated for President of the United States," he told the caucus, "would have far greater difficulty in winning in November with those contested Taft delegates than otherwise." In reply to pleas that the convention should accept the majority opinion of the credentials committee, he objected: "If we were to feel that we were bound automatically to accept the decisions of our committees here, there would be no reason for us to come to the convention at all. We could leave the nomination entirely up to committees."

Nixon's appeal crystallized sentiment; the delegation voted 57 to 8 in favor of casting the state's unit vote for the "fair play" resolution. From that moment the drift toward Eisenhower became a stampede, and Nixon's future was assured.

Until the last transcendent moment of triumph, there is only one other fleeting glimpse of Nixon on the convention stage. Just before General Douglas MacArthur delivered the keynote address, Congressman Hillings passed along an order to the California delegation:

"Don't cheer or applaud the general—in case of a big ovation, he might become a compromise candidate for President. This is orders from headquarters."

Delegates assumed that "headquarters" meant Warren, and most of them obeyed. Among the handful that ignored the instructions were some who lost no time in demanding an explanation. In this way Warren learned of the order issued by Hillings, who was angrily upbraided; Hillings in turn revealed that the "orders" came from Nixon, whose fertile imagination had conceived the stratagem and thereby overreached itself. The immediate sequel was that Nixon was barred from the inner conference rooms in the Warren headquarters.

III

Eisenhower was nominated July 11 on the first ballot.

At midafternoon the convention recessed until 6:30 p.m., and two secret strategy meetings were called to settle the question of the vice-presidency. There was a kind of rhythmically paced pantomime in what followed.

Weeks beforehand Nixon's name had begun cropping up in political columns, and at one time or another he had been approached by all three factions. Brownell said subsequently that Nixon not only was right geographically, but was the tailor-made bridge between the Eisenhower and Taft factions. He was considered right, moreover, on the two basic domestic issues, corruption and Communist subversion. While remaining nominally aloof, Nixon had settled his status with Dewey in May, at the same time having made it clear to Warren and Knowland that he was prepared to support Eisenhower when opportunity permitted.

During the convention publisher John Knight of the *Chicago Daily News* had said flatly in his signed column that Nixon would be in second place on the ticket. Senator Lodge, in order to prevent strategic defections, had felt it necessary to issue a statement that vice-presidential possibilities were not being discussed at Eisenhower headquarters, but Reston of *The New York Times* flatly called this a "strategic denial" after a careful check indicated that Eisenhower personally was impressed with Nixon, and his managers saw great advantages in having the Californian on the ticket.

On July 10, Nixon had again been sounded out unofficially, but he continued to dismiss hints of this kind with the observation that he was willing but "such things don't happen." Privately, however, matters had gone beyond the stage of coyness. The Nixons spent most of the night of July 10 in their room with Chotiner, going over and over the question of whether he should accept "if this thing is offered to me." The objections, such as they were, came from Pat Nixon, but there was nothing but encouragement from Chotiner, who argued pragmatically that Nixon had nothing to lose from defeat and everything to gain from victory.

It was under these circumstances that the first of the two caucuses took place July 11 in General Eisenhower's suite at the Blackstone Hotel. Present were the members of the "inner circle"—Governor Dewey, Senator Lodge, Herbert Brownell, Arthur Summerfield, and Senator Carlson. Eisenhower demurred when asked to name his preference for the vice-presidency, but finally gave them a list containing seven names in approximately this order: Nixon, Lodge, Governor Thornton, Governor Langlie, Governor Driscoll, Knowland, and Stassen.

The second meeting, immediately afterward, at which some thirty or forty weary leaders of the Eisenhower movement showed up, took place across the street at the Conrad Hilton Hotel. These were the men who had carried the burden of the struggle for months. They were bone-tired. As chairman and spokesman of the preconvention campaign organization, Lodge called the meeting to order. Dewey did not appear, but among those who joined the group were J. Russell Sprague, New York national committeeman, former Senator Sinclair Weeks of Massachusetts, Senator James H. Duff and Governor John S. Fine of Pennsylvania, Arthur Summerfield, Sherman Adams, Governor John Lodge of Connecticut, Paul Hoffman, Brownell, Barak T. Mattingly of St. Louis, and Roy Roberts, president of the *Kansas City Star.*

While the earlier meeting of the inner circle had been in progress, Senator Taft had telephoned to say that he had a commitment to Senator Everett Dirksen of Illinois and wanted to propose his name. Dewey, who had been the target of a vitriolic attack by Dirksen the previous day, had scowled, and the subject was dropped. At the larger meeting the first name proposed was that of Taft himself, together with an assurance that he would accept. There was a silence. Sprague said heavily that he could assure them the Republicans could not carry New York with Taft on the ticket. Another in the group said he had been asked to propose Dirksen's name; the Illinois senator was vetoed flatly by the governor of Iowa and there was no discussion.

Conversation throughout was desultory. Most of those in the room were exhausted. After a silence Nixon's was the third name tossed into the hopper. No one offered objection, and Hoffman, as chief spokesman for the Citizens for Eisenhower movement, was invited to put his group on record.

"I told them that everything I had heard about Senator Nixon was good," the former ECA chief said later. "I looked on him as one of the Republicans who had an enlightened view on foreign affairs, and I thought that a man of his views should run with General Eisenhower."

Hoffman inferred that the Dewey forces were prepared to make a fight for Nixon if necessary, but a consensus developed without debate. Eisenhower's list of seven was not produced or mentioned. The choice of Nixon was dictated in the end not so much by party wheelhorses in a smoke-filled room (although it was that too), but by the logic of events.

The U. S. Chamber of Commerce, starting in 1946 with the "Had Enough?" slogan, had compounded an issue out of communism and corruption. Its line was accepted as the last desperate hope of the GOP. Nixon was not only geographically right, but he was ideologically right. He was associated with anticommunism because of his role in the Hiss case; he had identified himself with the anticorruption issue by his part in the Senate inquiry into Democratic National Chairman William Boyle and Republican National Chairman Guy Gabrielson. He was young, had a good war record, and his 1950 plurality had been the largest of any senator elected that year. He had just the right attributes for the hustings in a year like 1952 as the running mate of a national war hero who was the image, not of politics, but of patriotism and integrity.

Once it became clear that Nixon was generally acceptable, the members of the caucus made it unanimous, cheered their own decision, and got back word from General Eisenhower, "That's fine with me."

While his future was being thus decided, Nixon, who had been up most of the previous night, had left the convention hall with Chotiner and Brennan and gone to a room at the nearby Stockyards Inn for a sandwich and a brief rest. He was dozing, shirtless and unshaven, when the telephone rang at 3:45 p.m. In a pause after he answered, Nixon heard Brownell's voice speaking in thrilling accents into another phone.

"Hello, General," the voice said, "I wanted to tell you that the committee has unanimously agreed on Nixon."

Immediately thereafter Brownell repeated the news to the thirty-nine-year-old senator from California and concluded, "Can you get over right away, Dick? The general would like to see you."

Nixon threw on his rumpled clothes, borrowed a car from the motor pool, and picked up a motorcycle escort complete with screaming sirens for the trip to the Blackstone. The meeting with the general was hardly more than a formality. However dazzled by the sudden turn of events, Nixon had no hesitancy in assuring Eisenhower that he would be "proud and happy" to join his crusade.

The sequel was ceremonial. By 5:30 he was back in the convention hall, still needing a shave, still in his wrinkled convention suit, but flushed with excitement as he responded to the cheers of the delegates.

In spare moments Nixon scribbled notes for his acceptance speech in a leather-bound notebook carried in his wallet—notes that he did not get to use when the moment came. By that time he had been joined by his wife, who had been getting a solitary snack at one of the convention restaurants when the news of his selection was first flashed.

To preserve the appearance of party harmony in California, Knowland made the nominating speech, and there were seconding speeches by Governor Alfred E. Driscoll of New Jersey and Governor Frank A. Barrett of Wyoming. On a motion by Governor Fine of Pennsylvania, it was Nixon by acclamation, the storybook climax of the American schoolboy's dream.

IV

In Nixon's debut on the national scene, notwithstanding the elements of high drama, there was one morbid overtone, a factor calculated to serve his immediate ends but fated to haunt his political career long afterward. It was the argument that beat Taft, the hoarse assurance of the convention touts that Taft could not win. This was a whisper that had been circulated for months. It finally took root, just as it had taken root more than a century earlier when Henry Clay hammered in rage and frustration against the same deeply felt but irrational belief.

There were probably a majority of convention delegates in 1952 who saw nothing in General Eisenhower to command their trust, who owed Taft both love and loyalty, but who were supporting the general because they had been sold on the Taft-can't-win slogan. To many of them Eisenhower was, as Rovere put it, a "parvenu, an amateur, a boob, and a heretic of sorts." It was part of Nixon's destiny to belong spiritually to Taftism but to join in repudiating what his instincts taught him to embrace. Had he done otherwise, he could not have been Vice-President. In his acceptance speech, tacitly acknowledging this inner conflict, he lauded Taft as "one of the really great senators" and pointed out that Republican victory at the polls in November would give Taft a place of power in the highest councils of government.

The irony of Nixon's position came to be appreciated only in later years when he pre-empted on the national stage the place that Taft vacated, and when his own name took the place of Taft's in the morbid refrain. He himself had told friends early in 1952, "I don't say Taft can't win, but I do say that I'm not sure he can win." As time went on, the stronger Nixon's place in the Republican hierarchy, the oftener was heard the whispered caution: "The question is whether Nixon can win."

CHAPTER IX

————◆————

The National Hustings

I

Except for a historical fluke—the expense-fund affair—Nixon's part in the 1952 campaign might have run true to the Throttle-bottom tradition. Although he had the makings of a better-than-average campaigner, he was still only a candidate for Vice-President. To this political reality he accommodated himself without quibble. Eisenhower became in his lexicon "the top guy."

But from the first, in terms of issues and ideology, the campaign fitted him like an old shoe. He had cultivated the party wheelhorses of the GOP and knew their thinking as they knew his. He had spent six years cataloguing and sharpening and testing the points at which the Democrats were vulnerable. He had rehearsed the techniques of sloganeering and the mass manipulation of public feeling.

In the 1952 campaign Nixon was a finished technician, as those who saw him in action were quick to acknowledge. Professionals might analyze his performance in terms of showmanship and a masterly sense of crowd psychology, but for the ordinary grass-roots auditor the overwhelming impression was one of passionate sincerity. On the platform, with his dark hair, dark eyes, beetling black eyebrows, and heavy jaws, he was the embodiment of dedicated tenacity. His voice was low and vibrant except when he laced into the opposition, and then it could take on the hard metallic bite of an avenging prosecutor. He seldom smiled, but when he did smile to put people at ease, his manner was charmingly, boyishly ingratiating.

Though not quite six feet tall, Nixon was built like an athlete, well proportioned and rugged. For years in college and during campaigns and periods of pressure he had been able to get along on six hours' sleep, catching up with twenty-minute catnaps when occasion offered. He never smoked, ate sparingly on the whole, and seldom drank coffee or liquor.

"Food never has meant much to me—it's incidental," he told an interviewer. "I like hamburger, chili, Spanish dishes, hash and so on, better than steak. I guess I'm not a gourmet."

He threw himself into the campaign with characteristic vigor. The day after his nomination there was a hasty series of protocol and housekeeping sessions in Chicago to chart staff and time schedules. Nixon joined in these private and group sessions with Eisenhower, with Taft, with congressional leaders and national committeemen, with Summerfield, Governor Fine, and others. On his arrival in Washington July 13, he was already dedicated to the "wonderful candidate" he had eulogized in his acceptance speech. He told interviewers: "I want to familiarize myself thoroughly with everything the general has said. I must conduct my own campaign activities in complete harmony with the general."

Although it was agreed that he would carry a heavier burden than most vice-presidential candidates, he insisted he would make no plans until he had talked over everything in detail with Eisenhower. In formulating the issues, however, he showed no hesitation.

The campaign battleground, he declared even before the Democrats had nominated Adlai Stevenson and John Sparkman, would be the Truman record and "communism at home and abroad."

Before taking his family to California for a short vacation, Nixon set up his own headquarters in the Washington Hotel. There he installed Murray Chotiner as his national campaign manager, with a staff consisting of George MacKinnon, Ruth Arnold, Glenard P. Lipscomb, and Edward A. ("Ted") Rogers, the last-named a television director on leave from his job as assistant manager of the Hollywood office of the Dancer-Fitzgerald-Sample advertising agency.

Two weeks later, July 27, en route to California, Nixon stopped off in Colorado for his first strategy huddle with Eisenhower. That visit proved to be mainly window dressing. It was Sunday, and after driving from Denver out to Fraser where Ike was fishing in relative seclusion, Nixon got little more than a desultory and unsuccessful lesson in trout fishing. Then, with scarcely a pause, Nixon spoke at a civic reception in San Francisco, at a Republican convention in Columbus, Ohio, at a harmony rally of the California state central committee in Sacramento, and at the Illinois State Fair in Springfield.

Early in August he flew back to Denver, where the Eisenhower headquarters had been established on the second floor of the Brown Palace Hotel. Nixon installed himself in an eighth-floor headquarters, with a compact staff setup under Congressman Pat Hillings and his secretary, Rose Mary Woods. It was here, in day and night sessions lasting until August 18, that the intensive precampaign planning took place.

Back in Washington August 21, Nixon revealed that the basic strategy evolved at the Denver conferences with Eisenhower was "to stencil Trumanism" on the Democratic nominee. In addition he told the *Kansas City Star,* whose publisher, Roy Roberts, had helped pick him as the nominee, that he had selected four main issues: peace, corruption, communism at home, and the pocketbook. His advisers told the *Star*'s staff writer that there was no question but that the Alger Hiss case would be a major part of the campaign, and there was no reluctance on Nixon's part to elaborate on the Communist issue.

"The administration has dragged its feet," he said, "has condoned corruption and communism until forced to act. . . . The most devastating thing that can be said about the Truman record is that he has lost 600 million people to the Communists. I will repeat that over and over. The administration has failed to develop a program which will bring the security resulting from a real peace. Eisenhower is the only man who can develop such a program. . . .

"There's one difference between the Reds and Pinks. The Pinks want to socialize America. The Reds want to socialize the world and make Moscow the world capital. Their paths are similar; they have the same bible—the teachings of Karl Marx."

And as if to foreshadow what was to be not only the great crisis of the campaign but the greatest crisis in Nixon's life, the

Kansas City Star interviewer reported: "The Californian said he and his wife, *with no other sources of income except his salary as senator,* are as familiar as most Americans are with the household budget crimp resulting from 'the twin pincers of high taxes and high prices.' " (Italics supplied.)

Even before the campaign got under way, McCarthyism was a sensitive issue. Nixon made an effort on August 22 to hedge by telling William S. White of *The New York Times* that, in advance of the Wisconsin primary, he would not endorse either "the views or the methods" of Senator McCarthy if he were to speak in the state. Reaction in Republican circles to this cautious disavowal was so violent, however, that Nixon found it necessary to say in a public statement that he and General Eisenhower believed the Republicans must gain control of Congress "to carry through the program of cleaning up the mess in Washington." He then laid down the party policy in these words:

"This means we must elect sufficient congressmen and senators to organize the Congress. For that reason I intend to campaign in the various states . . . for the election of Republican nominees —this means all states where I campaign."

Most of what followed was foreshadowed in the preliminary warm-up. The heat of battle produced no real innovations. There was an understanding with Eisenhower that the general would build his appeal principally on the moral plane. Nixon was left at the unheroic level of "practical" politics, with the task of deflating the opposition, of hammering away in his best *ad hominem* style at Democratic weaknesses. Thus, for pupils of the Chotiner persuasion, the GOP had it both ways—a campaign that, high and low, covered the whole political rainbow from the pot of gold to the kitchen sink.

Nixon stated the position frankly September 2 when he launched a four-day trial run at Bangor, Maine. Warning that he would make "Communist subversion and corruption the theme of every speech from now until the election," he added grimly: "If the record itself smears, let it smear. If the dry rot of corruption and communism, which has eaten deep into our body politic during the past seven years, can only be chopped out with a hatchet—then let's call for a hatchet."

In a series of hard-hitting speeches in New England, he proceeded to reject the idea of a "nicey-nice little powder-puff duel";

to chide Stevenson for "referring to the Communist menace in America as phantoms"; to charge that for every administration scandal that had been revealed "there are ten which haven't yet been uncovered"; to assert that respect for public servants "can only be restored by a thorough housecleaning of the sticky-fingered crew now contaminating the national capital"; to declare that General Eisenhower had pledged himself to try to "liberate" Iron Curtain nations while Stevenson had offered nothing more than a "negative policy of containment"; and to warn that the American people would condemn themselves to "ultimate national suicide" if they voted to continue the Democratic administration in power.

II

Having concluded some forty speeches on his New England tryout, Nixon paused briefly in Washington to consolidate his itinerary, and on September 17 was again in California after another flying visit to Eisenhower in Denver.

By that time, General Eisenhower was beating the drums of probity, promising with puritanical zeal to end "shady and shoddy" government by driving "crooks and cronies" out of Washington. Nixon himself was getting extra mileage at rallies out of his charge that Truman's had become a "scandal-a-day" administration.

Ahead of Nixon on his return to the West Coast was a major whistle-stop tour of fifty cities in eleven Western states, a tour that he began the next morning by declaring the Truman administration had refused or failed to do anything effective about a "dangerous fifth column," a "ruinous tide of inflation," and a "cancerous condition" of dishonesty in public office.

That same day, September 18, as Nixon chugged placidly up the San Joaquin Valley, the crisis over his private expense fund broke. It was heralded by a full-page *New York Post* headline reading:

SECRET
NIXON
FUND

In substance the story reported that, during his term in the Senate, a group of Californians representing major business interests had contributed $18,235, or about $870 a month, to help pay political expenses that Nixon would otherwise have had to pay out of his own pocket.

It is one of the anomalies of contemporary politics that the fund affair has not since ceased to be a controversial subject, yet in all the vehemence of charge and countercharge, no one ever attempted to deny the facts. The money *was* collected and disbursed exactly as the original story alleged.

Nevertheless, *Look* magazine called it the beginning of a "smear campaign without parallel," long after it had become evident that the only possible "smear" addressed itself to the ethical question whether a public servant ought to be supported under any circumstances by such a subsidy. If the ethical question has validity, it is timeless, a fact which may explain why, like Macbeth's "damned spot," it will not "out" with the passage of time. It is for this reason that the circumstances surrounding the revelation deserve a place in the permanent record.

The story had its beginning with a disgruntled Republican, a Los Angeles county official who had found himself pressured into contributing to the fund and who grew weary of the exactions. Early in September 1952 he took his story to Dan Green, pro-Democratic publisher of the *Independent Review.* Green in turn tipped off three Los Angeles reporters, Ernest Brashear of the *Los Angeles Daily News,* Leo Katcher of the *New York Post,* and Richard Donovan of *The Reporter,* who undertook to document the story. By the time they had traced the fund to the bank on which checks were drawn and inspected some of the canceled checks, they were ready to confront the fund's trustee, Dana C. Smith, a Los Angeles lawyer who had for several years helped handle Nixon's campaign finances.

Brashear had of course discussed with superiors on the *News* his efforts to run down the story, and he had every reason to expect them to welcome it, since the *News* was supporting Adlai Stevenson. However, the general manager, Robert Smith, with a major scoop well within his grasp, chose for reasons of his own to share the story; he arranged that word of the fund's existence be relayed to Peter Edson, nationally syndicated and highly respected columnist of the Newspaper Enterprise Association, a subsidiary of the pro-Eisenhower Scripps-Howard chain. In this manner, a journalistic cross current was set in motion.

On Sunday, September 14, Edson was a member of a panel interviewing Nixon on "Meet the Press." As it happened, he had already heard rumors about the fund before Smith's tip reached him, so after the broadcast he asked the senator privately to tell him about "the fund we hear about." Nixon took the question in stride and referred Edson to Dana Smith; next day the columnist put in a long-distance call, got the facts from Smith, and wrote a straightforward, noncommittal account of it that went out in the mail September 17.

From the point of view of public-relations handlers, who are inclined to measure successes in terms of one-upmanship, this release of the bare bones of the story in Edson's column before anything else had appeared in print constituted a perverse kind of vindication, a sufficient evidence of good faith. Any subsequent publication in "hostile" form could therefore be interpreted as an attempt to distort the facts for malicious reasons. From that point of view an inquiry going beyond the facts into motives or into ethical values was nothing more than a base political "smear."

Meanwhile, on Monday, September 15, the day after Edson spoke to Nixon in New York and forty-eight hours before his column was distributed, Brashear, Katcher, and Donovan visited Dana Smith, confronted him with their documentation, and expressed an interest in hearing the rest of the story. At that time Smith had already heard from Edson, and according to Donovan he was glad to talk about the senator, about the philosophy that went into the building of the special fund, and about the desire of Nixon's wealthy sponsors not to "own a senator" but to "see that Dick" was denied none of the things that a senator's station in life required.

Smith explained with impeccable candor that the donors had no selfish designs on their candidate. For years, he said, the government had been selling centralized control of all phases of American life, and individualists had been rendered impotent at the polls.

"Our thinking," said Smith, "was that we had to fight selling with selling, and for that job Dick Nixon seemed to be the best salesman against socialization available. That's his gift, really— salesmanship."

One of the reporters asked whether Governor Warren did not have similar qualifications.

"Frankly," Smith said, "Warren has too much of the other point of view, and he never has gone out selling the free-enterprise system. But Dick did just what we wanted him to do."

Smith explained that the contributors to the fund had elected to back Nixon after convincing themselves that he had a "sound" voting record in the House and seemed to have a grasp of original American political and economic principles.

"After Nixon's election [to the Senate]," Smith said, "we did not stop thinking about him. We realized that his salary [$12,500 plus a tax-free $2,500 for expenses] was pitifully inadequate for a salesman of free enterprise trying to do a job for his people in California. We took the position that we had got Dick into this and that we were going to see him through.

"He told us he needed money for such things as long-distance phone calls, for ten thousand Christmas cards, for airmail stamps on thousands of letters that couldn't be franked, for recordings that could be used on free radio time in California but that cost something to make, and for trips to California—he ought to make the trip at least three or four times a year.

"Well," said Smith in conclusion, "between the time of his election to the Senate and his nomination as Vice-President, we gave him between $16,000 and $17,000, which I disbursed." (The exact amount turned out to be $18,168.87.)

And Smith summed up the results from his point of view with a smile.

"Here we had a fine salesman who didn't have enough money to do the kind of selling job we wanted, so we got together and took care of some of those things. Between fifty and a hundred people put up the money, and we put a limit of five hundred dollars per person on the amount anyone could give in a single year . . . just so no one could say that we were buying a senator."

When the names were finally made public, there proved to be seventy-six contributors, including Herbert Hoover, Jr., who later served an unhappy hitch as Undersecretary of State.

These were the ingredients of the story as it made its first appearance September 18 in the *New York Post*. Only six other dailies in the United States published the story simultaneously, two of them using Edson's column. As a footnote on journalistic history, and a commentary on the resilience of political loyalties, the *Los Angeles Daily News* suppressed its own story and buried

Edson's on an inside page. On Friday the 19th, according to a survey of seventy leading dailies, five were still suppressing the story entirely, while fourteen of the remaining sixty-five were content to keep it tucked out of sight on inside pages. Some ardently Republican newspapers carried their crusading zeal for purification so far as to break into print with denials and explanations before they published the original account of the fund.

After the uncertainty of the first twenty-four hours, the fund story mushroomed into a national sensation. Some apologists for Nixon have pleaded that editors were slow to grasp the significance of the story, hence the delayed reaction; others have tried to infer that the story was intrinsically devoid of public interest and that it had to be built up in some presumably sinister way by the press. Such pleadings ignore two factors: the instinctive self-interest of the 690 newspapers supporting Eisenhower in hushing up anything resembling scandal; and the concomitant self-interest of the Democratic party in exploiting the story, whatever its merits. It took time for these opposing forces to assert and align themselves. Actually, the expense-fund story might never have reached nine out of ten voters had not the radio and television networks fulfilled the function that a free press forsook.

First word that the fund story was to be published reached the Nixon special at midnight, the 17th, shortly after his kickoff speech at Pomona, but a hurriedly called conference in the senator's private car led Rogers, Chotiner, and the staff to dismiss it as of no consequence. Next morning the first hint of trouble came when more newsmen, smelling a story, boarded the special. By early afternoon on the 18th, after secluding himself from the press all day, Nixon felt it advisable to issue a short statement outlining his version of the affair.

By Friday tensions were building up ominously. Welcoming delegations at way stations showed signs of skittishness. Telegrams and phone calls reached the special in increasing numbers, asking questions, offering advice. One California newspaper, the independent *Sacramento Bee,* was ready with an editorial stating the issue in icily challenging terms:

> The man who the people of the sovereign state of California believed was actually representing them is the pet and protege of a special interest group of rich Southern Californians. To put it more

bluntly, Nixon is their subsidized front man, if not, indeed, their lobbyist.

Under these pressures Nixon grew edgy. He had heard nothing from the Eisenhower special, and all his political training argued for closing ranks in the face of danger. In this frame of mind his first public reaction to criticism, as painted in a colorful word picture in the *Los Angeles Examiner,* was shrill and tendentious. Early Friday afternoon, whistle-stopping at Marysville, standing in the bright sunshine, Nixon exclaimed in excitement as the election special was about to pull out, "I heard that question, over there," pointing to a heckler.

The getaway whistle blew, but the senator cried, "Hold the train! Hold the train!" The engineer got the signal and Nixon went on, "I heard that question. He said, 'Tell them about the $16,000.' "

The crowd yelled and the candidate continued, "You folks know I did the work of investigating the Communists in the United States. Ever since I have done that work, the Communists and the left-wingers have been fighting me with every smear they have had.

"I want you folks to know something. I'm going to reveal it today for the first time.

"After I received the nomination for the vice-presidency, I was warned that if I continued to attack the Communists and crooks in this administration, they would smear me, and, believe me, you can expect that they will continue to do so.

"They started it yesterday. They said I had taken money— $16,000. What they didn't point out was this: what I was doing was saving you money. The expenses of my office were in excess of the amounts allowed under the law. Rather than using the taxpayers' money for these expenses, what did I do?

"What I did was to have those expenses paid by people back home who were interested in seeing that the information about what was going on in Washington was spread among the people of their state."

The crowd gave him a big hand. Nixon, talking rapidly and with full voice, went on.

"What else would you have had me do? I'll tell you what some of them do. They put their wives on the payroll. That's what Sparkman did. I don't believe in putting my wife on the payroll,

and taking your money and using it for that purpose. I think
most of you will agree on that. Pat Nixon has worked in my office
night after night, and I can say this and say it proudly, she has
never been on the government payroll since I have been in
Washington.

"Would you want me to do what some people are doing?
Take fat legal fees on the side? During the time I have been in
Washington, I have never taken a legal fee, although as a lawyer
I could legally but not ethically have done so. And I'm never
going to do so in the future because I think that's a violation of
a trust which my office has.

"You can be sure that the smears will continue to come, and
the purpose of these smears is to make me, if possible, relent in
my attacks on the Communists and the crooks in the present
administration.

"As far as I am concerned, they've got another guess coming.
What I intend to do is go up and down this land, and the more
they smear me the more I'm going to expose the Communists
and the crooks and those who defend them until they throw them
all out of Washington."

III

News of the Nixon fund reached the Eisenhower campaign
train Thursday as it was rocking westward across Iowa. To avoid
upsetting the general before a major speech, staff members withheld the story from him that day but gave it intensive study. The
implications were not lost on veterans like Adams, Lodge, and
Summerfield—practical politicians all—and at first they took
heart from the lack of local newspaper reaction. However, by the
time the "Look Ahead, Neighbor" special had passed through
Omaha, the rest of the country had begun to be heard from, and
a pall of gloom settled on those in the general's staff who looked
ahead.

The crusade against the "mess in Washington" had been catching on. Being against corruption, anybody's corruption, had all
the orthodoxy and fire of damning war from a bomb shelter. They
had caught the scent of victory, but if theirs turned out to be a
glass house instead of a bomb shelter, if they had in truth a culprit
one step from the top of the ticket, the momentum had obviously
gone out of their drive. If the Democrats could make the imputa-

tion of scandal stand, it might even be that the fire had gone out of Ike's whole campaign.

While the Democrats were calling on the Republicans to drop Nixon, advisers on the Eisenhower special weighed the implications of such a move. A number could see no other course. Telegrams reaching the train ran three to one against Nixon. Some, like Summerfield and Senator Karl Mundt, were flatly in favor of taking Nixon's side; argued that calling on the Republican national committee at this juncture to pick another nominee would be risking a catastrophic split in the party.

One of those who kept cool, and thereby placed Nixon in his lasting debt, was Sherman Adams. On Friday, while others were urging Eisenhower to hurry up and do something—anything— right away, Adams advised caution. First, to gain time, the general released a statement; facts, he said confidently, would show that the senator "would not compromise with what is right." Adams then telephoned Paul Hoffman in Pasadena, and ordered him to put fifty men onto an immediate analysis of the legal and financial aspects of the fund. Finally, to have a standby within reach if the worst should come, he phoned Senator Knowland in Hawaii and asked him to join the Eisenhower special at once.

While the debate swelled, Eisenhower, after Friday's *pro forma* release, clamped his jaws in silence, shrinking from an act of judgment, unwilling either to absolve or condemn Nixon by fiat. On the 20th, as the gloomy train neared St. Louis, the general called newsmen together for an off-the-record talk in the press car. Alluding to a private poll in which the reporters had voted overwhelmingly that Nixon would have to be dropped, and conceding that the fund was by no means a closed incident, the general said he wanted all fair-minded people to be convinced, as he was, that the vice-presidential nominee was innocent of anything crooked or unethical.

"I don't care if you fellows are forty to two against me, but I'm taking my time on this," Ike said, thinking back to the Patton incident of World War II. "Nothing's decided, contrary to your idea that this is all a setup for a whitewash of Nixon. Nixon has got to be clean as a hound's tooth."

All the while the hound's-tooth doctrine was taking form, Nixon had been in an agony of suspense. He realized after the first flush of defiance that he was in desperate trouble. It was not enough to debate proprieties with hecklers and trainside skeptics; what he had to deal with was a cargo of doubt as immense as the electorate.

Nixon was faintly incredulous when word of the hound's-tooth doctrine was relayed to him, not so much on moral as on purely pragmatic grounds. In his primer of politics (which in the end turned out to be defective), parties defended their own against all comers, and anything less than unqualified support amounted to perfidy or stupidity or both. Yet in the face of his rage and stupefaction, he could see the base of his support being eroded. The *New York Herald Tribune* called for his withdrawal from the ticket, and the *Washington Post* likewise. The press as a whole was lining up two to one against him. Stassen wired, advising him to resign for the good of the party, and Dewey, reporting a growing consensus that Nixon should step aside, agreed that the senator's only chance lay in a successful television report to the country.

It was Sunday the 21st before a plan for handling the crisis was agreed on. After four days of painful irresolution, Nixon was still sitting tight, still awaiting a call from the head of the ticket, having made up his mind earlier that he would have nothing to gain by haggling with subordinates. During the day in Portland he was by turns despondent and determined. He kept one speaking engagement, and back at the Benson Hotel afterward listened attentively to the arguments pro and con at a succession of staff huddles. In his mind, it was poor politics to talk of resigning; he took the position that, if he got off the ticket, the force of the Eisenhower crusade would be mortally undercut; and to remain as the nominee without destroying the momentum of the GOP campaign, he had to have an immediate opportunity to explain and defend his use of the expense fund.

The evening was well advanced before Eisenhower in St. Louis finally telephoned Nixon in Portland. Allowing for self-serving shades of exaggeration and vainglory in subsequent accounts, the senator handled himself adroitly in this conversation. He was at once composed and impatient, deferential and assertive. He offered to withdraw if that was what Ike wanted; he suggested everyone concerned ought to hear his side of the story; he discussed the practical perils of a withdrawal. Finally he delivered a lecture on the folly of procrastination, called for a quick, firm decision, and concluded with an earthy admonition that in politics a time comes when you have to fish or cut bait.

From Eisenhower's point of view, quite clearly, the upshot of the telephone conference was that Nixon either had to be pushed off the ticket—an act of *force majeure* against which the general's whole temperament rebelled—or else had to be given an opportunity to vindicate himself. Nixon's stubbornness therefore led to a long-distance strategy conference between Summerfield and Senator Fred Seaton at the general's headquarters and Chotiner and Rogers at Nixon's. They took their cue from Eisenhower's parting advice to his running mate, "Let's wait and see what all the facts are."

By midnight, what emerged from their talks was a strategy of full disclosure, including a nationwide radio-television appearance by Nixon on Tuesday, the 23rd. Chairman Summerfield had first argued that the party treasury lacked the $75,000 for a broadcast on such a scale—it eventually included some 800 radio and TV outlets on NBC, CBS, and Mutual—and tried to persuade Nixon to use the time of a commercial sponsor. In the end, after three groups of Eisenhower backers had pledged the money, the commitment was made, and eventually enough in the form of small contributions flowed in from listeners to pay the entire cost.

In a series of moves the stage was then set for the broadcast. Dana Smith made public one of the letters soliciting money which he had circulated September 25, 1951, ten months after the fund was set up. A *Los Angeles Times* headline referred to this as the "original letter setting up fund need," and the press generally did not stress the fact that it was an attempt to find new contributors, long after the fund had begun work. This was followed by a list of seventy-six contributors. As a holding action Nixon issued a statement repeating he had "never received one penny of the fund for personal use," and insisting it "represents a normal, legitimate, open matter of permitting constituents actively to support the political activity of a candidate."

The audit of the Dana Smith trusteeship which had been ordered by Hoffman from the top-drawer firm of Price, Waterhouse & Co. certified that the books showed receipts of $18,250 and various travel and public relations expenditures totaling $18,168.87. A legal opinion that had been requested from the law firm of Gibson, Dunn & Crutcher on orders from Adams held that there was no violation of the Corrupt Practices Act.

Nixon and his party flew from Portland to Los Angeles for the broadcast. As the crisis dragged on, Nixon's feelings can only be a matter of conjecture. For the most part he kept his own counsel, a lone wolf in this as in most other aspects of his career; but some on his staff were aware the vice-presidential nominee deeply, powerfully resented Eisenhower's keeping him in suspense. Friends said, "It was hell. We took sleeping tablets at night to get some rest; Benzedrine by day to keep going."

There are political pragmatists, however, who believe it was Eisenhower's timing that turned defeat into victory. Had he rushed forward prematurely with a defense of Nixon, he could not have escaped charges of a partisan whitewash. The result then would have been widespread disillusionment. In the actual event it was the uncertainty about the outcome, and the attendant emotional build-up that gave Nixon his audience of 58,000,000 and made his appeal effective.

Nor was the mood of uncertainty in any respect counterfeit. Dewey telephoned again shortly before air time. He had polled leading figures in the campaign—and by implication Eisenhower himself—and felt impelled to warn Nixon that there was substantial sentiment for his withdrawal. The senator later described the message as a "blockbuster." In a matter of minutes he had to choose between a last-ditch fight and the public humiliation of surrender.

Controversy has surrounded the circumstances under which the broadcast was prepared. Charges were made, as if it really mattered, that there were elaborate staging, rehearsal, and production, but the evidence suggests otherwise. Nixon ignored the bustling that went on all day in the studios and the big advertising agencies under contract to the GOP. He began the day with a swim and a long walk with William P. Rogers, the volunteer assistant who was later to become attorney-general. His board of strategy included, besides Rogers, his manager Murray Chotiner, publicity adviser, James Bassett, Representative Pat Hillings, and Ted Rogers, the radio-television advertising technician on his staff, who made physical arrangements for the broadcast.

At intervals during the day Nixon worked on the outline of his talk, a revised version of which finally covered five sheets of yellow paper in his own handwriting. At four o'clock he was urged to rehearse but refused, and even after his arrival at NBC's El Capitan theater studio with Mrs. Nixon, fifteen minutes before air time, he declined to tell technicians whether he would remain seated throughout. He was explicitly aware, even though others may not have been, that his best prop, his surest ally, was the spontaneity, the suspense, the "sincerity," he had so often advocated for political performers.

He sat down at a table in a stock library set, with his wife in frozen immobility nearby, and when the cue was given, he launched into the most controversial performance of his career.

To sophisticates the "Checkers speech," as it became known, was unbearably corny, the worst of political hokum and soap opera combined. It began with an air of injured innocence— "I come before you tonight . . . a man whose honesty and integrity have been questioned"—and went on using his old mastery of debating techniques to score points with a recital that ran the gamut of classic melodrama: family mortgages . . . borrowed money . . . the purchase of two houses . . . the respectable Republican cloth coat . . . his daughters' little cocker spaniel, Checkers . . . Navy service where the bombs were falling . . . the audit and the legal opinion . . . the unjust accusation . . . the Eisenhower crusade . . . communism . . . the mess in Washington . . . the check for $10 from the young GI's wife . . . the poor little rich boy . . . and finally:

". . . I know that this is not the last of the smears. In spite of my explanation tonight other smears will be made.

". . . I don't believe that I ought to quit, because I am not a quitter. And incidentally Pat is not a quitter . . . but the decision, my friends, is not mine.

". . . For that reason I am submitting to the Republican National Committee tonight through this television broadcast the decision which it is theirs to make. Let them decide whether my position on the ticket will help or hurt.

"And I am going to ask you to help them decide. Wire and write the Republican National Committee whether you think I should stay on or whether I should get off.

". . . and, remember, folks, Eisenhower is a great man. Folks, he is a great man, and a vote for Eisenhower is a vote for what is good for America."

The senator was no sooner off the air than it became apparent that the speech was a political triumph. The sophisticates were in a minority. For the rest of the populace, the high moral tone and the air of candor with which he bared the intimacies of his financial problems proved irresistible. Tens of thousands of telegrams and phone calls jammed the wires and isolated Nixon for hours from the rest of the country. Five days later Republican headquarters in Washington reported the receipt of 300,000 letters and telegrams signed by a million persons and running 350 to 1 in favor of Nixon. Other thousands of messages poured into other Republican centers.

Eisenhower was impressed, but once again he infuriated his running mate by withholding a final blessing. He had watched the telecast in a private room at the Cleveland Public Auditorium where a crowd of 17,000 was waiting to hear him speak. Throwing away his script he faced the crowd that had been chanting, "We want Nixon, we want Nixon," and declared, "I have been a warrior and I like courage. I have seen many brave men in tough situations. I have never seen any come through in better fashion than Senator Nixon did tonight."

Then, instead of slamming the door on the whole controversy, he read the audience a telegram inviting Nixon to meet him for "a face-to-face" talk at Wheeling, West Virginia, to help him "complete the formulation of my personal decision."

"It is obvious," said the general firmly, "that I have to have something more than one single presentation, necessarily limited to thirty minutes, the time allowed Senator Nixon."

Nixon's first reaction to the general's request was an explosive negative. All along he had lived in dread of the spectacle of his being summoned to the bar of judgment. Eisenhower had temporized for five days, unable or unwilling to make up his mind; and to both Nixon and Pat, trapped in the twilight of his irresolution, the strain was unbearable and there seemed no end in sight. Moreover, 107 members of the 138-man Republican national committee who could be contacted in a quick poll had voted unanimously that Nixon should stay on the ticket. That decision, together with the indubitable success of the broadcast, made it from his point of view almost sadistic to keep him on the hook.

When Summerfield finally got through to Los Angeles by telephone, Chotiner informed him that he had just finished tearing up a telegram of resignation for the general. He said Nixon was flying that night, not to Wheeling as the general had asked, but to Missoula, Montana, for his next scheduled speaking engagement. Chotiner assured Summerfield that Nixon would come to Wheeling only on one condition—a guarantee that he was to stay on the ticket and that Ike would use the occasion to reinforce his blessing with a public embrace.

The next morning, the 24th, at dawn, the assurances reached Chotiner in Missoula; and when Nixon's plane landed at Wheeling later that day, it was all over in a matter of minutes. Brushing protocol aside, Ike ran up the ramp, and there followed the denouement that was to become a folklore classic.

"General, you didn't have to do this," said the surprised Nixon.

"Why not?" said Ike, beaming. "You're my boy."

And Nixon, the self-possessed political machine, wept on Senator Knowland's shoulder. The benediction, precious as it was politically, could not at once obliterate the unspeakable humiliation of having been, after all, in the sight of the world, summoned to judgment.

Yet that night Nixon managed to make political hay out of his own seven-day agony. He told the audience at Wheeling a "lesser man" than Eisenhower would have called the charges a smear from the start and would have refused to listen to them.

"Let me say this," said Nixon. "I am glad General Eisenhower didn't do that."

Emphasizing that the general had risked the success of his campaign and his whole political future, Nixon praised him for having said, in effect, "Dick, take your case to the American people; bring out all the facts; tell the truth; and then we will make the decision as to what should be done."

"Folks, if he will do that with me," declared the senator, "just think what he is going to do when he becomes President. It is going to be the cleanest, the most honest government America has ever had."

IV

The fund episode transformed Nixon, in Stewart Alsop's words, "from a youthful would-be Throttlebottom into the really major political figure he has been ever since." Even so, the triumphal telecast did not lay all the ghosts. Notwithstanding his explanation, there remained certain indigestible facts: that real-estate men gave 36 per cent of the fund, manufacturing and distribution interests gave 19 per cent, and oil interests another 19 per cent; and that Nixon's votes on housing, on corporation taxation, on labor, and on oil issues tended uniformly to favor their interests.

In the cold afterglow of the campaign, it was apparent that some of his arguments were specious; some of his facts were subject to challenge; some of his assertions left unanswered questions.

It was specious, for example, to assert as he did that "not one cent . . . went to me for my personal use." Nixon himself told Peter Edson that, had it not been for the fund, he could not have made the down payment on his house in Washington. It stood to reason that the burden of staying in politics had been lifted from Nixon's shoulders by the fund, and his standard of living was thereby conspicuously improved. Other congressmen reserved part of their salaries to pay political expenses. It is wholly irrelevant to say that some members of Congress put their wives on the payroll to get this extra money. This is the classic fallacy *"tu quoque"* (you're another) and does not alter the fact that Nixon was able to maintain a better standard of living than otherwise and thus did indirectly turn the expense fund to his personal use.

It was likewise specious to argue, as Nixon did repeatedly, that his purpose in accepting the gift was to save the taxpayers money. None of the expenses covered by the fund could have been legally charged to the taxpayer. In the Price, Waterhouse audit several items are specifically stated to be "in excess of allowance."

Apropos of the same line of argument, the senator never during the controversy alluded to the fact that his regular office allowance in Congress was $70,000 a year, all of which he spent.

A fundamental question was raised by the statement in Dana Smith's letter of solicitation that the fund would "not provide in any way for people who are 'second guessers' to make any claim on the senator's particular interest."

In effect, the expense fund thus became, not a public subscription open to all well-wishers, as a campaign fund is, but a closed corporation. It was not illogical to ask why the contributors should want to be so exclusive unless they could perceive individual or group interests that the object of their benefactions might serve.

For obvious political reasons the controversy was handled in a way that omitted the key question: Is it morally right for a United States senator to accept gifts from private interests having a large financial stake in matters on which the senator speaks and votes?

Nixon may have been right in assuming that he was guiltless or that his guilt, if any, was not personal but institutional. Congress, while righteously high-minded about conflicts of interest in other branches of government, has been notoriously lax in fixing its own standards. Nixon's simplest defense was to plead that his conduct was no more venal than that of his contemporaries. Moreover, after the Nixon disclosure several other Republican West Coast politicians admitted proudly that they too enjoyed private subsidies.

By a tenuous adaptation of this defense, it became possible to shift the moral issue entirely into the political sphere. Republicans seized upon the fact that Illinois businessmen had contributed to a fund which Governor Stevenson had used to supplement the income of employees who could not otherwise have afforded to work for the state. A second and larger Stevenson fund came to light and was never explained. In the rough and tumble of a political campaign it was easier to cry *tu quoque* than it was to resolve the fundamental ethical values that had been called into question.

Not the least serious aspect of the Checkers broadcast was Nixon's statement that he had never so much as made a telephone call to a federal office on behalf of a fund contributor. The *Washington Star* on September 24, the day after the broadcast, reported that Nixon's office had interceded on behalf of Dana Smith himself in a Justice Department case in which a firm owned by Smith's family was asking a tax rebate of more than half a million dollars. Moreover, the legal opinion from Gibson, Dunn & Crutcher from which he quoted in the Checkers speech acknowledged that, after interviewing "a number of contributors," it had learned that "in two instances the contributor had contacted Nixon to request his assistance in connection with matters pending before a department or agency of the government." Whether these inquiries were in the slightest measure reprehensible was not subsequently determined.

Politicians have an instinctive distrust of abstract moral considerations. The hound's-tooth doctrine as it was applied in the Eisenhower-Nixon crusade distinguished sharply between the abstract and the pragmatic in behavioral values. It defined morality as something different from politics, so that "moral" cleanliness was simply personal and had nothing to do with policy. Nixon was adjudged wholly "honest" by his GOP peers because it was evident that he had not been guilty of anything so crude as a confusion of public and private money. The challenge had not been posed in those terms, and when it was answered in those terms alone, it was not answered at all.

Nixon was not alone in his eagerness to turn away from the moral issue. Eisenhower let the final tableau at Wheeling stand as a symbol of flagrant betrayal. In his Cleveland speech the previous night, reacting to the Checkers extravaganza with spontaneous goodwill, he had assured a nationwide audience that he would obviously need "more than one single presentation of thirty minutes." No one ever again heard a reference to that promise. No one among the millions who heard it was ever told what other "presentation" the general received. The dealers in expediency moved in overnight, and Chotiner carried things off at his end with a high hand. No one has ever been told what unresolved doubts, what high-minded reservations, Eisenhower might have had or what assurances he might have required. So far as the record goes, the rest is silence.

No final assessment of the affair is yet possible. History will write the verdict in the larger terms of Nixon's whole public career. This much is certain. Nixon was not bribed. The fund did not in any conscious way compromise his integrity or independence.

As William V. Shannon summed it up in his biographical sketch: "He was not a man of independent views entering politics in the conventional way and then 'bought off' by the vested interests. This would imply a moral tension and a dramatic fall from virtue which never took place. . . .

"A man can be compromised only if he makes a conscious choice between his own moral standard and that of others. When the standards coincide, there is no need for choice and no sense of guilt. . . . Arthur Balfour, the British statesman, once remarked of an opponent that 'his conscience is not his guide but his accomplice.' It would be melancholy if such a phrase were ever applied to an American President."

So far as the 1952 campaign was concerned, Nixon proved by his conduct in the fund crisis that he was fully entitled to wear his laurels as an accomplished campaigner. Inwardly frightened but sustained by the conviction that he was wholly innocent, he handled himself and his party and press relations with coolness and toughness. He kept the political realities in sane perspective, and he acted on them, when the timing was right, with boldness and adroitness.

Nixon was right in predicting there would be other "smears." Richard Wilson, *Look* magazine's Washington bureau chief, compiled a painstaking documentation early in 1953 on five different efforts that had been made to accuse Nixon of improper conduct. These cases were : (1) a suit against Dana Smith for a gambling debt in which Nixon was falsely accused of being involved; (2) a charge that Nixon had given a false statement in order to chisel on California property taxes, a charge which was shown to be false when investigation disclosed another Richard and Pat Nixon; (3) a statement by the Democratic national committee that the Nixon family owned real estate valued at a quarter of a million dollars, the implication being that Nixon had used his position in public life to acquire valuable real-estate holdings covertly—this story did not stand up under investigation; (4) an attempt to show by means of two forged letters that Nixon received more than $52,000 in 1950 from the oil industry, an intrigue which collapsed when Nixon insisted on a full investigation by a Senate committee; (5) an attempt going back to 1945 to suggest that, while engaged in Navy contract termination work, he had shaken down the ERCO Company for a loan, a story which also collapsed under investigation.

Some of these charges were circulated while the campaign was in progress; others cropped up later. In no case did they have a perceptible effect on the electorate in general.

V

With a one-day rest after the rendezvous at Wheeling, Nixon plunged straight back into the campaign. Starting September 26 at Ogden, Utah, his itinerary took him by chartered airliner across

Colorado and into Oklahoma and Texas. Adhering to the Chotiner dictum that once an attack had been answered the subject should be dropped, Nixon refused to dwell on the fund issue, but pounded away instead at his favorite charges of administration shortcomings.

By now the cynics had coined a new label for his campaign wares: K-1, C-3—so called for Korea, communism, corruption, and controls, his four main topics. Observers noted two changes in the wake of the fund episode: the crowds were more curious and often more enthusiastic, and for a few days Nixon soft-pedaled corruption and gave major emphasis to the Republican issue that seemed to have the greatest popular appeal, the war in Korea.

On Ike's train the high-level treatment of the issues had found itself. As early as September 2 Eisenhower and his speech writer, Emmet Hughes, had joyously hit upon the refrain that was to lend the coloration of good, clean, rollicking moralism to the rest of their campaign—the refrain that Truman's administration had degenerated into one that could only "stumble, fumble, and fall."

Although the rest of the campaign was a downhill run, Nixon maintained a strenuous schedule to the end, making as many as a dozen speeches a day. As a new-found celebrity he began to draw crowds of up to 20,000. A writer for the *Wall Street Journal* said his technique combined "youthful sincerity and charm, a folksy touch and a hard-hitting attack on the Truman administration."

From day to day, through September and October, his speeches varied hardly at all except for a personal tour de force October 13. This was a nationwide television appearance recounting in detail his part in the Alger Hiss investigations of 1948.

For Nixon's friends the speech was exactly what they had been hearing for nearly four years and what they wanted to hear in coast-to-coast accents. For his critics, among them the *Washington Post,* the speech's dominant note was its lack of restraint, its effort to "make the nation's flesh creep." The *Post,* pointing out that all through World War II the War Department continued to draft known Communists, took particular umbrage at Nixon's statement that General Eisenhower "never had an instance of infiltration into his command." The paper, although supporting the Republican ticket, called the senator's remarks "dangerous demagogic nonsense" and reminded him with asperity that his "sudden rise to national prominence is one of those quadrennial accidents that come about because our parties do not take the vice-presidency as seriously as they should."

Nixon used this major broadcast to elaborate on a theme that was part of his stock in trade throughout the campaign, the theme which he summarized in these words:

". . . We can assume because of the cover-up of this administration in the Hiss case that the Communists, the fellow-travelers, have not been cleaned out of the executive branch of the government."

He also dwelt heavily on an issue that he had introduced largely on his own initiative and used with only occasional assistance from others in the party—the fact that Stevenson had filed a deposition as a character witness when Hiss was being tried for perjury. Nixon said, "There is no question in my mind as to the loyalty of Mr. Stevenson," but he contended that the Democratic nominee had disqualified himself for public trust by "going down the line for the arch-traitor of our generation." He charged that Stevenson gave the statement after all the facts were known, that he acted voluntarily, that he used his prestige as governor of Illinois on behalf of Hiss, and that Stevenson had never expressed indignation over Hiss's alleged treachery.

Ten days later he was saying in Minneapolis, "I do not question Mr. Stevenson's right to testify for his friend, Alger Hiss, for I am sure he really believed Hiss was a man of loyalty, veracity, and integrity when he came to his defense in 1949. But Mr. Stevenson was dead wrong. . . . If Stevenson were to be taken in by Stalin as he was by Hiss, the Yalta sell-out would look like a great American diplomatic triumph by comparison."

In the minds of Democrats especially, these were dirty blows. Stevenson and Hiss could scarcely have been called "friends." The governor had known Hiss briefly in 1933 in the Department of Agriculture, in 1945 at the United Nations Charter conference, and in 1946 and 1947 in connection with duties at the United Nations. They had never visited each other's homes. When Stevenson was asked by a United States commissioner to give an affidavit—at the same time that Justices Reed and Frankfurter and a number of other leading men were asked for statements—

he was aware that he could either make a statement voluntarily or be forced to do so by subpoena.

Nevertheless, as the leading architect of the K-1, C-3 formula, Nixon showed no scruples about employing this variant of the basic attack. He developed other and more direct variations of the central theme. He called Stevenson "a weakling, a waster, and a small-caliber Truman" who had been put in the Illinois governor's mansion by a political organization infested with "mobsters, gangsters, and remnants of the old Capone gang." He referred to him as "Adlai the appeaser . . . who got a Ph.D. from Dean Acheson's College of Cowardly Communist Containment."

In the month leading up to the election, he charged that:

"Adlai Stevenson, if elected . . . would continue the policy of appeasement. . . ."

". . . Every problem facing this country is connected with the Truman administration's failure to deal with the threat of communism."

". . . The word of Truman and Acheson, as well as that of Acheson's former assistant, Adlai Stevenson, gives the American people no hope for safety at home from the sinister threat of communism."

"I charge that the buried record will show that Mr. Truman and his associates, either through stupidity or political expedience, were primarily responsible for the unimpeded growth of the Communist conspiracy within the United States. I further charge that Mr. Truman, Dean Acheson and other administration officials for political reasons covered up this Communist conspiracy and attempted to halt its exposure."

What these words conveyed to Nixon must remain problematical; the inference, from the fact that he continued unabashed with this line of attack, is that he interpreted them as professional political brickbats, nothing more. His opponents took a much more embittered view. To them, his sleight-of-hand juggling of words conveyed an impression that Truman, Stevenson, and the Democrats generally had been guilty of treason.

Nixon apologists have always denied this, and it is true that the record contains no instance in which the senator went as far as his contemporary, McCarthy, did. However, for Truman,

Speaker Rayburn, and other leading Democrats, Nixon's use of innuendo was unforgivable, and they held he went too far on at least one occasion. That was at Texarkana, October 27, 1952, when, according to an Associated Press dispatch, he told a Texas-Arkansas crowd: ". . . that President Truman and Adlai Stevenson are 'traitors to the high principles' of the Democratic party. He said they tolerated and defended Communists in the government."

There is general agreement that Nixon, so far as his own party and its candidates were concerned, played not only an energetic but a percipient role in the '52 campaign. The ballots on November 4 gave the Republican ticket 33,936,234 votes, or 55.1 per cent of the total, compared with Stevenson's 27,314,992 votes. To the victors went thirty-nine states and 442 electoral votes.

It was wholly an Eisenhower victory, as witness the hairline margin by which Republicans took control of House and Senate, but to Nixon followers it had other portents. He had come a long way in six years, and the White House stood squarely across his horoscope.

His campaign methods, after his emergence on the national stage, were more rather than less bitterly controversial. From the vantage point of 1956, *Newsweek*'s analysts reported that the Checkers broadcast, although regarded as a triumph at the time, had come to be viewed by Washington political theorists as a case of winning the battle and losing the war. Conceding that the conflict of interest was equivocal and that Congress as an institution was no less at fault than its individual members in a variety of matters like the expense fund, Nixon's melodramatic defense suggested a basic lack of sophistication.

Moreover, the harsh bite of his anti-Democratic oratory, in the opinion of some public-opinion analysts, had left permanent scars; had hurt him. What stuck in the craw in those quarters was that, not content with running against the Kremlin, he could not resist a temptation to impute to his political opponents secret Communist sins that he would not name. The "Tricky Dick" legend persisted. The 1952 result was to focus on him, as on McCarthy, an inchoate mixture of anger and hatred and fear.

CHAPTER X

First Ebb Tide, 1954

As a campaigner, riding a wave of popular revulsion against wartime urgencies and stringencies, Nixon had gained a series of impressive victories. Then came the ebb tide, and in 1954 he found himself for the first time playing a lead in a more turgid drama.

As the 1952 crusade lost momentum the outlook for the Republicans became equivocal. Disillusionment set in; there was dissatisfaction over continuing budget deficits, over high taxes, over the business recession, over the evident fact that the general had not worked miracles in the White House, and over the no less evident refusal of the Cold War to go away.

Superficially the political climate in which the Republicans had risen to power seemed little changed. McCarthyism was still riding high; the senator had intimidated the State Department, the U. S. Information Service, the Commerce Department, and the Pentagon, and he was threatening to outflank the White House itself. His momentum was formidable, and he bestrode the Senate like a colossus.

Nevertheless McCarthyism had reached its climax. Slowly at first and then in a brisk reversal of public feeling, it lost favor, as successive charges, denunciations, hearings, challenges, and investigations produced, not Communist spies, but more headlines. When Edward R. Murrow dramatized the senator's pretensions in a television report, the bubble burst, coast to coast; the tyranny that had set neighbor whispering against neighbor was over. The

Eisenhower administration, to preserve its self-respect, found it necessary in March to go to the mat with the senator on the Army's behalf, and on April 12 there began the agonizing thirty-six days of Senate hearings that broke his power.

At the time the extent of McCarthy's repudiation was not clearly visible, although Nixon himself as an administration spokesman said March 13 in a nationwide broadcast: "Men who have in the past done effective work exposing Communists in this country have, by reckless talk and questionable methods, made themselves the issue rather than the cause they believe in so deeply."

In retrospect that lean understatement was the breaking point, and by campaign time all that remained of McCarthyism were the overtones and echoes of a slogan. Nevertheless in a congressional contest lacking other issues McCarthyism carried over irresistibly into Nixon's oratory. Even after seven years the Cold War enjoyed a fearsome mystique; communism was still a word to make the voters' flesh creep, still good for a fling on the hustings. After all, it was the issue on which Nixon had cut his political teeth and on which he had nurtured his ambitions. It was as natural as breathing for him to trust the Communist plonk to see him through again, and he turned hopefully to K-1, C-3, not yet aware that the old formula had lost its old impact.

His choice of a dead issue was remarkable enough in view of his general reputation for political sagacity, but all the more so in view of the circumstances. As early as October 18, 1953, Eisenhower had told a news conference that he hoped the whole security issue of Communists in government would be "a matter of history and memory by the time the next election comes around." He deplored the fear of communism in government and "the suspicion on the part of the American people that their government services are weak in this regard." Moreover, Nixon had himself ruled out the corruption issue in a Lincoln Day speech at Oakland, California, where he declared flatly that the Eisenhower administration had finished "cleaning up the mess" in Washington.

One of Nixon's hardiest perennials—the charge of errors in Far Eastern policy under Truman—came within an ace of being destroyed by his own carelessness when he made an off-the-record appearance April 16 at the annual convention of the

American Society of Newspaper Editors. This was the moment when Dien Bien Phu was tottering and the crisis in Indochina was moving toward a climax. A questioner asked, after Nixon's speech, whether the United States ought to send troops to prevent a Communist take-over if the French should decide to withdraw. Nixon's answer, not intended for attribution but promptly spread worldwide owing to the gravity of the issue, was couched in these terms:

". . . I do not believe that the presumption or the assumption which has been made by the questioner will occur and I recognize that he has put it as a hypothetical question. . . . However, answering the question directly and facing up to it, I say this: the United States is the leader of the free world and the free world cannot afford in Asia a further retreat to the Communists. I trust that we can do it without putting American boys in. I think that with the proper leadership we can do it without putting American boys in. But under the circumstances, if in order to avoid further communistic expansion in Asia and particularly in Indochina, if in order to avoid it we must take the risk now by putting American boys in, I believe that the Executive Branch of the Government has to take the politically unpopular position of facing up to it and doing it, and I personally would support such a decision."

The intimation that an administration that had condemned Truman for Korea would consider fighting a new war in the jungles of Indochina broke like a thunderclap. In the ensuing hubbub, the State Department first called U. S. intervention highly unlikely; Nixon was obliged to deny any intention of floating a trial balloon on behalf of the administration; on April 20 Secretary of State Dulles threw cold water on the idea, and a chastened Nixon told a Cincinnati audience that the administration's prime objective was to "keep us from having to send American boys to fight in Indochina or anywhere else"; on April 25 Washington authorities turned down the French request for air support from a U. S. carrier; on April 26 Eisenhower announced, as the Geneva conference began, that we were trying to arrive at a *modus vivendi* on Indochina; on April 28 Nixon told the U. S. Chamber of Commerce that the administration intended to avoid sending troops to Indochina or anywhere else "if we can." On May 7 the Communists overran Dien Bien Phu and four days later Dulles scrubbed out the issue by declaring that Indochina, after all, was not essential to the security or welfare of the United States.

After his ASNE venture into foreign policy-making—an astonishing contretemps, actually, in view of the fact that he attended Cabinet and National Security Council meetings regularly—Nixon began a tactical withdrawal with the cautious statements of April 20 and 28. By June the storm had subsided and the campaign was taking form; following his customary strategy he made a bid for the initiative, using as his platform a fund-raising dinner in Milwaukee. There, on June 26, he took it upon himself to set forth the terms on which he would fight the fall campaign. Not content with a forthright defense of the administration's record, instead of redefining in a substantive way the respective foreign-policy positions of the parties he reverted to a barefaced *ad hominem*. Pointing an accusing finger at his old enemy, the Truman administration, he charged solemnly:

"To sum it up bluntly, the Acheson policy was directly responsible for the loss of China. And if China had not been lost, there would have been no war in Korea and there would be no war in Indochina today."

Administration officials promptly let it be known that this intrusion of foreign policy into partisan politics could not have come at a more embarrassing moment. Dulles was by no means unaware of the measure in which the administration had fallen down on its foreign-policy promises—the "unleashing" of Chiang Kai-shek, the "liberation" of the captive East Europeans, the unification of Korea, and the defense of Indochina—and he deplored charges that might give the Democrats partisan leverage. Moreover, on the very day the speech was made, Eisenhower and Dulles had begun a crucial conference with Prime Minister Winston Churchill, attempting to unify Anglo-American policy, and the British statesman was already fearful that internal squabbling would make the United States unfit for world leadership. Ironically, as Reston reported in the *Times,* Nixon managed to emphasize "almost every point of difference between Washington and London," at a moment when everyone else in the administration was exerting himself to harmonize these relations.

Republican politicians, however, ignored the administration's distress, and by early July the Nixon speech was regarded as settled campaign policy for most of those whose seats were at stake in November. The administration setback in Indochina was to be pinned on the Trumanites—a legacy of betrayal and defeat from which there was no escape. Nixon blandly ignored his own words (echoing one of his own 1951 speeches in the Senate) before the Governors' Conference at Lake George July 12, when he said: "In 1917, what was communism? Nothing but a cellar conspiracy. . . . Today they control . . . a third of the globe. . . . The great gains have been obtained through the tactic of internal subversion [and] revolution. For example, China was won to the Communist side by Chinese, Czechoslovakia by Czechs, Hungary by Hungarians."

It was no time to make a fetish of consistency. At a meeting of Republican strategists September 1 in Cincinnati, Nixon warned bluntly that it would behoove all to "run scared." He repeated the party line that had been laid down two years earlier—that the White House would give backing to every Republican congressional nominee over any Democrat. He brushed aside dissension over whether a Case in New Jersey was "too liberal" or a Meek in Illinois was "too conservative."

"We've got to get forty-eight votes in the Senate," he said, "and let's get that into our heads."

As for the specter of defeat, he warned grimly: "If that happens this year, we are done . . . we might as well fold up our tents and go away."

Against that background Nixon left Washington September 15 to fight for the election of another Republican Congress. His team was in trouble, its back to the wall. The polls almost unanimously foreshadowed a Republican defeat. Although not himself a candidate, he shared fully the party's sense of desperation, a hangover of the 1952 fear that another national defeat would mean the disintegration of the Republican party.

Starting in mid-September, one of 146 Republican barnstormers beating the bushes for votes that year, Nixon made a valiant effort to stem the anti-Republican tide. In 48 days he traveled 28,072 miles, visited 95 cities in 31 states, made 204 speeches, and held more than a hundred news conferences.

Wherever he went he followed his usual policy of working from a master text and adding only a few strokes of embroidery for local color. It was a tested formula consisting of roughly equal parts of three ingredients—Korea, communism, and corruption, with occasional references to the economy and economic controls. According to Loftus of *The New York Times,* a typical day consisted of 500 miles of travel, three speeches, three press conferences, three political conferences, hundreds of handshakes, dozens of photographs, reading and answering mail. Sometimes he made as many as six speeches in a day.

After the first few times the speeches were delivered with clocklike efficiency. He neither needed nor used a script. So expertly had he contrived the planned spontaneity that the interruptions for applause and laughter were as predetermined as the movements of the solar system. Crowds, none of them discourteous, were in nearly all cases considered large compared with the size of the towns. Women attended in unusually large numbers. His speeches ran twenty to forty minutes, and he never failed to command rapt attention.

His drumfire of attack drew heavily on the arguments and charges that he had rehearsed in '50 and '52.

St. Louis, September 17:

[The Democrats] either did not understand the magnitude of the [Communist] threat, or ignored it.

Omaha, September 20:

[The Eisenhower administration is] kicking Communists, fellow travelers, and bad security risks out of the federal government by the thousands. The Communist conspiracy is being smashed to bits by this administration. . . . Previous Democratic administrations underestimated the Communist danger at home and ignored it. They covered up rather than cleaned up.

Lansing, September 21:

. . . The issue is the inexcusable actions of a few leaders of the previous administration who by underestimating the danger of Communist infiltration, by ignoring the warnings of J. Edgar Hoover and the FBI, and by covering up rather than cleaning up when disloyalty was brought to their attention, rendered a terrible disservice to their country and discredit to their party.

New Bedford, September 27:

We have driven the Communists, the fellow-travelers, and the security risks out of government by the thousands. I stand by the statement.

Washington, D. C., October 18 (foreshadowing the plonk he was to favor in 1958):

> They [the people] realize also that the alternative [to a Republican Eighty-fourth Congress] is a Congress unfriendly to President Eisenhower's administration, under the thumb of the ADA left wing, which captured the Democratic party at Chicago in 1952, and which is masterminding the current campaign. The people know from bitter experience that this clique is notoriously soft on the Communist threat at home and is blatantly advocating socialization of American institutions.

Lest it appear that excerpts of this kind might misrepresent Nixon's views, as being out of context, it might be well to present his own complete statement of the K-1, C-3 formula as it appeared in the pro-Eisenhower *New York Herald Tribune,* October 4, in the first of a series of fourteen articles by administration spokesmen:

> The KOREAN[1] conflict ended after costing the United States 142,000 casualties, and $15,000,000,000 from the national treasury. Subsequently, President Eisenhower had made it plain he would never carry this country into war without full consultation with the Congress. On more than 100 occasions the President and the State Department in those twenty months have conferred with leaders of both parties and both houses.
>
> The world is at peace for the first time in twelve years. We must not underestimate the threat that will exist to the peace of the world as long as the international outlaws of the COMMUNIST CONSPIRACY are on the loose. We believe, however, that this Administration's policy of strength militarily, firmness diplomatically, and coolness in crises is the one which has the best chance of gaining our great objective of peace without surrender.
>
> At home, we live in fullest assurance that all possible safeguards have been built against the kind of SUBVERSION which made a shambles of domestic security in the locust years during and after World War II. Together, this Administration team has evolved a hard-hitting program that forged potent legal weapons designed to destroy the Communist conspiracy.
>
> We have dealt effectively with CORRUPTION. No appointee of the Eisenhower administration has become tinged with scandal and the American people can be sure that corruption of any type will not go unpunished in this Administration.
>
> CONTROLS which patently were unable to control runaway inflation have been lifted off the backs of harassed consumers, workers and business men alike. Our dollars today are firm dollars; pur-

---

[1] Capitals supplied.

chasing power has held steady for twenty months after a skyrocket ride that had sent living costs up almost 50 per cent between 1945 and 1952.

Nixon employed a series of meretricious platform gimmicks that enraged the Democrats and were of questionable value in the final tally. One of these was the charge, first heard in Van Nuys, California, October 13, that "when the Eisenhower administration came to Washington on January 20, 1953, we found in the files a blueprint for socializing America. This dangerous, well-oiled scheme contained plans for adding $40 billion to the national debt by 1956. It called for socialized medicine, socialized housing, socialized agriculture, socialized water and power, and perhaps most disturbing of all, socialization of America's greatest source of power, atomic energy."

What Nixon did not say—and what few news stories reported —but what Nixon's press officer said when queried was that the Vice-President was not referring to any specific documents in using the term "blueprint," but was using figurative language to describe the philosophy and proposals of President Truman. The fact that there was no blueprint did not deter Nixon from continuing to use the figure of speech.

A second gimmick, used first at Butte, Montana, October 22, was his announcement that he had in his possession a "secret memorandum" sent to California leaders of the Communist party, directing them to "fight out the issues within the ranks of the Democratic Party." Following his usual practice of equating the Communist and Democratic parties by this type of reverse English, he charged that this alleged document proved the Communist party was "determined to conduct its program within the Democratic Party." Thus, by foisting the Communists willy-nilly on the Democrats, he tried to persuade audiences the latter had been infiltrated and rendered fatally suspect.

Another ploy grew out of Republican party efforts to prove statistically that all subversives had been weeded out of the federal government. Over a period of months, in this "numbers game," the figures on ousted security risks rose progressively from 1456, to 2200 to 2429 to 2486 and eventually to 6926. Using this figure Nixon told a Rock Island, Illinois, rally October 21: "The President's security risk program resulted in 6926 individuals removed from the federal service. . . . The great majority of these individuals were inherited largely from the Truman regime. . . . Included in this number were individuals who were members of the Communist Party and Communist-controlled organizations."

He even went so far as to assert November 1 in Denver that "96 per cent of the 6926 Communists, fellow travelers, sex perverts, people with criminal records, dope addicts, drunks, and other security risks removed under the Eisenhower security program were hired by the Truman administration."

Nixon's statistics did not stand up under examination. The record showed that in Truman's last full year 32,345 employees were fired for cause by the Democrats; and in Eisenhower's first full fiscal year, the government fired 21,626 employees for cause. Moreover, toward the end of the 1954 campaign Philip Young, the Eisenhower-appointed chairman of the Civil Service Commission, testified that he knew of no single government employee who had been fired by the Eisenhower administration for being a Communist or fellow traveler. Later Young revealed that an analysis of 3746 employees who were dismissed or who resigned for security reasons from May 1953 until mid-1955 showed 41.2 per cent had been hired by the Eisenhower administration itself. Still later a Senate investigating committee reported that 53 per cent of those ousted as security risks had been hired by the Republicans.

The Democrats also took vehement exception to Nixon's charge, repeated in successive campaigns, that they had been blind to the danger of Communist subversion and had covered up rather than cleaned up. They cited FBI reports showing that at the beginning of the Hoover administration some 50,000 Americans voted the Communist ticket. At the end of Hoover's administration, at the depth of the depression in 1932, the Communist vote had risen to 103,000. By 1950, after seventeen years of Democratic rule, Communist party membership totaled just under 53,000; and by the beginning of 1953 when Truman left office, the number according to J. Edgar Hoover's FBI had dropped to 24,796.

Meanwhile from 1933 until the end of the Truman administration an impressive list of antisubversion laws had been added to the statute books: the McCormack Foreign Agents Registration Act; the Hatch Act, which among other things made it illegal for a federal employee to be a Communist; the Nationality Act of 1940, whose purpose was to prevent the naturalization of Communists; the Voorhis Act requiring registration of alien-controlled organizations; the Smith Act, under which Communist leaders were prosecuted and imprisoned; the Atomic Energy Espionage Act of 1946, which tightened up the original espionage act (1917) with respect to atomic secrets; and the Internal Security Act, which required the registration of Communist and Communist-front organizations.

Adlai Stevenson continued to be a favorite Nixon target. As the Vice-President opened the final week of the campaign at Pocatello, he insisted that communism was still the paramount issue and that communism and socialism were leftishly related. He charged that Truman and Stevenson were leaders of the left wing of the Democratic party, that a Democratic victory would mean "a sharp turn to the left, back down the road to socialism," and that five Democratic Senate candidates in the West—Neuberger, O'Mahoney, Taylor, Carroll, and Yorty—were all members of the left wing of the party.

At the Beverly Hills city hall October 28 Nixon used his talent for the oblique turn of phrase to make a particularly invidious insinuation about Stevenson.

"Mr. Stevenson has been guilty, probably without being aware that he was doing so," said Nixon, "of spreading pro-Communist propaganda as he has attacked with violent fury the economic system of the United States and praised the Soviet economy. He said recently, 'While the American economy has been shrinking [this was at a time when there were signs of a business recession in the U.S.], the Soviet economy has been growing fast, which is one of the most important facts in the world situation. In the long view it is probably a more important fact than the development of Soviet military power.'

"Whatever Mr. Stevenson's purpose may be," the Vice-President continued, "such statements of praise for the Soviet economy do the cause of the free world great damage. His dislike for our own economic system is his own business, but when he links such criticism with praise of the rapid growth of the Soviet economy, he is performing a grave disservice to us and the rest of the free world."

Taken in context, Stevenson had spoken, not in praise of the

Soviet system, not in "violent fury" against the American system, but in an effort to arouse the American public to support a more rapid expansion of the American economy. The bland insinuation that Stevenson "disliked" the American system was, like Nixon's college football efforts, offside. The innuendo was false, a trick of language to plant suspicion, the same trick he used on numberless other occasions to arraign the motives of an opponent.

In that instance as in others when Nixon, the spieler, let his eagerness to please an audience carry him into deep waters, he later found himself recanting. In April 1958, speaking before the American Newspaper Publishers Association, he boldly adopted the Stevenson thesis which he had viewed with such sinister distaste four years earlier.

"The Soviet economy is growing faster than ours," Nixon conceded on sober second thought. "We must recognize that economic competition between the free world and the Communist world may well decide the world conflict. . . . We hear much today of the great strength of the Soviet Union. I have never been one to discount this strength. It would be fatal to underestimate it. . . . We cannot afford to stand still. . . ."

Whether Nixon's platform style was an invidious departure from normal political patterns was then as always a matter of opinion. Cabell Phillips of *The New York Times,* describing the Vice-President as the chief strategist and "one-man task force of the GOP," found that as a political performer Nixon portrayed "in an almost filial sense the reflected image of Eisenhower." To convey this image, in the remarks on corruption which formed a part of nearly every speech, Nixon would conclude sternly, hand upraised in a gesture of affirmation: "I say to you that this administration from top to bottom is based upon the integrity of President Dwight D. Eisenhower."

As for Democratic charges that Nixon was offside in his methods, Phillips took a somewhat more detached view after watching the Vice-President in action. "Like most politicians," he wrote, "Mr. Nixon talks in hyperboles, makes sweeping generalizations of sometimes dubious validity, and is adept at planting the dark and ominous inference. But he does it with extraordinary finesse. . . . He is indeed, 'terrific,' as defined in current political usage."

It would be unfair to suggest that Nixon alone was responsible for the tone of the Republican campaign. In reality, he may have been somewhat more moderate than the party high command. State and national GOP committees minced no words in accusing the Democrats of pro-Communist sympathies. In Iowa, in Thomas E. Martin's Senate race, a leaflet addressed to "MR. VOTER" went on to assert: "If you like graft, corruption, pinkos, left-wingers and actual communists in your government, Vote Democratic."

An Indiana leaflet used in the Adair race showed drawings of Lenin, Stalin, and Malenkov and trumpeted: "We shall force the United States to spend itself to destruction," a wholly fictitious quotation coined by the Jenner forces. It warned, "12 billion dollars of *Your* Taxes Given to Russia by Democrats," and pleaded, "Vote Republican for your own security—for protection of Home—Farm—Church!" In states as far apart as Utah and Rhode Island, posters blossomed out almost simultaneously with the slogan: "The SON you save may be your OWN"; and the casualty lists in three wars were laid at the doorstep of the Democratic party, with the implication that the Democrats were bloody warmongers. Senator O'Mahoney in Wyoming was labeled Foreign Agent 783 because he had registered as legal counsel for a foreign client.

The stridency of the campaign reached its climax in a series of radio spot announcements distributed by the Republican congressional committee for use on local radio stations as paid advertising. Here is one verbatim text:

> Crier: Oyez! Oyez! Oyez! Listen to the record of the Fair Deal, and the New Deal, the Double Deal!
> Different Voices: Communists and spies infiltrated the top spots in our government!
> Voice B: Traitors stole the secrets of the A bomb and gave them to Russia!
> Voice C: Traitors stole the secrets of the H bomb and gave them to Russia!
> Voice D: Government spending went up and up! Taxes went up and up! Casualty lists went up and up! Fair Deal cronies avoided millions in income tax payments!
> Announcer: Yes, this is the record of twenty years of Double Deal—a record of communism and corruption. It must not happen again! America's future is at stake. Vote Ike a Republican Congress and endorse his crusade against communism and corruption. Vote Republican in November!

In the last hours of the campaign Nixon went all out against Stevenson. The Illinois Democrat had suggested that Eisenhower must have spoken "thoughtlessly and carelessly" in affirming that American prosperity had been achieved only at the price of war and bloodshed; and had charged that, after failing to "control a campaign of slander" against the Democrats, the President "evidently has embraced it now." In answer the Vice-President first fired off a telegram October 30, in which he told Stevenson:

> You have been following your usual tactics of covering up the record and failing to answer the facts by screaming "smear, slur and slander." Your principal target seems to be me. All I have done since September 15 is to cite the hard facts from the record so that the American people can make an intelligent choice on election day between going forward with the Eisenhower program, or electing a congress which has been committed by the Democratic national chairman to go back to the policies of Harry Truman. . . .
>
> I suggest that in your speech tonight to the American people, instead of answering with your usual quips and with the shopworn cry of 'smear,' you discuss this record.
>
> It is clear that the issue today is exactly what it was in 1952. We have the same spokesmen, yourself, Mr. Mitchell, and your A.D.A. bedfellows calling for the defeat of President Eisenhower through the election of an anti-Eisenhower Congress. . . . I am confident that millions of Democrats, as in 1952, will realize in 1954 that your clique of starry-eyed opportunists with your feet in the clouds, and your heads in the sand, does not represent the true principles of the Democratic Party. . . .

The next day the Vice-President followed up with a statement calling Stevenson's criticism of Eisenhower "one of the most vicious, scurrilous attacks ever made by a major political figure on a President of the United States."

Asserting that this proved again that 34 million voters were right when they found Stevenson "unfit" to be President in 1952, Nixon proceeded to indict the "Stevenson–Truman–anti-Eisenhower–A.D.A.–leftwing campaign" for what he called "the most despicable political tactic—that of the 'big lie.' " Then in a crisp condensation of his treatment of the issues, he gave his version of the "big lie technique":

> BIG LIE I: The Eisenhower-Dulles foreign policy has failed.
> THE TRUTH: The Truman Administration got us into war. The Eisenhower Administration got us out.
> BIG LIE II: Depression and recession.

THE TRUTH: This is the best peacetime year in America's history.

BIG LIE III: The President's security program is not necessary.

THE TRUTH: Ninety-six percent of the 6926 Communists, fellow-travelers, people with criminal records, narcotics addicts, and other security risks removed by President Eisenhower were hired by President Truman.

BIG LIE IV: There is corruption in this Administration.

THE TRUTH: There is no unpunished corruption and we are cleaning up the "sordid mess" of the Truman Administration, probably the most corrupt in America's history.

BIG LIE V: A Democratic Congress will support the President better than a Republican Congress.

THE TRUTH: The Eisenhower program, which brought peace to America and honesty, loyalty and solvency to government, could not have been put through if Democrats controlled the Eighty-third Congress. Democrats voted against the Eisenhower program 60 percent of the time in the last Congress. A Democratic Congress means a return to the Truman socialization policies.

While these last-minute blows were being struck, President Eisenhower showed his gratitude in a "Dear Dick" letter dated October 28 in which he said feelingly:

Whenever my burdens tend to feel unduly heavy, I admire all the more the tremendous job you have done since the opening of the present campaign. You have personally carried a back-breaking load of hard, tedious, day-to-day and state-by-state campaigning. And in doing so you have been undismayed by problems of time, distance and physical effort. . . . No man could have done more effective work. . . . Whatever the outcome next Tuesday, I can find no words to express my deep appreciation. . . .

The voters showed their lack of appreciation November 2 by lodging control of both houses in the Eighty-fourth Congress with the Democratic party. The House vote showed the following shift in national totals:

	Republican	Democratic
1952	28,399,286	28,336,127
1954	20,033,673	22,175,228

The 1952 elections had given the Republicans control of the House by a majority of eight votes, 221 to 213. As a result of the '54 election the Republicans lost eighteen seats in the House, and control shifted to the Democrats, 232 to 203.

The Republicans had controlled the Senate in the Eighty-third Congress by the narrow margin of 49 to 47. When the

Eighty-fourth Congress convened, the lineup was reversed: 49 Democrats, 47 Republicans.

Repercussions continued to be heard for months. Nixon's explanation was conveniently at hand. In the summer of 1953 he had told a reporter that a controversy over McCarthy "would cause a very decided split among Republicans and could well lead to a defeat for us in the 1954 election." On November 12, 1954, a news magazine quoted him in a long interview:

> . . . Early in the campaign the McCarthy issue hurt the Republicans in the sense that it divided the Republicans. It made it more difficult to obtain contributions . . . created some apathy in Republican organization ranks. . . . My reports are . . . the fall-off in Republican support was due to a certain extent to the disappointment of some of the Republicans over the handling of the McCarthy issue. I will not make that statement as being my opinion.

The Vice-President's supporters, as a salvaging operation, made a hypothetical case for him by insisting that a Republican debacle had been averted only through his efforts. The Democrats were in no mood to accept this catchpenny rationalization. In their view the Republican campaign had been based on imputations of treason, and their resentment focused most bitterly of all on Nixon. In January Democratic national headquarters exhibited a "chamber of smears," in which excerpts from thirty-one Nixon speeches occupied a prominent place. The Vice-President had equated the New Deal with socialism and socialism with communism, and the *New Leader* of January 24 reported that, as a result, it had been "many a year since the relation between the two parties had been as bitter and dangerous as it is now."

The end of the 1954 campaign marked a turning point of sorts for the Vice-President. He had tested his maximum powers as a campaigner and failed. For the first time he had no victories to offer his own party, and he had nothing but enmity to expect from the opposition. He had ridden the tide of postwar Republicanism up to the crest and down, and he was widely blamed for the Republican party's reckless flirtation with the treason issue. That flirtation had been no invention of typewriter pundits. The question posed by McCarthyism early in 1954 had been whether it would become the Republican party line to accuse the Democratic party of countenancing treason. There had been strong voices urging President Eisenhower to adopt such a tack.

That moment was, without exaggeration, crucial in American history. Had the President acquiesced, had he permitted Republican politicians to accuse fellow citizens of treason, there could have been only one result, an irreconcilable division rendering the democratic system unworkable. The supreme danger, said columnist Walter Lippmann, was that: "McCarthyism would become the policy not of a faction but of the party . . . that administration leaders like Brownell, Nixon, Chairman Hall, would adopt McCarthyism as the party line for winning the election."

Nixon was thus deeply involved in the decision. The evidence suggests timidity and vacillation in GOP ranks, and such odium as may have attached to Nixon derived mainly from the fact that he temporized instead of aligning himself boldly with the President in opposition to the McCarthyites. Nixon did pay lip service, certainly, to the Eisenhower credo by insisting at one point "there is no difference between the loyalty of Democrats and Republicans," but in Lippmann's optimistic conclusion that the political climate had moderated in the wake of the election, his acknowledgments for the improvement went explicitly not to Nixon, but to Eisenhower.

CHAPTER XI

Coronary Crisis

I

Nixon was plunged into a situation of unparalleled stress on Saturday, September 24, 1955, when President Eisenhower suffered a heart attack while vacationing in Denver. Instantly it was apparent that the presence of a heart patient in the White House could not but cause a subtle alteration on the Vice-President's status and prospects, and to the chagrin of his enemies his conduct in the immediate crisis proved unexceptionable.

In the late summer, after the Geneva Summit Conference and the adjournment of Congress, President Eisenhower had hurried out to Denver. As week succeeded week, with only cursory office hours for routine matters, the President's vacation became a subject of widespread critical gossip. A foreign ministers' conference to discuss German unification and European security was scheduled for October 27; no sign of preparations for that. Rough outlines of the 1957 budget took form with only casual policy guidance. A decline in farm income, subjecting the administration to new pressures from the back country, was largely ignored. Although there was nothing approaching a major crisis, the presence of the Chief Executive was sorely missed after he had spent more than seven weeks away from the national capital.

Gossip was abruptly stilled by the news of the President's illness. There was a hush as the country took time to assess the facts and their implications.

The Vice-President was in Washington when the news was flashed, one of the few senior officials not traveling on pleasure or administration business. In the *Washington Evening Star* he had read and dismissed a matter-of-fact report that the President had suffered a digestive upset. He had attended an early afternoon wedding reception and had just returned to his home in the fashionable Spring Valley section of Washington when James Hagerty, the President's press secretary, telephoned. It was then 3:30 p.m., nearly twelve hours after the President's heart attack and soon after his removal to Fitzsimons General Hospital on the outskirts of Denver. As Robert Donovan reconstructed the story, Hagerty broke the news without ceremony: "The President has had a coronary."

"Oh, my God," Nixon gasped.

Afterward, in describing his feelings, Nixon said he went dead inside. Even the next day when he talked to newsmen, he still felt overwhelmed.

"I find it rather difficult," he told them, "to express, in words, feelings that are so deep."

Following Hagerty's call he sat alone for several minutes pulling his thoughts together. Hagerty had said he was leaving at once for Denver to insure the liveliest candor in the telling of the story and thus minimize damaging repercussions. Nixon then phoned Deputy Attorney General Rogers and asked him to join the Nixon family for dinner. Nixon's secretary, Rose Mary Woods, recalled that the Vice-President also telephoned her at the wedding reception, told her of the President's illness, and asked her to stand by in her apartment to take calls on a phone that rang there when the Nixon phone did not answer.

Rogers dined with the Nixons, but shortly afterward, when the clamor of the telephone and a group of newsmen outside made talk impossible, he and the Vice-President slipped out the back way unobserved and hid out at Rogers' home. Some time later they were joined there by General Wilton B. (Jerry) Persons, the senior White House staff member in Washington.

It was at this meeting, late in the evening of September 24, while Hagerty was flying to Denver, that the general outlines of administration tactics for handling the crisis were first laid out.

Nixon with Rogers' concurrence took the lead in urging a "business as usual" keynote for the government's operations. The Nixon-Rogers thesis was an echo of the view expressed earlier that same evening by Treasury Secretary George Humphrey, the strong man of the Cabinet, who had announced that Secretaries Dulles, Benson, and Weeks would leave with him the next day on schedule for economic and trade talks with the Canadian Cabinet at Ottawa.

Informally, by telephone conversation and in private get-togethers, a consensus of the Cabinet was quickly achieved. To reassure both the country and the world, government departments and the White House staff would carry on in routine fashion, within the framework of policies already established.

After a sleepless night at Rogers' home, the Vice-President emerged Sunday morning to join his family in church services at Westmoreland Congregational Church. Afterward he invited a half-dozen reporters into his living room to make the administration's plan explicit.

"Under the President's administration," he said, "a team has been set up in Washington which will carry out his well-defined plans. The business of government will go on as usual, without any delay because of the President's temporary absence."

As part of the strategy of emphasizing this continuity, Nixon refused all speculation about possible enlargement in his own role. In telephone consultation with Hagerty and others, it was also agreed that, until more was known about the coronary and its aftereffects, those in the topmost political echelon would do well to avoid comment on the political consequences of the President's illness. Nixon called questions in that category "not worthy of discussion," but the aim of course was to batten down hatches all around for fear of an enervating whispering campaign.

As another psychological attack on the problem, Nixon proposed Sunday night in a second meeting at Rogers' home that a meeting of the Cabinet should be called for the following Friday, in addition to the National Security Council meeting already scheduled for Thursday; from a public relations viewpoint, he pointed out, a gathering of the Cabinet would dramatize the orderly functioning of government with an emphasis not otherwise possible. A decision was postponed until the Secretaries could be polled.

II

During these first days, while the President's health mended steadily at Fitzsimons Hospital, Nixon was under immense strain. By the time presidential assistant Sherman Adams returned Monday from a European vacation, Nixon was being referred to in *The New York Times* as the "fountainhead" for the actions taken up to that point. When reporters told him it had been suggested he move to Blair House, across Pennsylvania Avenue from the White House, he maintained a discreet and total silence.

The first question after the President's attack was whether the functions of government could be legally carried on if he should be incapacitated for a considerable time. As early as Sunday, the 25th, Hagerty indicated that the Attorney General's office would be asked for a legal opinion as to whether certain presidential powers might be delegated. Although no such opinion was ever requested, the question remained, and to the extent that Nixon was a hypothetical recipient of any such delegated powers he was feared or courted, attacked or defended.

By midweek—after having assumed urgent proportions three days earlier—the question of the delegation of powers had all but been abandoned. The medical crisis had been surmounted; the bulletins from Denver were highly optimistic. Dr. Paul Dudley White, the Boston heart specialist who had been called in, predicted the President might be ready for conferences in two weeks and should be ready for normal activity in two months. He disposed of fears about permanent injury to the President's heart; if the recovery continued, he said, there would be no reason why Ike could not run for re-election in 1956!

Administration officials quickly adjusted themselves to the presumption that theirs was a caretaker role, a holding operation. Nixon met from time to time with Cabinet members and White House personnel; he canceled fifteen speaking engagements scheduled for October, abandoned plans for a Middle Eastern trip, and announced he would make no overnight trips away from Washington, thus holding himself in constant readiness to assume the presidency in case of need.

With his usual sense of the political realities, and with Rogers' able guidance, Nixon handled himself circumspectly throughout this tense period. While avoiding the appearance of inaction or irresponsibility, he likewise avoided any move that might have been interpreted as an overt grab for power. On Saturday and Sunday nights he met with Rogers and Persons. On Monday he had luncheon at the White House with Adams, Persons, and Rogers; and on Tuesday these same four were together with Brownell for luncheon in the office of Treasury Secretary Humphrey. The Washington gossip mills whispered that the Vice-President was moving with somewhat more speed and audacity than the situation required, but no one in authority testified to that effect.

Over the first weekend, when the extent of the President's illness was obscure, the status of the Vice-President had seemed a matter of paramount concern. Those whose first thought was to safeguard the continuity of the Administration by exploring the succession issue underwent a quick change of heart when the medical bulletins took an encouraging turn.

It was in these second thoughts that political considerations asserted themselves, and so forcefully that by the 28th Nixon himself was discounting the need of a legal opinion. His political sixth sense warned against going too far too fast. However prudent it might have been to set forth the legal nature of the succession problem in the event of the President's incapacity—as Eisenhower himself did define it later in a two-and-a-half-page letter—those in the President's official family instinctively recoiled from any step that would give Nixon greater authority or even give an impression that greater authority would soon be his. Their reluctance was due not necessarily to any personal animus or distrust, but rather to the fact that Cabinet officers owe their appointments and their loyalty to the President, and any reshuffling of power is more likely to result in a loss than in a gain of power for them.

Predictions of a savage struggle for power were not fulfilled but this did not prevent gossip. Sherman Adams, it was reported, felt himself to be the logical caretaker of the President's interests and had undertaken to whittle Nixon down to size. There was talk that the crisis had generated new ambitions on the part of Humphrey, Brownell, Dewey. The vice-presidential luncheon in Humphrey's office launched a mixed cargo of speculation—that Nixon had been summoned by the real *junta,* Humphrey, Adams, and Brownell; that Humphrey alone wished to demonstrate his power and insisted Nixon come to him; that the presence of

Adams and Brownell was a surprise to Nixon; and that he was suffering agonizing doubts about the kind of game his three teammates were playing. At this same time it was Humphrey who in the privacy of the Cabinet meeting appealed for cooperation among the departments to forestall rumors of conflict.

At the NSC meeting on Thursday, the 29th, for which twenty-three officials gathered in the Cabinet room and over which Nixon presided, it was agreed that Sherman Adams would take charge of the Denver White House and thus, in effect, become the principal agent for the President. This decision marked the end of Nixon's paramountcy in the crisis. After the Security Council meeting he refused to delineate his own position or even to say that he would remain as the principal official in Washington.

"I prefer to let the facts speak for themselves," he said.

When asked about his role in the decision-making process, the Vice-President took pains to expound the concept that would govern him the following day in presiding over the Cabinet meeting.

"Neither the Security Council nor the Cabinet," he said, "are decision-making bodies. They provide the President with advice and consultation on the decision he must make. They are bodies for an exchange of views . . . and coordination of action being taken . . . within the framework of existing policies. The Vice-President . . . functions primarily as the presiding officer, a chairman to see that items on the agenda are moved along effectively and efficiently. . . . Decisions constituting new policy have been made in the past and will be made in the future by the President."

Nixon's own words suggest the anomaly of saying, as some have tried to, that the Vice-President "presided" in any substantive sense at official meetings during the emergency. From the very outset it was understood no new policy could be adopted; every Cabinet member was therefore free to interpret existing policy in his own way, and what he reported at Cabinet meetings was by way of a gentleman's agreement and not subject to the Vice-President's review. The terms of reference made Nixon's role wholly powerless and ceremonial, for, so long as the Chief Executive had life and sanity, he alone possessed the ultimate power of decision.

III

The worst of the crisis was over in six days. Nixon's idea of a Cabinet meeting as an exercise in dramatics won approval, and the departmental Secretaries gathered with eight staff members at the White House September 30. Nixon ran the show, which lasted two and a half hours, with the efficiency of a Broadway producer: a moment of silent prayer; a solemn report on the current Mediterranean crisis from Mr. Dulles; then the heart of the problem—plans for allaying the nation's and the world's uncertainty about the continuity of affairs in Washington.

According to the minutes, the Vice-President began by pointing out that routine matters must not be allowed to pile up in a log jam awaiting the President's return, but at the same time, no federal agency should on its own authority take action on matters which would call for the establishment of new policies. Important measures should be channeled through the Cabinet or the NSC in accordance with standard protocol.

With his usual political prescience Nixon urged all present to lose no opportunity to remind the public that this was the Eisenhower administration at work, not somebody else's administration. His advice alerted them to a danger that was to become explicit in the months preceding the '56 campaign, and forecast, before the Democrats had coined the slogan, the possible hazards of campaigning on behalf of a "part-time president."

As a matter of record, the Attorney General saw no legal obstacle to the course being followed. He invited Cabinet members to provide him with a list of routine papers normally passing over the President's desk, with the idea of lifting part of this burden from the White House permanently. He also offered the draft of a press release which was revised and issued at the close of the session. The release did no more than summarize the "business as usual" policy, and by its very silence on the thorny succession issue left it to be resolved by higher authority.

As they rose to adjourn, Secretary Dulles took it upon himself to say what had been apparent to most: that Nixon had been under great strain and deserved an expression of appreciation for the manner in which he had conducted himself. All applauded, and all agreed that an awesome crisis had been surmounted.

CHAPTER XII

Post-Coronary Intrigue

I

For Nixon the winter of 1955-56 was dominated by a question of obsessive prominence: whether President Eisenhower could or would run for re-election. If it was a time of spiritual torment for Ike, it was no less so for the Vice-President. At any moment he might be President, or a presidential candidate, or a second-term Vice-President, or none of these at all. As days ran into weeks his field of maneuver shrank steadily; yet his hands were tied, for a single false move at so trying a juncture could have proved his entire undoing.

Eisenhower flew from Denver to the White House November 11 and drove to his Gettysburg farm on the 14th to continue his convalescence. By then the first hasty assumption that he would be invalided out of office had been almost universally discarded. His recovery had matched his physicians' best hopes, and, whatever the actuarial tables might argue, the President's physical condition warranted serious consideration of a second term.

White House aides, notably Adams, Brownell, and Summerfield, maneuvered to keep the question of Eisenhower's future alive, and the mass media wore the subject threadbare with speculation. GOP Chairman Leonard Hall took an audacious course from the first, insisting Eisenhower and Nixon were still his candidates, insisting he knew of no change in the party's plans for the next election.

For Eisenhower the first psychological reaction at Denver had been one of buoyancy and he had accepted his limited regimen of work gratefully. When he reached Gettysburg, however, the depression that often follows a coronary thrombosis set in. The weather for the most part was cold and wet and his only outdoor exercise consisted of an occasional jeep ride. His doctors kept him on a starvation work ration, and he paced the floor at home with a golf club for a stick, chafing at inaction but determined to be a good patient.

Nixon saw him infrequently and only in the course of official business. The first of these occasions was just before Thanksgiving when the principal members of the White House official family were summoned for a two-day meeting at Camp David, Maryland. On the morning of November 21, the President drove over from his farm nearby, and Nixon was flown up from Washington in an H-19 army liaison plane. That day there was a long session of the National Security Council; the party remained at the camp overnight, and the following morning the President presided over a full-dress Cabinet meeting, with Nixon in his usual place as consultant and observer. The sessions were without incident; and twice again during the five weeks of his convalescence at Gettysburg, the President drove over to Camp David, once for an NSC meeting December 1 and again for a Cabinet meeting December 9. By December 12 his strength was so far recovered that he spent two full days in his White House office.

Five days before Christmas he returned to the White House, restless and bored, telling his staff: "Don't give me mush; I want the hard ones now." On December 28, immediately after the family holiday gathering, his doctors sent him to Key West to enlarge his outdoor regimen—unhurried walks in the sun and a careful ration of practice shots off a golf tee.

All this time Nixon waited.

II

The President flew back to Washington January 8. It was his good fortune and the country's that during the crucial four months of his illness the government had not been troubled by a major crisis. As the new Congress met, there was the prospect of a balanced budget, an uneasy peace in the world, and a national economy producing at the rate of $400 billion a year.

Nevertheless, the time was at hand when decisions could not be long postponed. The President acted with characteristic deliberation. After dinner on January 13, with elaborate secrecy, he met in his second-floor study with a group of intimates, reminded them that he must soon declare his intentions, and asked each in turn to discuss the factors having a bearing on his decision. Present were four from the Cabinet: Dulles, Humphrey, Summerfield, and Brownell; five from the White House staff: Adams, Persons, Hagerty, Howard Pyle, and Tom Stephens; besides Cabot Lodge, Leonard Hall, and Dr. Milton Eisenhower. Nixon was conspicuously absent. The President sat with his back to the fireplace, listening soberly as each member of the informal roundtable assessed the odds. Not surprisingly, the unanimous view was that the President's work was unfinished; that, if final medical tests were satisfactory, he should run for a second term.

Eisenhower thanked them and kept his own counsel.

It was more than a month before the decision was made. The crucial X-ray of Eisenhower's heart was made February 11, and the word three days later was that his health ought to enable him to continue leading an active life for five or ten years. Between February 15 and 25, the President submitted his strength to a more strenuous and final test on a quail-hunting expedition at George Humphrey's plantation at Thomasville, Georgia.

Nixon, along with Hall, Adams, Persons, Hagerty, and one or two others finally learned the President's decision on February 28, the day before the news conference at which the President announced that, if the Republican convention nominated him, "my answer will be positive; that is, affirmative."

That announcement meant the issue was half settled, no more. The Vice-President still had no assurance whatever that he would be welcome a second time as Eisenhower's running mate. His future was distinctly unclear. Even before the President's illness there had been rumblings of opposition; doubts and misgivings generated in 1952 by the secret fund episode had not been altogether dispelled. Criticism of his campaign tactics in 1946 and 1950 persisted, and the violently partisan line he had chosen in '54 did nothing to reassure some of those in the ardently pro-Eisenhower wing of the GOP.

While the President was still convalescing at Denver, Senator
Knowland had come close to outright repudiation of his fellow
Californian. In what was interpreted as a backlash of the 1952
convention bitterness, the Senate's minority leader, without alluding to the Vice-President directly, had growled portentously, "I
do not consider a Pepsodent smile, a ready quip, and an actor's
perfection with lines, nor an ability to avoid issues, as qualifications for high office."

Following the President's heart attack an amorphous movement
to eliminate Nixon from the 1956 ticket had taken form. The
pollsters found some evidence of Nixon's unpopularity with the
general public; surveys in 1955 had shown him as not only much
weaker than Eisenhower but also as weaker than Stevenson. Aside
from these doubts, some party leaders felt it would make for a
healthier convention to permit an open contest for the vice-
presidency.

During the winter there were reports that Nixon was to be
downgraded by a maneuver in which President Eisenhower took
a hand. In February, just before announcing his own decision,
the President called Nixon to the White House for a fatherly chat.
He pointed out that no Vice-President in modern history had
succeeded a living President. He suggested that the Vice-President's career had been to some degree handicapped by his never
having occupied an important administrative office. He invited
Nixon to consider whether his long-range interests might not be
better served if he stepped aside at the expiration of his first term
to accept a Cabinet post, perhaps Secretary of Defense.

On the face of it, Eisenhower was seriously considering the
idea of a less controversial running mate. Nixon was dismayed,
but for once his wife refused to share his concern. For Pat, the
torment of the 1952 fund crisis had had a traumatic effect. It
was after that campaign that she asked Nixon for the first time
to consider retiring from politics. She reverted to the subject
early in 1954, an occasion made memorable by the fact that the
Vice-President then committed to writing a promise not to seek
re-election. After the 1954 campaign she had spoken of her
desire again.

Now, the moment of truth had come, and the decision was his
alone. Pat's attitude was by no means an inconsiderable factor

as he brooded over his predicament, moodily weighing the factors that might force him to jump before being pushed.

Throughout this period the President was noncommittal. He did bridle angrily at a press conference suggestion that he might "dump" Nixon, but there appeared every reason to believe he was carefully weighing the arguments pro and con. To leave Nixon off the ticket would, in some quarters, be interpreted as a confession of weakness, but his retention might cut into the President's following among Democrats and independents who liked Ike but disliked Nixon.

As late as March 7 Eisenhower took a neutral position, telling his news conference that he had asked Nixon "to chart his own course and tell me what he would like to do." Reston reported in the *Times* the following weekend that Adams and Brownell were "master-minding" a White House "holding operation" to head off the Vice-President, and added: "Mr. Nixon does not like this and he is not without power to influence the outcome. . . . President Eisenhower could, of course, come out flatly against Mr. Nixon, and that would end it. But he is not yet sure he wants to do that and besides he does not like direct action."

Nixon also interpreted the March 7 statement as a covert repudiation. To test his ground he let two or three intimates know he was preparing to call a news conference at which he would announce his retirement from politics. Whatever his motives or his real intentions—and he has said they were perfectly straightforward—party wheelhorses reacted in vehement protest. At their insistence and on the plea that his exodus would create doubt about Eisenhower's ability to win again, he agreed to postpone a decision. That delay ended all talk of withdrawal. Later, in trying to rationalize this apparent indecision, he reverted to his fundamentally determinist philosophy.

"Once you're in the stream of history," he said, "you can't get out."

At that moment a minor incident threw its weight into the scales. In the New Hampshire presidential primary March 13, as a result of 87 telephone calls by Senator Styles Bridges, 22,202 voters took the trouble to write Nixon's name on the ballot, 40 per cent as many votes as Eisenhower polled. In Manchester during the fall campaign Nixon harked back to that write-in, and told an airport news conference that it had been an important factor in his decision to try for a second term.

"Coming as it did," he said, "without any solicitation on my part and without any appearances in the state, it had a very great impact on me."

It was Nixon himself who eventually forced a decision when he found himself threatened with involvement in a congressional investigation having unsavory possibilities. A Senate subcommittee probing corruption and influence-peddling in military procurement issued a subpoena April 25 for Murray Chotiner, Nixon's campaign manager and friend. Democrats wanted to establish that Chotiner had used his administration connections on behalf of clients.

On April 26, when Chotiner failed to appear as requested, risking a contempt citation, and before any testimony from his lips might conceivably compromise the Vice-President, Nixon called at the White House to tell Eisenhower that he had indeed charted his course.

Then, using the White House itself as a platform, despite the tradition that the President reserves that prerogative for himself, Nixon made what *Time* called "the most predictable announcement of the year."

"I informed the President," he said, "that in the event the President and the delegates to the convention reached the decision that it was their desire for me to serve as the nominee of the Republican party for Vice-President, I would be honored to accept that nomination again, as I was, and as I did in 1952."

The President's press secretary, James Hagerty, interjected on cue to reporters: "The President has asked me to tell you gentlemen that he was delighted to hear of the Vice-President's decision."

And the Vice-President, to explain why it had taken him so long to put his intentions on record, was happy to discuss the personal travail that he had undergone in the months just past. "I felt," he said, "that it was most important for me to make a decision which in my judgment and in the judgment of my associates was in the best interests of the success of the President in his campaign for re-election and for the continued success of the President's administration. Consequently, I had to weigh all the factors involved and to reach a decision which would put that primary goal first, and after discussing the matter with friends, associates, and, of course, the President, I have made the decision that I indicated today."

Musing over that statement later, a columnist said gently, "Even his partisans could smile at the Vice-President's implication that he had seriously considered stepping out."

Actually, of course, it was never within Nixon's power to make the decision single-handed. In the ebb and flow of headlines and maneuvers and statements, professional politicians never lost sight of the fact that Nixon was a party man, and in the last analysis it was his firm standing with the Republican organization that tipped the scales in his favor. He had worked hard to ingratiate himself with key members of the GOP national committee and with influential leaders of the state organizations. In the intervals between conventions he could count on their support, notwithstanding any intrigues against him that might be launched by either amateur supporters of the President or members of the White House staff.

When Nixon went to the White House that April day to declare himself in, he was not unarmed. Largely through the efforts of Victor Johnson, an old Republican pro, Nixon brought along private pledges of support from more than 800 delegates or prospective delegates to the San Francisco convention, a clear majority. He had other powerful support—from Leonard Hall, Dr. Milton Eisenhower, Dewey, and Sidney J. Weinberg, senior partner of the New York investment banking firm of Goldman Sachs, who had played a conspicuous part in bankrolling Eisenhower's political debut.

The countervailing weakness of Nixon's position made itself visible just six weeks later, June 8, when President Eisenhower was hospitalized a second time to undergo an ileitis operation. Again, the long-range outlook for the President's health became a subject of nationwide debate, and as a corollary the question of Nixon's fitness to be President was reopened. Even among those who accepted him uncritically in the role of Vice-President there were uneasy second thoughts about the possibility of his becoming President.

These doubts became more articulate during the summer. Influential leaders in the Citizens for Eisenhower movement, the more liberal faction of the party, headed by Lucius Clay and Paul Hoffman, cautiously refused to embrace Nixon's candidacy. They headed off a proposal from Weinberg in March that the name of the organization be changed to include Nixon, but refrained from opposing him openly. A petition from twenty-one GOP governors asking Eisenhower to run again omitted Nixon's name, and Governor Fred Hall of Kansas admitted that one of the signers had urged, "For God's sake, keep Nixon's name off it." Publisher John Knight acknowledged in his signed editorial column not only that Nixon had weaknesses but that there was a party division on the question of his renomination. Knight argued that "not all of his [Nixon's] career has been marked by the best judgment," and added, "If the tergiversating Republicans who are shying away from Nixon feel he lacks the proper qualifications, why don't they stand up and say so?"

Nixon showed his disdain of skeptics and critics by a gesture that fell just short of flamboyance. Knowing he had done his homework and nailed down the votes, he ignored intraparty carping by embarking on a whirlwind two-week trip to the Far East, thus revealing again his instinct for picking a battleground calculated to serve his public relations interest. It was perhaps no fault of Nixon's that the trip failed to pay political dividends; news coverage was sketchy; his Manila speech at the tenth anniversary celebration of Philippine independence aroused a spate of anger elsewhere in Asia, but the home front was interested chiefly in preconvention gossip. By July 10 Nixon was back, having neither gained nor lost by the gambit, ready for the showdown.

III

What finally dropped the nomination in his hands like an overripe plum was the lugubrious Stassen affair. On July 23, Harold Stassen, the President's administrative assistant on disarmament, called on Nixon to step aside voluntarily and permit the convention to install Governor Christian Herter of Massachusetts in second place on the ticket. Stassen's argument was simply that public and private polls showed Nixon was "unpopular" and would weaken the ticket by 6 per cent.

The implications of this move were complex and disturbing. It was assumed first that such a statement could not have come from within the White House family without the President's acquiescence. Indeed Stassen said he had consulted the President, in itself an alarming circumstance. It was likewise inferred that Stassen, as an experienced politician, would not be likely to risk such an undertaking without strong assurances of outside support, if not from the President himself, then certainly from other influential Republicans. Professionals scoffed at the revolt, but the outlook for Nixon remained unclear.

What had to be determined was the power and extent of Stassen's support. It was a macabre situation. The President remained aloof. So long as he did that, no one could be sure where the center of gravity was located. At no time did Stassen identify his secret supporters and those within the mysterious coterie proved themselves the most reluctant of reluctant dragons.

A second puzzle for both professionals and outsiders was Stassen's decision to act only a month before the Republican convention. The Nixon problem had existed before the President's illness, since when there had been ample opportunity to carry earnest private discussions into the open. While the President had been making up his mind about running again, there had been a strong feeling that he must be allowed to choose his running mate, but after he announced his decision without indicating such a choice, the situation was fluid. That would have seemed the logical time for Stassen's stop-Nixon move, and the fact that it had been so long delayed gave it a strange air of desperation.

Nixon was plunged into gloom. His backers spoke reassuringly but he was realist enough to know that anything could happen. Again his brooding fatalism asserted itself. He retreated to the solitude of Maryland's Eastern Shore, where friends reported him "eating his heart out" with apprehension.

The situation would have been less mystifying if Stassen's total unpreparedness had been known. He had returned in May from a long, unprofitable disarmament conference in London. With only the scantiest evidence by which to judge Nixon's political standing when he let himself be persuaded to lead the movement against him, Stassen felt he was being driven headlong by the pressure of time. As the fantastic story of his intrigue revealed itself ultimately, he did make an effort to see Nixon personally, to explain his action beforehand, and he likewise tried to reach both Leonard Hall and Christian Herter, but in a strange comedy of errors, he missed them all.

The GOP publication "Straight from the Shoulder" reacted to

the Stassen controversy in its next issue by remaining carefully noncommittal. It plugged the "Ike Bandwagon Ready to Roll" theme but avoided mention of the "Ike and Dick" placards that were being readied for the convention.

Politicians and pundits alike groped for explanations. In the view of columnist David Lawrence, Eisenhower had made it clear that Stassen was acting as an individual "and not as a member of the President's official family." Sorting through the rumors that were making life miserable for Nixon's friends, Lawrence said, "The finger points to a 'left wing' coterie in New York City which put up money for the polls with the avowed object of developing statistical data to force Mr. Nixon out of the race." Others said bluntly the Stassen polls were "phony."

The anti-Nixon movement gained fresh impetus, at least psychologically, when Adlai Stevenson at the Democratic convention threw open to all candidates the contest for the vice-presidential nomination. Those on the Stassenite fringe argued that the Republican convention by adopting the same device could clear the air of whatever appearance of disunity had been created.

In the last-minute maneuvering, General Clay was active behind the scenes, trying to find an acceptable alternative for Nixon. Sherman Adams suggested that Eisenhower might extricate the party from its dilemma by reverting to the face-saving formula of 1952—a list of "acceptable" candidates with Nixon's name first. Nixon told Dewey he would not demur; Brownell, however, called the idea "plain crazy," and Stassen in the end angered the President and killed the idea of a list by predicting it would be issued.

It was not until the convention was in session that the showdown came. Although not himself a delegate, Stassen had applied to the chairman, Representative Joseph W. Martin, Jr., for permission to address the convention, but had given no hint of his intentions.

As the struggle was reconstructed later by Fletcher Knebel for *Look* magazine, Stassen asked to see the President Wednesday morning, and Eisenhower instructed Adams to talk to him first. Hall joined Adams and the two of them spent almost an hour with Stassen.

"Harold," Hall said finally, "for weeks you've been forecasting legions on white horses. They never materialize. You haven't got any delegates."

When Stassen still refused to surrender, Adams handed him an ultimatum: he could see the President if he agreed to second Nixon's nomination.

In the end, that's the way it was. Stassen gave the President his personal assurance that the vendetta was off, and Eisenhower lost no time in calling a news conference to announce that harmony had been restored. Stassen's humiliation was Nixon's triumph. All opposition turned as empty as delegate Terry Carpenter's mythical "Joe Smith." The President may have been as reluctant to accept Nixon as he was to endorse him, but once the vote had been taken, he showed no further trace of vacillation.

IV

Onlookers who had watched Nixon's star in the ascendant recalled his remark, March 14, 1955, at a meeting of GOP workers: "The Republican party is not strong enough to elect a President. We have to have a presidential candidate strong enough to get the Republican party elected."

It would be a fair inference that Vice-President Nixon related the Republican party's handicap to an estimate of his own future, and concluded that another application of Eisenhower stardust was the secret of his own ultimate ability to rise above the party.

Stassen's intrigue, however, left a distinct aftertaste, bitter to some in the Old Guard. In effect, it drew the battle line for 1960.

Stassen belonged ideologically to the Eastern internationalist wing of the party which had won at every Republican national convention since 1940. Philosophically, these were the moderates. It was this wing that had produced Eisenhower, but some of its leaders doubted whether in terms of basic political doctrine Nixon could be relied on to hold fast to the canons of Eisenhower Republicanism. True, as Vice-President he served Eisenhower with notable loyalty but even that fact had its disturbing implications. To some it argued an unstable intellectual fiber, an unprincipled readiness to bend with the winds of expediency. Others in the Eisenhower wing of the party were skeptical because, on his own, Nixon had too marked a tendency to move toward the Republican right, and still others simply questioned whether he could win.

The "dump Nixon" movement of 1956, ill-timed and abortive as it was, seemed to foreshadow a more articulate challenge at the next Republican national convention.

CHAPTER XIII

———————◆———————

Coasting with Ike, 1956

I

THE 1956 campaign began in an atmosphere of political uncertainty. The nominating conventions had been lackadaisical performances on both sides, and the state of the President's health remained of such paramount concern that a search for "issues" in the usual sense would have been academic.

A good deal of water had gone over the dam since Eisenhower had discounted communism as a major political issue in the United States. In the interval McCarthyism had been killed off. The question in the minds of Democrats was whether Nixon and the Republican Old Guard would agree that the security issue had been disposed of, or whether the Vice-President, for lack of anything more popular as a debating ground, would return to his charge that the Democratic party was soft on communism.

Nixon's role, it was tacitly conceded, was the major imponderable, since Eisenhower clearly would not tax his strength with the kind of campaign he had waged four years earlier.

Washington columnists as early as December '55 floated reports that the President's illness had caused Nixon to reconsider his posture on the national scene. The stridency of his ambition, it was said, had mellowed because, to his surprise, his speeches were no longer mere exercises in semantics but were widely read as the utterances of a man who might well be President. His new status sobered him, so the legend went; and to prove it there were reports that he had cast about for speech writers to help modulate his public pronouncements.

Reports of the "new Nixon" did nothing to mollify leading Democrats, including Harry Truman. The former President, still fuming over the Vice-President's 1954 tactics, seized the initiative by charging that Nixon had called him a traitor in speeches "all over the West." That put the Republicans on the defensive. Chairman Hall of the GOP National Committee, rising to champion Nixon, offered to donate $1000 to charity in return for proof that Nixon had ever said, "Mr. Truman was a traitor, or Mr. Stevenson was a traitor, or if you find where he said the Democratic party is a party of treason."

His counterpart, Paul M. Butler of the Democratic National Committee, acknowledged Hall's offer with a heavyfooted show of disdain, accusing him of "splitting hairs" and "resorting to technicalities" in an effort to "clean up the Vice-President."

Butler no doubt reflected the general feeling of the Democratic party when he asserted that Nixon in 1954 had repeatedly made remarks "deliberately contrived and intended to leave his listeners with the impression that the Democratic party and its leaders have been guilty of treason." He called the Vice-President the "leading practitioner of a cruel and malignant political weapon—the not-quite-libelous smear." He charged that Hall's thousand-dollar offer was an "advertising gimmick" designed to obscure Nixon's innuendoes, and asserted that the latter's "slick smears are part of the Republican political strategy, the hate offensive that was planned in cold blood."

The Roman Catholic liberal weekly *The Commonweal* agreed editorially that Mr. Hall's thousand dollars was probably safe "if only on a technicality." The technicality, of course, was that Nixon "implies rather than charges; he imputes rather than accuses," said *The Commonweal,* "but the effect is much the same." And the publication then proceeded to levy against the Vice-President the same moral indictment that has characterized non-Republican opinion of Nixon throughout his public career.

The sad part about all this is that Mr. Nixon himself sometimes seems genuinely confused. . . . Apparently he is a man who very much likes to be liked, and he does not understand why, after the campaign is over, people do not simply forgive and forget. He can-

not seem to get it into his head that there are some things one cannot do if political life is to go on peacefully after an election is
finished. One can criticize, slash hard, accuse opponents of stupidity,
blindness, inefficiency—any number of things. But it is impossible
to imply that one's opponents deliberately betrayed the interests of
the United States, and then expect to be able to work with these
men after the campaign is over as if nothing had happened.

Right now, for example, a good case could be made that, *vis à
vis* the Russians, the United States is in worse shape than it was in
1952. Considerable evidence is available to indicate that the Soviet
Union is out-maneuvering us in the field of foreign policy, and solid
indications exist that our military position has deteriorated rather
than improved since the Republicans took office. The Democrats
are entitled to make all these points, we think, as convincingly as
possible. What they are not entitled to do is to imply that our wors-
ening position is due to secret softness toward Communism by
Secretary of State Dulles, or to the deliberate hiring of "security
risks" by Mr. Nixon, or to a fondness for traitors by President Eisenhower. Such tactics would make American political life impossible,
because they would transform politics into a war of extermination.
Yet this point seems to be the one Mr. Nixon has always failed to
grasp.

In the end the fears of Nixon's detractors, Democrats and pub-
licists alike, proved largely groundless, for 1956 was the year
of the big switch, the year in which Nixon offered himself to a
wary electorate as the Little Lord Fauntleroy of the hustings.

The campaign was slow getting under way, and Nixon made
his preparations with the deliberation of a veteran. By September
9 he had scheduled a pulse-feeling excursion into thirty-two states;
and having so set the stage, he met privately at the White House
with President Eisenhower to agree on the line each would follow
on the stump. He told newsmen next day, as he prepared to begin
work on his basic speech, that his mission would be to counter
Democratic "distortions" of the record, "vigorously and aggressively so that people will know that they have something to fight
for." And with a nostalgic genuflection to the Chotiner influence
of other days, he added, "You can't win by wishy-washy milk
toast."

It was not exactly a rocking-socking-fighting mood; something
more like a synthetic, Sunday-best facsimile, but it was symptomatic. As to the capital cloakroom jargon of the moment—talk
of the "new Nixon" as something less bloodthirsty than the slug-
ger who had infuriated opponents in earlier campaigns—he re-

mained smoothly noncommittal. The individual, he said, "is least qualified to judge whether he is new or old."

The curtain-raiser for the campaign was a folksy, enthusiastic picnic for 600 key party workers September 13 at the Eisenhower farm at Gettysburg. The President played host under a big tent in a pasture; he circulated busily in the crowd, shaking hands, lined up with his guests at a buffet table to eat fried chicken standing up, and shared star billing with Nixon on the speaking program.

In tone if not in the substance of his apparently discursive remarks, Ike set the keynote for the campaign. Saying, "I feel fine," and looking it, the President threw away his prepared notes and delivered an informal pep talk in which he took for himself the role of defining basic guideposts for the Republican party. Then, alluding boldly to the issue of his own health, as he had from the beginning, he went on to assure the assemblage: "There is no man in the history of America who has had such a careful preparation as has Vice-President Nixon for carrying out the duties of the presidency, if that duty should ever fall on him."

In the light of that statement there could be no blinking the fact that Nixon was a central figure in the campaign, if not its central issue. The Vice-President in turn reflected the shifting scale of values; he defined his primary responsibility in the terms which by now had grown familiar to audiences from coast to coast, even to the solemn assurance of which he seemed never to tire: "You don't win campaigns with a diet of dishwater and milk toast!"

He went on to deny that the Democrats were the party of the poor and that Republicans were only for the rich and big business; he ridiculed charges that the Eisenhower administration was shot through with corruption; he accused Stevenson of political fakery for voicing a hope that the draft might soon be ended, and twitted the Democratic nominee for his failure to give the Supreme Court's school integration ruling his four-square endorsement.

Ike and Mamie beamed at the platform sallies; the guests were noisily, cheerfully partisan; and the picnic set a tone of genial party strife, a far cry from the desperate climate of mistrust that had prevailed two years earlier.

II

Nixon's actual campaigning began early on the morning of September 18. The scene was the Terrace Dining Room of the Washington National Airport. Present to signalize the occasion was President Eisenhower himself, breakfasting with the Vice-President and a group of other GOP campaigners. Nixon had ahead of him six weeks of the most arduous hedgehopping and whistle-stopping, 33,000 miles in thirty-two states.

Ike was in a rosy, confident mood, and he was ready with a characteristic homily.

"The record itself is sufficient, if it is made sufficiently clear to all Americans," he assured the Vice-President. "And that should be our campaign." To make his message wholly clear, the President added benignly that there was "no need to indulge in the exaggerations of partisan political talk" nor to "claim perfection."

That was the official enunciation of the party line.

The President was on hand with a parting salute because it was the least he could do for a man undertaking that most difficult of all missions—the task of stating another man's case for him—but he was there on his own terms, not on Nixon's. However reluctant Eisenhower was to do his own stumping, whether for reasons of health or otherwise, he undertook to lay out the ground rules for the struggle, rules that did not encourage the Chotiner-Nixon style of in-fighting.

This White House policy line may have had much to do with Eisenhower's personal success as an office-seeker, but the effort to identify his faith in the household virtues with political virtue in general was a profitless miscalculation that year for the Republican party.

In the circumstances, however, the professionals had to accept the President's battle plan as a calculated risk. They had barely won control of Congress in '52, riding the Eisenhower coattails, and they had lost heavily in '54 after an all-out slugging match. The reasonable inference was that there was no magic in the party name or image, and that even slugging had its limitations. That being so, what remained in their arsenal was the Eisenhower magic. If that could still win, it had to win on its own—even if only on a diet of dishwater and milk toast—and it had to win for both itself *and* the party.

For lack of another issue, the President's health continued to hold the center of the stage. The Republicans might not have preferred it that way but it was not theirs to choose. And the focal point of that issue, quite logically and inevitably, was Vice-President Nixon. The voter had only to ask himself—or be invited to by a Democrat—whether a Republican ticket deserved to win if the man who might succeed to the presidency was of questionable fitness for the highest office in the land. So long as the question could be asked, it had to be answered.

Opinion about Nixon was still divided. One of the Vice-President's avowed admirers, Richard Wilson, wrote in *Look* that his biggest problem was still "to overcome the impression in some groups, particularly those who think of themselves as intellectuals, that some undefined tricky quality in Nixon makes him unsuited for the presidency." The *Madison* (Wis.) *Capital Times* argued with frank belligerency that the problem was "how to exploit Nixon's unquestionable capacity for smear-type campaigning and at the same time project the image of Eisenhower as a unifier and pacifier above the political battles."

The origin of the 1956 strategy—whether it was conceived by the Vice-President alone or in concert with administration and party advisers—has never been revealed. At any rate, the Republican high command let itself be persuaded that the task of the campaign was to exorcise the old, controversial Nixon personality. If the Vice-President was to be propped up as the spokesman and filial image of an ailing administration, the first essential was to provide him with a veneer of statesmanship and Eisenhowerism.

Nixon embraced the strategy skillfully. He was billed as the traveling salesman of Republicanism but his chief product was no longer to be the party. His tactic, when the precinct workers yelled for the taste of raw meat, was to offer instead the composite Eisenhower-Nixon personality, whose spirit infused and transcended the grosser aspects of partisanship.

The campaign was hardly more than a few days old when the *Wall Street Journal* cited, as an example of his "political craftsmanship," the fact that Nixon had "carefully set out to undo Democratic attempts to picture him as just a party hatchet man, and to appear before the voters as a man of Presidential timber."

Nixon had fortified himself for the ordeal. Five days before the Terrace Dining Room pep talk, he had secluded himself in a room at the Mayflower Hotel. There with pencil and pad, he analyzed, outlined, revised, and laboriously, brick by brick, laid out the text of his "basic speech."

"He just climbed into his pajamas and thought and thought and wrote and wrote," one of his press secretaries told Richard Rovere. "He doesn't want ghost-writers. Oh, we help with research, and we give him ideas now and then, and sometimes we throw in a phrase or a sentence we think might be helpful. But it all goes through that meat-grinder of a mind he's got, and believe me, it comes out an entirely different grade of hamburger. He has his own vocabulary and his own rhythms, and none of us can really catch them. And he'll never use anything that doesn't sound like him."

What came out of the meat-grinder was, in essence, a slogan coupled with a name: "Eisenhower; peace, prosperity, progress." It was a text liberally sprinkled with eulogies to "the greatest leader of the atomic age," "a man who ranks among the greatest of the legendary heroes of this nation," "a man of destiny, both at home and abroad." It reached a climax urging every American to rise above the petty squabbles of partisanship:

> And finally may I tell you, as you go out and work in this campaign to keep [name of state] in the Eisenhower column, you are working for an administration that has brought peace and prosperity and progress to America and you are going to be working for a man whom every American can proudly hold up to his children as one who has faith in God, faith in America, and one who has restored dignity and respect to the highest office in the land.

On the first leg of his tour, from Washington to southern California and the Pacific Northwest, Nixon's quest for votes fell into a smooth-running pattern. At the first stop after the President's send-off, in Indianapolis, he promised to stick to the high road, but warned the Democrats not to get rough.

"Let's get one thing straight right now," he said. "Where our opponents misrepresent and distort the record and where they vilify the President of the United States, I shall consider it a duty and a privilege to set the record straight." The rest was oratorical window dressing.

By the time he hit Oregon, Nixon had so polished the basic speech that he could deliver it backward. It was a subdued, mellow performance, with just enough nips at the Truman policies to stir up the crowd but none like his snide 1952 assurance that "nothing would please the Kremlin more" than Stevenson's election.

At each airport Nixon walked down the ramp from his DC-6B with his arm around wife Pat, for a greeting from a beribboned delegation of ranking Republicans in the vicinity. Then off in a motorcade to the rally. The speech drew good crowds and seemed to go over, although to be sure the audiences were to a large extent claques of the faithful who needed no persuasion.

From city to city and state to state the main body of the speech remained constant, and as the phraseology grew shopworn with repetition, the correspondents coined their own titles for the familiar clichés. The "Old Shoe" was his statement that the United States "has prosperity and peace to boot"; the "Weight-Lifting Act," his line that "every man can hold up Dwight Eisenhower to his children as a man who has faith in God, faith in America"; and the "Bush-Leaguer" identified his assertion that "Adlai Stevenson just isn't in the same league with President Eisenhower."

A correspondent who accompanied the Vice-President on both 1956 campaign swings admitted that, as he listened day after day, a preconceived dislike had been intensified. "There was something completely synthetic about Nixon's appearances," he said. "He never debated the issues, simply brushed them off with slogans and cliches. After a while you only felt him saying to himself: 'How can I make this crowd *like* me?' Granting that all politicians want to be liked, Nixon's effort was too transparent; it made him look bad."

On this as on other trips, both Nixons worked with tireless intensity. Their chartered airliner had been fitted with a beaverboard compartment at the rear where they could have privacy to read, nap, or write without interruption. For Nixon, one of the advantages of plane travel was that, with every seat booked, there was no room for that self-invited pest, the local politician who might want to hitch a ride to the next stop. Toward the end of the trip Nixon did shift to a train part of the time and he made no secret of his distaste for the company of these political reliquiae of the whistle-stop era. When a reporter asked whether he preferred planes or trains, he answered shortly, "Planes, of course; more privacy, and you can get more work done."

Normally his tours booked every hour of every day solidly. On one occasion, however, there was an enforced layover of several hours, and a group of weary staff members and reporters took advantage of the break to go for a swim in the hotel pool. Suddenly, in the midst of the laughter and horseplay, Nixon in his bathing suit stalked into the patio, dived in, swam the length of the pool several times, climbed out, and disappeared in the direction of his room. All this without so much as a glance right or left or a word or a smile to anyone in the party.

For Mrs. Nixon, as for her husband, every thought was dedicated to the campaign. On one occasion in Cheyenne, Nixon was suffering from a virus attack and the speech was an ordeal; words came with difficulty, his face was ashen, and he fought for control. Later, as the party boarded a midnight plane, a correspondent standing beside Mrs. Nixon expressed sympathy for the Vice-President's having to carry on at such a cost. "Oh," she exclaimed defensively, "but it was a *good* speech!" Whatever her private feelings, she gave no outward sign of wifely anxiety.

III

By October 1 the Vice-President's preoccupation with the pounding rhythms of the campaign was being interrupted by raucous protests from Republican headquarters in Washington. Willard Edwards reported in the *Chicago Tribune,* after private conversations with Nixon in his flying office, that the party high command had begun sending messages begging him frantically to slug it out with Stevenson and deploring the lofty level at which he had been operating. In response to their advice to "engage in verbal street-fighting, slashing, ripping, and swinging from his heels," the Vice-President let it be known that he had no intention of becoming a "political Jack the Ripper."

To verify the report, Edwards telephoned Washington at a stop on the tour and confirmed not only that Nixon was running his own show but that panicky Republican leaders were imploring him to assume again the role of hatchet man.

"He's paying us no attention," a high Republican official growled. "He's got his own mimeograph machine and he won't let us lay a hand on the crank."

What had stirred the party high command to a sense of panic were the private polls indicating an easy victory for Eisenhower and Nixon but a depressing outlook for House and Senate candidates in many areas. Nixon admitted that, in probing for "soft spots," he had found many; but to him the cold fact of politics was that the Republicans were a minority party, and Eisenhower could not win without Democratic votes. His appeal was therefore bipartisan in those states where voter registration showed the Republicans to be outnumbered, and the tactics that he had favored in earlier years were no longer appropriate.

Nixon worked subtly and persistently to divide the Democratic party against itself. One of his popular arguments at closed meetings of party workers was that UAW President Walter Reuther, whom he called the "smartest labor leader in America," was the "man to beat" in November, rather than Stevenson. After he had exploited the possibilities of this line privately, he arranged that a Michigan reporter should hear one of his briefings. The result was a *Detroit News* story in which Nixon praised Reuther's "cleverness" and suggested that the UAW leader sat at the center of a nationwide spider web, the "source of the big money and organizers" capable of winning for the Democratic party.

At the other extreme, in a Milwaukee news conference he went so far as to make backhanded amends for his controversial 1952 allusion to Truman as a "traitor to the high principles" of the Democratic party. Explaining the charge, Nixon said, "I believe that in the Democratic party there is a great cleavage between the great principles on which the Democratic party was founded —Jefferson and Jackson, principles which recognize the dignity of the individual, the sovereignty of the states—and the new theory which some of those who are now quite influential in the Democratic party hold to, that the answer to most problems is through federal government action.

"I think that when Mr. Truman and Mr. Stevenson and others went along with this new theory rather than the one that is traditionally considered to be the special province of the Democratic party, I believe they left millions of Democrats without a home. In other words, I believe that they deserted their party rather than the party deserting them."

The stratagem may have been well conceived, but if it paid off the evidence was scanty. In fact, it was a question how much or whether the final outcome was affected at all by the foot-pounds of selfless energy and devotion he poured into the struggle. On

the whole it was a tepid campaign because there was no fundamental or vital issue dividing the country that year. During October the campaign was enlivened, if only sporadically, by Adlai
Stevenson's proposal to suspend nuclear bomb testing; but the
fallout danger had not yet been recognized for what it was, and
the public was not ready for the proposal.

By and large the test ban never became an issue. Eisenhower,
having perhaps some prescience that the proposal contained its
own built-in logic, treated the subject gingerly. Nixon began with
similar caution, calling it first "unacceptable," but warming to the
subject progressively when he found audiences responsive. At
Philadelphia October 3 he called the test ban proposal "extraordinary . . . appalling . . . catastrophic nonsense . . . the height
of irresponsibility . . . naïve . . . the most dangerous theme of
the campaign." By October 17 at Buffalo he was accusing Stevenson of "playing dangerous politics with American security" and
referring to "the ridiculous H-bomb proposal" as a "major political error" on Stevenson's part.

Except for that indiscretion, Nixon's new personality was proof
against all temptation. When Congressman Dewey Short, intro-
ducing him at a rally, assured Nixon: "You're among friends—
take off your gloves and sock them," the Vice-President could
only pretend not to hear. In Ohio, where GOP workers openly
deplored his mellow mood, he was challenged directly to defend
his "high-level" campaign. For the first time, publicly at any rate,
he deserted the Chotiner fear-and-scare psychology of winning
political converts. He told a news conference:

"The problem this year is different from that in 1952. I always
conduct a hard-hitting campaign on issues, and avoid personalities. In 1952 we were giving the people reasons to throw out a
group, and now we are giving them reasons to keep an administration in. What I am doing now is to appeal to swing voters,
whom we must have to win. It is essential to have a type of campaign persuasive to independents and Democrats."

IV

Nixon's first cross-country swing was followed by a second,
and simultaneously by a burst of energy on Eisenhower's part.
Their theme remained the same—that the American people had

never been happier or more prosperous. They refused to grapple with the possibility that the world had achieved, not peace, but an uneasy truce.

As the campaign drew to a close Nixon was saying, "our opponents are having great difficulty finding issues." Actually he was on the defensive, painting a synthetic state of euphoria and having difficulty avoiding issues. In the Midwest he refused to mention Agriculture Secretary Ezra Taft Benson, farm parity prices, or flexible price supports. At Cornell University, where a group of college editors hammered hard at suggesting that there was inconsistency between his voting record and his current campaign speeches, he answered in platitudes. On McCarthyism, when asked if he favored a resumption of Senate probing, he could only insist the Eisenhower administration had taken the security issue out of politics.

It was Nixon's good fortune that the public was as little interested in the issues as he was in discussing them. His appeal continued to be essentially emotional or evangelistic. He avoided mention of the Republican platform or the program the party would put forward if elected. His argument from beginning to end was that President Eisenhower was the greatest man alive and should be re-elected to assure continued peace, prosperity, and progress. It was not a thesis to set the countryside afire, but Nixon was no longer a firebrand. His was a more modest role.

A newsman in Buffalo captured the tone of the Vice-President's 1956 campaign. Questioning a staff member, he pried out an admission that Nixon had explicitly vetoed the use of Cadillacs or other big cars in his campaign motorcades!

In the upshot, it was an easy Eisenhower victory. The margin was more than nine million popular votes: 35,590,472 for Eisenhower; 26,029,752 for Stevenson.

But the fears of party professionals had been well grounded. The Democrats held their control in the Senate, 49 to 47; and picked up another two seats in the House. Thus, notwithstanding a presidential sweep of landslide proportions, the Republican party could not win at the state and district level. It had tried the hard sell without success in '54, and it had no better results in '56 using both a soft sell and the Eisenhower magic. From the Vice-President's point of view, looking ahead to 1960, the returns were ambiguous.

CHAPTER XIV

The King Canute of '58

I

FOR NIXON the campaign of 1958 was at once his best and his worst. On the one hand, Communist subversion, the issue on which he had risen to prominence, was hardly mentioned; to the degree that his silence helped bury the issue, and so helped to allay fears of an irreconcilable schism in our national political life, the Vice-President won approbation. On the other hand, the Republicans suffered their worst congressional defeat since 1936; to the degree that his efforts to prevent a debacle were unavailing, his reputation as a winner was compromised.

For campaign purposes the image of the "new Nixon" of 1956 was transformed into the ideologically "newer Nixon" of 1958; but after the votes were counted, there came a realization that Nixon without his favorite issue was a poor match for the gigantic tides of national feeling that he was undertaking to manipulate.

In fairness, it would be unrealistic to imagine that any individual could have redirected the massive undercurrents favoring the Democrats. Nixon could have been fully aware of the odds against him and could still have been a pawn of circumstance. Politically he had a gun at his head. The man in the White House was the first lame-duck President to be categorically retired under the Twenty-second Amendment; when this constitutional inhibition was compounded by considerations of health—a mild cerebral stroke November 25, 1957, together with the earlier history of ileitis and a coronary occulsion—it was clear that little could be expected from a party leader in Eisenhower's state of physical and political debilitation. If there was to be, nationally, an authoritative voice of Republicanism, it had to be Nixon's.

Other factors intensified the Vice-President's disadvantage. A recession starting late in 1957 had spiraled downward during the winter until unemployment stood at more than five million, most of the layoffs occurring in industrial areas where they took on a high degree of political visibility. The Eighty-fifth Democratic Congress, seizing upon the recession as proof that the tight-money retrenchment policies of the Republicans were strangling the economy, took the initiative on a series of pump-priming measures not likely to alienate voters. Finally, the Dulles policy of brinksmanship was still producing equivocal results—in the Middle East, where a revolt in Iraq foreshadowed new and unpredictable turbulence, and American Marine intervention in Lebanon dramatized no-one-knew-what threats to Western interests; and also in Asia, where a new Communist Chinese feint at Quemoy again brought war talk to the surface.

For whatever causes—and they were many—the GOP was in trouble. On that point the pollsters were unanimous. To a politician of Nixon's experience, the omens could hardly have been worse. At intervals during the campaign, defensively and at times compulsively, he acknowledged his forebodings.

In his keynote speech at Indianapolis September 29, he plunged straight into the subject: "We would just be kidding ourselves if we did not recognize right now that we Republicans have the fight of our lives on our hands this November. . . .

"Some of my Republican friends have even urged me to do as little as possible in this campaign so as to avoid being associated with a losing cause. My answer to that kind of talk is—poppycock! . . . We will lose if we continue to backpedal. . . . We aren't going to win by giving the voters a diet of dishwater and milk toast. But we can win if we start slugging. . . ."

But he had lost some of the old enthusiasm for slugging, and he continued to shadowbox with defeatism. In Garden City, Long Island, October 23, he repeated: "Many friends have warned me of the political risks involved in being associated with a losing campaign. . . . What happens to me in this campaign is relatively unimportant. What happens to the Republican party is more important. . . . Win or lose, it is unforgivable to lack the courage to fight for the principles we believe in."

That same week in Baltimore, when asked on a televised press conference whether he had not become so "controversial" that he could not win in 1960, he avoided a direct answer, showing his preoccupation with the impending defeat and its impact on his own future by saying that "regardless of how it might affect my political future, there is no choice—and I accept this choice, incidentally, gladly—there is no choice but to fight as hard as I can for those principles and for the election of men who will support the President and his principles, and I intend to continue to do that regardless of the political consequences."

II

In laying out the general plan of the campaign, his handling of the issues developed fresh nuances. Instead of standing foursquare on the Eisenhower father image, as he had two years before, he reworked his material in a fashion that pushed Ike gently into the background. Emphasis shifted from the President to the corporate body of the administration with which Nixon could identify himself. One passage in which Eisenhower had been ballyhooed in 1956 as the man who had got us out of one war and kept us out of others came out thus in the modified pitch: "This administration got the United States out of one war, kept it out of others, and has kept the peace without surrender of principle or territory."

On civil rights and school integration the Vice-President took a strictly tactical position. Arguing that state and local voting trends were governed by local social patterns, he said civil rights were not worth stressing in an off-year since the issue would have little influence on the makeup of the new Congress, but he predicted the Republicans could capitalize on it profitably in 1960. On one occasion, however, in New York, October 23, he made an exception to his rule with a statement denouncing Adlai Stevenson for criticizing Eisenhower's lack of leadership on civil rights. In a *tu quoque* argument, he asked how Stevenson proposed to enlist the support of Southern governors in extending school integration, boasting, "We have done more in six years of this administration than they talked of doing in twenty years," and concluded: "The fight on this issue is one that must be made within the Democratic party itself."

Again, as a hedge against recession vote losses, and in what was for him an unprecedented move to broaden the base of the party, Nixon refused to join Republicans like Goldwater of Arizona and Knowland of California in campaigning against labor; he warned that the GOP should not jockey itself into the "false position" of being opposed to the labor movement. In another departure from party orthodoxy, he argued in favor of making liberals as well as conservatives feel at home in Republican ranks; he told a Philadelphia breakfast rally there was need for both conservative and liberal points of view in a healthy party, thus breaking with Old Guardists of the Taft persuasion who fought to make the Republican party the fortress of standpattism.

Having by this exercise in semantics subordinated certain major points of friction, Nixon then proceeded to wage a new kind of campaign—a campaign in which he drove himself with cool, tireless, relentless efficiency, avoiding, as Douglass Cater observed in *The Reporter,* both the hard sell and the soft sell and concentrating on a passionless, colorless self sell.

One incident, otherwise wholly insignificant, reflected his sensitivity to public-relations values. At San Diego, October 1, in reply to Democratic criticisms of the defense program, he said that he found "very disturbing . . . the implication that we are so scientifically poverty-stricken and that our industrial machinery is so ramshackle that everything we are going to do in the next few years will be wrong and everything the Communists do will be right.

"That," he concluded, "is rotgut thinking."

To newsmen on the trip, most of whom by this time knew the basic speech almost as well as he did, the phrase "rotgut thinking" was new and picturesque, a throwback to earlier fighting campaigns, and the sort of thing that lent itself readily to a quick puff and a bold headline. On the strength of that one phrase, the San Diego speech got a heavy play in the press, and the reaction sounded a tremor of alarm. Republicans who liked to hear Nixon "pour it on" welcomed back the "old Nixon," the rocking-socking campaigner. Democrats and some commentators recoiled, however, pointing an accusing finger at the political roughneck who always seemed to be a little offside.

As if he had touched a live wire, Nixon dropped the word "rotgut" from his vocabulary. The staff member who had first incorporated it in a memorandum fell into disfavor and shortly afterward left the Vice-President's entourage. It would be an exaggeration to say that the incident caused Nixon to panic, but intimate observers were aware that he was shaken by the criticism. From the beginning of his political career words like "rotgut" seemed to have a purely ornamental quality in Nixon's campaign oratory. He employed them as one employs colored baubles to decorate a Christmas tree, with a sense that they were at once part of the dime-store world of reality and at the same time no less a part of Saint Nicholas's legendary world of fantasy. On this, as on more than one occasion in his career, his basic sense of security was profoundly shaken by the discovery that where the lives and reputations of men are at stake words cannot be juggled about like colored tinsel.

III

Nixon's efforts to find a substantive issue for 1958 met with repeated frustration. Perhaps his best hope and his biggest disappointment was the foreign-policy issue on which he was badly crossruffed in mid-October. At that time the outlook at Quemoy was still equivocal, still tense because of the continuing sporadic Communist bombardment. Although Harry Truman had come out flatly in support of President Eisenhower's policy on both Lebanon and Quemoy, the Democratic Advisory Council took a highly critical tone in a report challenging Republican foreign policy. In the ensuing flurry of charge and countercharge Nixon took a beating.

The Vice-President as the chief campaign policy-maker took it upon himself to leap forward October 13 with an *ad hominem* statement denouncing the Democratic party's "sorry record of retreat and appeasement" and comparing the Eisenhower administration's performance on foreign policy "with the record of failure of the seven years that preceded it" and the "defensive, defeatist fuzzy-headed thinking which contributed to the loss of China and led to the Korean war."

"In a nutshell," he said, "the Acheson foreign policy resulted in war and the Eisenhower-Dulles policy resulted in peace."

At the State Department the next morning Secretary Dulles was holding a news conference. The situation in Asia was precarious; Dulles had no wish to compound his difficulties with the indiscretions of campaign oratory, so when he was asked whether current aspects of foreign policy should be debated on the stump, he called the practice "highly undesirable" and added, "I would hope that both sides would calm down on this aspect of the debate."

Nixon did not take kindly to the rebuke and on the 15th Dulles switched his position, obviously under pressure from the indignant Vice-President, to suggest there was need for a reply such as Nixon made to the weekend statement of the Democratic Advisory Council. That same day, however, President Eisenhower told his news conference: ". . . I do subscribe to this theory: foreign policy ought to be kept out of partisan debate. . . . I realize that when someone makes a charge another individual is going to reply. I deplore that. . . . America's best interests in the world will be served if we do not indulge in this kind of thing."

Nixon's first instinct was to defend his position. As he was about to board a plane for Los Angeles, he told a San Francisco news conference: "One of the reasons the Republican party is in trouble today is because we have allowed people to criticize our policies and we have not stood up and answered effectively. . . . I intend to continue to answer the attacks. . . . That's my view of a political campaign."

And then Vice-President Nixon digressed from the immediate issue to philosophize about the nature of his own job as contrasted with that of the President. Acknowledging Eisenhower's statement that attacks on foreign policy should not be answered, he said, "This, I think, is a proper position for the President." But he added, "For us who have the responsibility of carrying the weight of this campaign to stand by and to allow our policies to be attacked with impunity by our opponents without reply would lead to inevitable defeat. . . . If my view of a political campaign differs from that which the President has expressed, the difference is not because of any difference we have as individuals. The difference is because of the positions we hold. He's the President of the United States, a man who has to mobilize the entire country behind his policy, if that is possible. I am the Vice-President of the United States and have certain responsibilities in a political campaign."

On the record that tortured rationalization left the issue where it had been, with Nixon still charging that Democratic policies led to war. Whereupon, on the 16th, Eisenhower took the final categorical step that removed Democratic patriotism as a partisan issue. He sent Nixon a telegram saying bluntly:

> Both political parties have taken a common stand for a number of years on the essential foundations of a foreign policy. Both of us are dedicated to peace, to the renunciation of force except for defense, to the principles of the United Nations Charter, to opposing Communist expansion, to promoting the defensive and economic strength of the free world through cooperative action, including mutual aid and technical assistance.
>
> While in my view these, with rare exceptions, should not and do not lend themselves to political argument, the matter of administrative operation of foreign policy—whether or not agreed goals are in fact realized—has time and again been challenged both by ourselves in the past and very recently by some of our political opponents. . . . These actions, when criticized, should be supported by our side. No one can do this more effectively than you.

"At times," added the President dryly, "it is of course difficult to distinguish between policy and administrative operations. . . ."

At intervals throughout the remainder of the campaign Nixon continued to make angry noises and occasional oblique references to Acheson, but on October 21 at Baltimore he all but threw in the towel. After a bitter attack on the "radical leadership" of the Democratic National Committee and the Advisory Council, he went on to say:

"In answer to these attacks, I want to reiterate what I have said on many occasions in the past. I do not question the sincerity or patriotism of those who criticize our policies. Our differences are not in ends but in means.

"There is no war party in the United States. All Americans want peace.

"There is no party of surrender in the United States. . . .

"There is only one party of treason in the United States— the Communist party. . . .

"Our differences arise in the means which will best accomplish this purpose. . . .

"We believe that the policy of weakness and vacillation of the

previous administration which was developed under Mr. Acheson
. . . has been tried and found wanting.

"We have learned once and for all that in dealing with dictators
—first with Hitler and then in Korea—a weak policy is a war
policy, a firm policy is a peace policy."

After that, by further subtle shifts in his vocabulary, the Vice-
President accommodated himself to the White House policy line.
On the last day of October he was repeating, "A weak policy is
a war policy; a firm policy is a peace policy," and in a plea for
Democratic votes insisting the issue "is not between a Republican
foreign policy and a Democratic foreign policy."

Barely a month later, during a BBC television interview in
London, he frankly acknowledged having lost the round. A pan-
elist asked whether it was true that "you were gently rebuked
by the President for making foreign affairs an election issue."

"Yes," Nixon replied, "as a matter of fact it is true."

Again on the corruption issue, Nixon found himself on the
defensive for the first time because of the Goldfine–Sherman
Adams case and the revelations of the House Legislative Oversight Committee. By that time the Eisenhower administration
had been in office long enough to collect its share of influence-
peddlers and dubious-percenters, and when the President's assistant was found guilty of indiscretions, there ceased to be any
mileage in being against sin.

None of these disappointments prevented Nixon from continuing his fight. He worked twenty-four hours a day—an effort that
had genuine integrity regardless of his motives. He felt that he
was the underdog, partly because the President was not giving
him wholehearted support. At Salt Lake City, October 16, he
complained with restrained bitterness, "If all the members of the
President's Cabinet will in the last three weeks of this campaign
fight as effectively and as articulately" as Ezra Taft Benson,
thousands of votes would be shifted.

In the end, however, the campaign was colorless because it
lacked an affirmative, substantive issue—something to be "for."
And it found only one windmill left standing to tilt against—the
ephemeral "ADA left wing" of the Democratic party which never
materialized. Nixon had tried his lance against the "ADA clique"
in an earlier campaign, and had found one advantage—the gambit tended to stiffen the coalition of Republicans and conservative

Southern Democrats. So long as the ADA had been comparatively unknown and its reputation vaguely sinister, it had been a useful whipping boy, but in returning to the attack on it in 1958 Nixon drew a blank. This was the case partly because the ADA remained what it had been, a minor ideological splinter, and partly because it had lost some of its militancy—had in fact moved in behind Senator Lyndon Johnson of Texas on some issues—and its reputation for anticommunism by this time was so well known in most parts of the country that it raised no hobgoblins.

Toward the end Nixon was trying to recast the image of his campaign, saying: "The issue, very simply stated, is this—guarantee progress for America by electing more Republicans. Stop progress by electing more Democrats." Along with that appeal, the phrases that occurred most frequently were: "Democrats from the free-spending wing of the party, the radical group from the North and the West"; "runaway inflation which a Congress dominated by radicals will inevitably bring about"; "Congress dominated by radicals and labor politicians"; "nominees on the Democratic ticket . . . exposed as helpless captives of the same old radical wing"; "When you vote for more Democrats, you are voting to raise your taxes, cheapen your money, and to stifle new investment and enterprise"; "radical ADA wing"; "We have the fight of our lives on our hands."

In the homestretch he risked his political reputation still further by a series of optimistic forecasts that ran contrary to every poll and every independent sounding. In Wyoming: "I find increasing evidence that the political pollsters and prophets who have been predicting a decisive Democratic victory are in for the surprise of their lives on November 4." In Eau Claire, Wisconsin: ". . . Thousands of moderate Democrats will turn the tide in close races for the House and Senate in the Northern and Western states by voting for Republican candidates"—a bit of wishful thinking never to be fulfilled.

He sent all GOP candidates for House and Senate a secret telegram October 19, summarizing and cataloguing the ideas he had been expounding in his own barnstorming, and saying:

> . . . The tide that was running so strongly against us has taken a sharp turn in our favor. . . . If we make the fight of our lives and mount a massive offensive . . . we can turn what appeared to be

certain defeat into victory. . . . All Republican candidates and spokesmen should radiate optimism and should be on the offensive. . . . In a nutshell . . . why take a chance with a change? . . . I am convinced that if we hammer on this line from now to election day, we can blitz the opposition and shift thousands of votes in close races throughout the country.

IV

The outcome November 4 was what all others had forecast—an unprecedented midterm victory for the Democrats. They gained fifteen seats in the Senate, forty-six in the House, and nine governorships. The total popular vote for members of the House, which had favored the Democrats in 1956 when the Republicans were running with the support of Eisenhower by the narrow margin of 29,831,608 to 28,697,321—a difference of barely over a million—shifted in 1958 to give the Democrats a margin of more than five million: a total of 25,365,961 for Democrats to 19,943,882 for Republican candidates.

Philip Potter of the Baltimore *Sun,* analyzing the results, concluded that Nixon's herculean effort in twenty-five states to blitz the Democrats had been successful only in the cases of five out of the nineteen GOP Senate candidates for whom he spoke, of only one-third of the Republican aspirants for the House, and in the cases of three governors.

In Nixon's defense, as he himself pointed out at a Philadelphia rally, there were too many "turkeys" on the GOP list in '58; where the party had outstanding candidates, as in New York and Pennsylvania, they were able to win handily, with or without Nixon's support.

In his own analysis of the outcome, he told Earl Mazo that half the losses could be attributed to the fact that the issues "ran against us from the time of the second term inauguration. . . ." And he listed those issues as the budget, sputnik, the recession, and the Adams case, all of them calculated to keep the administration on the defensive. The Republicans themselves, he said, were responsible for the other half of the losses—by fighting among themselves in California and Indiana, by forcing the right-to-work issue in Ohio, and "in other states because of poor organization and failure to run stronger candidates."

The most remarkable aspect of his failure was that he achieved new levels of moderation but his moderation failed to get across.

His mellowness was suspect or went unnoticed. The "Tricky Dick" image persisted. His choice of Democratic "radicalism" as an issue he dismissed with an explanation whose cogency would be instantly apparent on Madison Avenue or in Hollywood.

"The President and I," he said, "used the term 'radical' to describe the economic philosophy of the Northern and Western wings of the Democratic party because we felt that the term 'liberal' has become so corrupted in recent years that it could not accurately be used in describing that philosophy. . . . We used it [radical] only as a descriptive term . . . the opposite of moderate. . . ."

Hence, in this view, the campaign was fought over a twist of semantics, not on the question of whether the Democrats were in an essential, abiding sense believers in a radical socio-economic philosophy.

It was the chairman of the Republican National Committee, Meade Alcorn, who summed up the meaning of the election at Des Moines, January 22, 1959, when he proposed a look at "some frightening figures."

"In 1950 the population of the United States was 150 million," he said. "Approximately 20 million people voted in the midterm elections for Republican candidates for Congress. In 1958 there were 175 million Americans and again 20 million of them voted for Republican congressional candidates.

"Through those same eight years the Democrats increased their congressional vote from 20 million in 1950 to 25.7 million in 1958.

"In other words, while we have stood still as the population increased, our opposition has steadily enlarged its vote turn-out.

"Despite the two great presidential sweeps of 1952 and 1956," Alcorn concluded, "the Republican party has not won what could properly be called a national party victory since 1946 when the 'had enough' temper of the country touched off a landslide."

It is certainly no more than coincidence that Nixon's public career spanned the twelve-year interval from the emotion-charged "had enough" landslide of 1946 to the electorate's bleakly un-emotional repudiation of the Republican party in 1958. In that interval he had risen from obscurity to stand at the threshhold of the presidency; three times, as Eisenhower surmounted grave illnesses, the Vice-President was no more than a heartbeat from the White House. In his climb he had built large reservoirs of gratitude in the state Republican organizations as a tireless cheer leader and money raiser.

The irony of it was that, at the pinnacle, he should have had to lead the Republican party to its worst defeat in two decades and at the same time see an attractive rival, a rival whose power base in New York was a match for his own in California, be propelled from nowhere into the race for the presidency.

PART THREE

PUBLIC SERVANT

CHAPTER XV

Congressman

I

TIME: January 3, 1947.

Setting: The Republican cloakroom in the House of Representatives.

New members waiting to take the oath were milling about striking up acquaintances, mentally fitting themselves into their new roles. A newspaperman, stepping up to one of the freshman legislators, asked the stock question.

"Do you have any bill you plan to introduce, or any pet project you intend to push for?"

The young congressman pursed his lips and smiled. "No, nothing in particular," he replied modestly. "I was elected to smash the labor bosses, and my one principle is to accept no dictation from the CIO-PAC."

The congressman of course was thirty-three-year-old Richard Nixon, fresh from his triumph over Jerry Voorhis, ideologically flexing himself for a career of public service.

Attempts since then to assess Nixon's record in the House have been inconclusive. His name was not identified with any policy, and his votes reveal no broad recognizable pattern. William S. White called his record in the House "obscure" except for his connection with the Hiss affair and put him down as a routine, orthodox-to-right-wing Republican "sufficiently unsoft on

179

most welfare and allied legislation to suit management-minded Republicans."

By a not too tortured process of tailoring his voting record, it has been possible to show him in a variety of postures—from liberal to moderate to reactionary—a fact which has been employed with success by both his friends and his political foes. Almost from the start Nixon showed a grasp of the opportunistic art of working on one side of the fence while a bill was being amended and perfected, and then switching to the other side or being conveniently absent when the measure came to a final vote. Among professionals this is considered vintage politics, a technique hoary with respectability, the only pragmatic answer to the opposition in districts where the turnover of congressmen tends to be high. By a careful distribution of votes and speeches on sensitive issues, it is possible to be on all sides simultaneously and thus relatively immune from partisan attack. The ethics of the system is a separate problem, usually disposed of by professionals with a shrug and a wink.

Early in his House career, Nixon was referred to by a Washington newspaper as "the greenest congressman in town." In the light of what happened, it would have been safer to reserve judgment. Nixon showed, in fact, a rare insight into the manipulation of power. One of his shrewdest moves was to help organize the Chowder and Marching Club, a group of fifteen junior Republicans who met every Wednesday for strategy conferences on bills, hearings, reports, and amendments.[1]

As a bloc the youthful marchers were big enough to command a degree of attention which would not have been accorded them as individuals; at the same time they were not big enough to excite hostility or reprisals. They provided one another with a degree of

---

[1] The club's charter members besides Nixon were: Kenneth Keating of New York, Norris Cotton of New Hampshire, and Thruston B. Morton of Kentucky, all of whom went on to the Senate; John J. Allen of California, who became Undersecretary of Commerce; Representatives John Byrnes of Wisconsin, Donald Jackson of California, Gerald Ford of Michigan, Glenn Davis of Wisconsin, and Walter Norblad of Oregon; John Lodge of Connecticut, who became ambassador to Spain; Charles Potter of Michigan, who went into business after his defeat for re-election to the Senate; Claude Bakewell, who became postmaster of St. Louis; Charles Nelson of Maine, who joined the political-science department of the University of Miami; Harold Lovre of South Dakota, who practiced law in Washington after leaving Congress; and J. Caleb Boggs, who was elected governor of Delaware.

protective coloration, and gave Nixon as their leader a base of operations and a first tentative step upward on the ladder of congressional influence. Without such a base Nixon and his associates as individuals might easily have been lost in the remote upper corridors of the House Office Building, ignored in committee assignments and steamrollered into impotence by the complex machinery of the House and its seniority system. The Douglas forces in the 1950 campaign charged that Nixon never took part in shaping legislation on the floor of the House; such a charge overlooked the fact that he was the center of a small power nexus, which exerted its influence on legislation during the drafting stage in committee, where most of the basic decisions were made.

In view of Nixon's interest in "smashing the labor bosses" and his success with the Communist-subversion issue in the 1946 campaign, he was especially fortunate in his committee assignments. Under the Reorganization Act of 1946 the congressional committee structure was radically modified at the outset of the Eightieth Congress; fewer assignments were available and competition for them was keen. Although only a freshman, Nixon applied for and got a place on the House Education and Labor Committee. In addition he was eligible for assignment to a minor committee; and although the Committee on Un-American Activities had been established since 1945 as a permanent standing committee of the House, it was still regarded as a lesser post.

There are conflicting reports on the circumstances under which Nixon took his place on the Un-American Activities Committee. At that time, owing to the earlier excesses of Martin Dies and succeeding chairmen, the committee's name was almost synonymous with bigotry and witch hunting. In 1947 its chairman was J. Parnell Thomas, who later went to jail, and its most conspicuous member was John Rankin, the inflammatory Mississippi racist. The committee's method of flailing about indiscriminately, smearing the innocent along with the guilty in the search for Nazis or fascists or Communist subversives, had subjected it to unremitting attack from the defenders of constitutional liberties.

Because of the committee's unsavory reputation Nixon is said to have hesitated about accepting a place on it. A fellow member of the Chowder and Marching Club, Donald Jackson, recalled that Nixon paced up and down his office weighing the decision, arguing on the one hand that it was an unpleasant, thankless assignment, that it might be politically the kiss of death, but that on the other hand it might be possible to correct the injustices and irresponsibilities in the committee's procedures and that therefore he might be under a moral obligation to undertake the assignment.

This picture of a man wrestling with his conscience is accepted with reservations by practical politicians. House committee assignments for the most part are made in response to an expression of preference. The Un-American Activities Committee at that time was an unrivaled forum for personal publicity and there were more Republican applicants than there were openings. For an almost unknown freshman to get such a plum could only mean that powerful influence had been exerted on his behalf.

Using these committees as springboards, Nixon was identified with three causes during his four years of service in the House: (1) the Taft-Hartley Act of 1947, and the 1949 struggle to amend it; (2) the Mundt-Nixon Bill; (3) the Hiss case.

Although he had lampooned Jerry Voorhis for his failure to push more of his own bills through to final enactment, Nixon made no conspicuous effort to sponsor substantive legislation. By long odds his most important proposal during four years in the House was the subversive activities control bill, commonly known as the Mundt-Nixon bill (H. R. 5852), which was introduced April 28, 1948, on behalf of Nixon's legislative subcommittee of the House Committee on Un-American Activities; it was reintroduced in the Eighty-first Congress after it had died in the Senate, and eventually became part of the McCarran Internal Security Act of 1950.

In 1947 Nixon introduced three individual relief bills and offered a resolution calling for a conference to revise and strengthen the United Nations Charter. In 1948 he introduced three resolutions, three private relief bills, and three bills of national significance, one giving the states control of tidelands oil, one amending the Social Security Act, the third amending the Servicemen's Readjustment Act. In 1949 he introduced eleven private relief bills, two resolutions, including one to commend FBI Director J. Edgar Hoover, and fourteen bills including several asking construction of post offices. In 1950, besides a dozen private relief bills, he introduced two resolutions and five minor bills, one of which, to facilitate servicemen's voting, was passed by both houses and signed into law.

II

Nixon's maiden speech in Congress was an outgrowth of proceedings before the Un-American Activities Committee. Early in the 1947 session a subpoena had been issued for the appearance of Gerhart Eisler, a notorious international Communist then being prosecuted for passport fraud, who eventually jumped bail and turned up in East Germany as a Communist gauleiter. Misled by Communist-front protests, Nixon had approached the hearing with some mental reservations but these were soon dissipated. Eisler, finding himself cornered, resorted to a one-man mob scene, demanding to make a statement, refusing to be sworn, shouting non sequiturs, challenging the authority of the committee—a colossal show of arrogance and a stratagem that paralyzed the hearing.

The committee lost no time in citing Eisler for contempt, and on February 18 the appropriate resolution was presented to the House for approval. Having a sure-fire subject and a sympathetic audience (in the end Marcantonio's was the only negative vote), Nixon, along with other committee members, seized the opportunity to test his oratorical skills. Speaking in "measured tones" and with the "intensely sincere" manner that was to be the hallmark of his platform personality, the young congressman reviewed Eisler's career and his frequent trips to the United States.

"There is a tendency," Nixon said, "to treat this case as one of a political prisoner, a harmless refugee whom this committee is persecuting. . . ." He proceeded to argue that Eisler's conspiratorial activities were too brazen to warrant such a belief, but then turned aside to question the loyalty of bureaucrats in the Immigration and Naturalization Service, who in 1943, during the Allied-Soviet wartime alliance, had reclassified Eisler from the status of "alien in transit" to that of "alien for pleasure," thus permitting him unrestricted travel inside the United States.

"It would certainly seem," Nixon told the House, "that an investigation should be made of the procedures and the personnel responsible for granting such privileges. . . . There is no place in the federal service in positions so closely related to the security of the United States, for governmental employees who follow the Communist line. . . ."

Thus in his first official statement Nixon found it possible, by cautious innuendo, to suggest that Communist sympathizers might be working secretly within the federal government.

III

Although Nixon was a very junior member of the Education and Labor Committee, his principal energies during his first session in the House were devoted to the enactment of the Taft-Hartley bill "to provide fair and equitable rules of conduct to be observed by labor and management." There is no evidence that he had a major hand in drafting the measure that was submitted to the House April 15 for debate, but there is no lack of testimony from Nixon's House colleagues that, in this as in all other matters in which he took an interest, he was one of the rare congressmen who "did his homework," studiously hacking his way through the mountain of paperwork that clutters the legislative process.

The proposition before Congress was that labor's status had advanced greatly since the enactment of the Wagner Act in the 'thirties; privileges accorded in the earlier legislation had made unionism powerful and should be matched with the responsibilities of power. A few diehards on the right favored punitive measures, and the labor movement in fighting off such extremism found itself in the position of opposing anything at all restrictive.

Midway in the second day of debate on the bill, the chairman yielded ten minutes to his fellow committee member, Dick Nixon, who began by deploring the "name-calling attacks" on the bill. Without alluding to his earlier promise to "smash the labor bosses," he pleaded for a "labor bill which is not class legislation but which is in the best interests of all the people of America." He reviewed the charge that, since VJ Day, the nation had suffered a loss of six billion dollars as a result of industrial strife, and then ticked off in his best debating style the list of Republican arguments that were still being paraded before the Congress twelve years later during consideration of the Kennedy-Irvin labor reform bill.

"Let us analyze the provisions of the bill," he urged in the passionless manner that blended sincerity, humility, and reasonableness, "having in mind the interests of American workers.

"Do they [the workers] object to the fact that the bill gives them the right to speak freely in their union meetings?

"Do they object to the fact that the bill gives them the right to vote freely in democratic elections for their officers and to organize and bargain collectively?

"Do they object to the fact that the bill protects their rights to strike over fundamental issues involving wages, hours and working conditions?

"Do they object to the fact that we have attempted to control violence, mass picketing, and other abuses which all good union leaders have decried? . . ."

When his ten minutes expired, Hartley yielded Nixon another half-minute, and the congressman went swiftly into a peroration describing the pending measure as a "bill of rights" for the American worker. Passage the following day was by a vote of 308 to 107, and after the Senate had worked its will and the two houses had compromised there were votes to spare when the House subsequently overrode President Truman's veto.

On July 9, possibly with an eye toward his Twelfth District sponsors, the Committee of One Hundred, Nixon inserted in the appendix of the *Congressional Record* an analysis of the Taft-Hartley bill entitled "The Truth About the New Labor Law." It was a skillful apologia, a matter-of-fact essay undertaking to reshape the political image of what he referred to as "the most controversial piece of legislation passed by the Eightieth Congress," but its essential bias was reflected in the fact that thousands of reprints were ordered by other Republican congressmen as the best answer to organized labor's criticism.

Although Nixon pleaded publicly for "fairness" and "the fundamental rights of the sixty million people in America who work for a living" he explicitly disclaimed pro-labor leanings, telling the House in 1949, "Whether you consider yourself to be in the so-called pro-labor group or in the group of those who are attempting to retain what we think are the good features of the present law, I think all of us will recognize that there should be some provision in the law making both unions and management responsible for their contracts."

Nixon took the line that, although the Taft-Hartley Act was not perfect and he would vote to amend it, labor nevertheless made great gains under it; he said, "Wages have increased, pensions have improved, there have been fewer strikes and work-stoppages, and labor and the general public have benefited by the law." He even went so far as to contend, "Management is always quick to point out the faults of labor. It should be as quick to recognize its own faults and to take remedial action. Management should give labor a stake in business and industry through profit-sharing plans and similar devices."

Despite this painstaking effort to strike a note of evenhanded impartiality in labor-management affairs, Nixon acquired a reputation as a subtle foe of labor's interests. Many Republicans were shaken by the Democratic victory in the 1948 elections, but when a House fight erupted in 1949 over the issue of repealing or amending the Taft-Hartley Act, it found Nixon standing his ground. Feeling against the act still ran high in the labor movement, and with the Democrats again controlling Congress the unions felt strong enough to demand repeal; the strategy of those favoring tighter control of unionism was to head off repeal by making minimum concessions.

In the debate beginning April 27 the issue narrowed to a choice between the Lesinski bill, which would have repealed the 1947 act, and the substitute Wood bill, which was in effect an amended version of Taft-Hartley. The ranking Republican on the Education and Labor Committee, Representative Samuel K. McConnell, Jr., of Pennsylvania, called the Wood bill nothing more than a rewrite "requiring scissors and paste, not genius."

Nixon by that time had enough committee seniority to get twenty-five minutes on the first day of the debate and shorter allocations of time on three other days. He fought hard for the Wood substitute, which was adopted May 3 by a margin of only fourteen votes, and was then killed the following day, on a motion to recommit, by an even narrower margin of three votes. With the death of the Wood bill, there was no further serious effort to amend the Taft-Hartley Act until 1958.

A week after his defeat on the Wood bill Nixon rose in the House to charge on behalf of the Republican minority that "administration spokesmen and certain national union leaders have been frantically resorting to . . . name-calling tactics . . . in a deliberate campaign of distortion and misinformation against the provisions of that bill," and to assert that the nineteen significant changes of existing law contained in the Wood bill were in fact "pro-labor amendments." By and large, as extreme claims of both sides proved false, his contention was not without validity.

IV

For ten years the Un-American Activities Committee had been an investigatory body and nothing more. It had produced no legislative recommendations whatever. Other congressional committees had shepherded into law various potent measures for dealing with subversion—the Smith Act, the Voorhis Act, the McCormack Act—and the Justice Department had used these along with earlier statutes to spread chaos in the ranks of the American Communist movement.

It was Nixon who transformed the committee into a functioning legislative organism. He began late in 1947 by winning appointment as chairman of a special legislative subcommittee. He then proceeded to hold a series of hearings in February, compiled two monographs on Communist operational tactics from the committee's voluminous files, and drafted a report outlining a proposed new attack on the Red conspiracy. Shortly afterward the Mundt-Nixon bill was introduced.

The principal provisions of the bill included: registration of Communist party members, identification of the source of all printed and broadcast material issued by Communist-front organizations; denial of passports to party members; denial of federal employment to members of the Communist party; discontinuance of tax-exemption of Communist-front organizations; deportation proceedings against aliens convicted of Communist activity; increasing the penalty for peacetime espionage to a $10,000 fine and a maximum of ten years' imprisonment; creation of a subversive activities control board which upon application by the Attorney General would determine whether an organization was a Communist-front or Communist-action group.

Although critics contended there was already ample legislation for prosecuting Communists, the Mundt-Nixon bill was reported out of committee unanimously. When it came up for debate May 14, honest opponents found themselves in an impossible position. Nixon had been appointed floor manager for the bill, and in the absence of a Democrat willing to head the opposition, that task devolved upon Marcantonio of New York, who was notorious for his Communist sympathies.

Nixon's House apprenticeship came to an end in the three-day debate that followed. A reading of the *Record* indicates he handled himself with the aplomb of a veteran. He followed the debate; he interjected a word of interpretation here, of explanation there. He was the committee member who answered the toughest charges of the opposition; he was the committee member who knew the bill to its finest detail. He treated Marcantonio courteously, even granting him extra time when the hour and a half allocated to the New Yorker ran out. He never became involved in acrimonious exchanges. He was sharp on occasion, but always in order to avoid irrelevancies.

At the end of the first day of debate Nixon took four minutes to speak. He said, ". . . There is too much loose talk and confusion on the Communist issue. By passing this bill the Congress of the United States will go on record as to just what is subversive about communism in the United States. . . . It will once and for all spike many of the loose charges about organizations being Communist-fronts because they happen to advocate some of the same policies which the Communists support. . . ."

In the eyes of traditionalists the bill was offensive on two general grounds. The first of these was that it represented little more than a digest of the views of a small nine-man committee and had been sent to the floor of the House without hearings, without thorough analysis by either federal officials or outside legal experts. The second objection was that the bill undertook to regulate not conduct but opinion and therefore, as a species of thought-control, was unconstitutional.

On the second day of debate, the Mundt-Nixon forces suffered a setback from an unexpected quarter, a setback which not only contributed to subsequent failure of the bill in the Senate but which was to have a series of ironic overtones. In the preconvention maneuvering of 1948 Dewey and Stassen had emerged as the principal GOP antagonists, and the paramount issue was whether to deal with the problem of Communist subversion by outlawing the Communist party. On May 15, in a meeting that proved to be the turning point in the struggle, Stassen and Dewey debated the issue in Portland, Oregon.

At that period Nixon was heavily involved with Stassen. He had begun his political career in 1946 by soliciting an endorsement from the former Minnesota governor, and he found the California Stassenites among his most energetic supporters. In preparation for the Dewey-Stassen debate, and knowing that while Dewey opposed the Mundt-Nixon bill Stassen favored it, Nixon had prepared a concise defense of the bill which Stassen in the end failed to use. Dewey, however, in his fiery defense of civil liberties and freedom of speech, pointed a finger of scorn at the Mundt-Nixon bill, declaring:

"Stripped to its naked essential, this is nothing but the method of Hitler and Stalin. It is thought-control borrowed from the Japanese. It is an attempt to beat down ideas with a club. It is surrender of everything we believe in."

Leading newspapers in all parts of the country joined in Dewey's protest. *The New York Times* predicted that the bill "could be used to impose restraints on freedom such as the American people have not known for one hundred and fifty years." The *Denver Post* wrote that the bill "would work against many innocent persons." The *St. Louis Post-Dispatch* said it "could be used to harass and even to prosecute any nonconforming individual or group." And the *Christian Science Monitor* anxiously reflected that it could set up ". . . the precedents and the machinery for a kind of political proscription which could be turned by any party in power against any minority."

In the Senate the Mundt-Nixon bill was referred to the Judiciary Committee, which in June did take the trouble to order a series of hearings. By that time protests against the measure had become so vociferous that its proponents were unable to round up enough votes to report it out of committee. Nevertheless from the point of view of Republican political strategists the Mundt-Nixon bill had established itself conveniently in the party's arsenal of anti-Communist weapons.

On March 7, 1950—barely two weeks after the Wheeling, West Virginia, speech that launched Joe McCarthy on his demagogic crusade—the Mundt-Nixon bill was resuscitated. By this time Nixon no longer had the field to himself. There were other similar measures by Mundt, Ferguson, and McCarran in the Senate and by Wood of Georgia in the House.

Two days after Nixon's bill went in the hopper, the Republican *San Francisco Chronicle* editorialized: "We are as whole-heartedly against the new Mundt-Nixon bill as we were against the old . . . [it is] completely backhanded and totally subversive of the spirit and letter of the Constitution."

Nevertheless, in the prevailing anti-Communist neurosis, few politicians dared vote against such a proposal in an election year; and when McCarran threw the weight of his power into the scales, Congress rammed through, over Truman's veto, an omnibus control bill that included not only most of Nixon's ideas but a tangle of provisos from other pending measures.

Nixon's defense of the bill in his 1950 campaign manual started from the premise that, while it would have been a mistake to outlaw the Communist party and drive it underground, the statute finally adopted would render communism harmless by requiring the movement to operate in the open. "The Communist party," he said, "can't stand the light of day." He insisted the bill "carefully defines the organizations which must register," and said the act would "take the procedure of identifying Communists and Communist-front organizations out of the field of name-calling and remove all uncertainty as to the organization's true nature by taking the procedure into the realm of legislative standards."

Notwithstanding this confident prediction, efforts to enforce the McCarran Act left a trail of frustration. In its 1958 summary to Congress and the President, the Subversive Activities Control Board reported itself still hamstrung by litigation. In eight years the Attorney General had brought twenty-four cases before the board. At his own request eight of these were eventually dismissed because the organizations had ceased to exist. Eight other respondents had been ordered by the board, after hearings, to register as Communist-front organizations, but all had appealed the ruling to the District of Columbia Court of Appeals.

Eight other cases were still before the board. These included five on which hearings had been completed but no decisions had been filed, and two cases of "Communist-infiltrated labor unions" on which no action had been taken. The twenty-fourth case— that against the Communist party of the United States—had been remanded once by the Supreme Court and twice by the Court of Appeals for further consideration. Unless and until the Supreme Court upheld the constitutionality of the act requiring the Communist party to register, enforcement of the statute was at a standstill, since under the act no organization could be compelled to register until all opportunities for appeal had been exhausted.

Thus after eight years of litigation, no order of the SACB had become final. Predictions that the Mundt-Nixon bill's philosophy would give the Attorney General dictatorial powers to subvert civil liberties had not been fulfilled, but other crystal gazers had been more nearly right. Ambiguities in the act trod so narrowly on the Bill of Rights as to open the door to a paralyzing parade of lawsuits. SACB officials took comfort in the thought that juridical harassment of the Red conspiracy had effectually tied up much of the party's funds and manpower, but from the point of view of general public policy, once Congress and the public stopped looking under the bed for imaginary Red witchcraft, the McCarran Act of 1950 scarcely measured up to the hopes of its sponsors.

v

Politically the climax of Nixon's career in the House was the Alger Hiss affair, the only dramatic and widely meaningful case in a decade of investigation by Congress. In the short space of 134 days, between August 3 and December 15, 1948, Nixon's name rocketed into the headlines; and as two Hiss perjury trials dragged through the courts in 1949 with sensation following sensation, the Californian became a national celebrity.

During the late summer of 1948, an American airlift fighting the Berlin blockade held the center of the world stage as Western diplomats conferred anxiously with the Russians in Moscow to try to reopen the overland corridors. Harry Truman was preparing for his apparently hopeless campaign battle against Tom Dewey and the Eightieth Congress. The Un-American Activities Committee, having failed to put the Mundt-Nixon bill on the statute books, found its fortunes at a low ebb.

At that juncture a new and provocative line of inquiry opened up. The committee on July 31 questioned Elizabeth Bentley, a confessed ex-Communist spy, who had not only testified before a New York grand jury and before a Senate subcommittee, but had actually told her story to the world in a series of newspaper articles. Her warmed-over report of spy rings that had infiltrated the federal government named names and was successful in making headlines. The committee was thereby encouraged to call another ex-Communist, Whittaker Chambers, who had been trying for years with indifferent success to convince Washington authorities that communism in government was a real and present danger.

The Hiss case had its origin in the testimony Chambers gave at a committee hearing August 3. The committee already had material on Hiss in its files, raw, unevaluated data that added up to nothing until Chambers came along. Nixon recalled later that the witness "made charges which at the time seemed fantastic— that he'd been a Communist, that he had worked with Hiss, White, Abt, Pressman, Witt, and a number of other people who were also connected with the government." Hiss, who had served briefly in the State Department during the New Deal and had since become president of the Carnegie Endowment for International Peace, promptly denied Chambers' charges and demanded an opportunity to be heard. He came before the committee August 5 and denied all.

"He was an amazingly impressive witness the first time," Nixon said later. "I would say that ninety per cent of those who were in the committee room were convinced that Mr. Hiss was telling the truth . . . when he said that he did not know Mr. Chambers."

At that point the case was almost dropped. Chambers was a man of considerable standing, one of six senior editors of *Time* magazine, but Hiss had had a phenomenal record in government service and came before the committee, not a confessed Communist like Chambers, but a man of redoubtable credentials. Nixon, however, took the lead in urging further investigation. Later, to explain his hunch, he called attention to a few lines of testimony that had seemed to strike a false note from the first.

Q. You say you have never seen Mr. Chambers?
A. The name means absolutely nothing to me, Mr. Stripling.

A mind trained in courtroom procedure and cross-examination could perceive that Hiss was not answering the question.

"I was a lawyer," Nixon said, "and I knew he was a lawyer and I felt that his testimony was just too slick. . . . As I read the testimony later I became convinced that if Hiss was lying he was lying in such a way as to avoid perjury, with a very careful use of phrasing. He never made a categorical statement. He would say, 'To the best of my recollection' over and over again. He never said, 'I have never known Whittaker Chambers.' He constantly reiterated when the question was put to him, 'I have never known a man by the name of Whittaker Chambers.' In other words, he was too careful in his testimony, too smooth. It was very possibly an act, it seemed to me."

Nixon proceeded cautiously. Together with Representative Charles J. Kersten, he went to see John Foster Dulles, then Dewey's foreign-policy adviser. Present also at the Roosevelt Hotel interview in New York were Allen Dulles, Christian Herter, and C. Douglas Dillon. It was the elder Dulles who in the end, after a long night of analysis, agreed that the weight of evidence against Hiss called for further investigation. Dulles reached that decision reluctantly, for on December 26, 1946, in response to an offer of a Detroit lawyer to provide evidence that Hiss had a Communist record, Dulles had written: "I have heard the report you refer to, but I have confidence that there is no reason to doubt Mr. Hiss's complete loyalty to our American institutions. . . . I feel a little skeptical about information which seems inconsistent with all that I personally know and what is the judgment of reliable friends and associates in Washington."

The question raised by Hiss's carefully qualified answers was of course whether he might have known Chambers under another name. In the end that suspicion proved to be the clue that unraveled the mystery. Nixon, having been appointed chairman of a special subcommittee to pursue the investigation, proceeded to question Chambers separately about a multitude of intimate personal details concerning his alleged friendship with Hiss between 1934 and 1938. He then cross-examined Hiss on this mass of corroborative detail. When answers coincided and when Hiss began dropping intimations that he might indeed have known Chambers by another name (eventually he was to identify Chambers as "George Crosley," a deadbeat freelance writer whom he had allegedly befriended), Nixon arranged for a confrontation which took place August 16 in the Commodore Hotel in New York City.

At that meeting, in a melodramatic performance in which he displayed an almost comic reluctance in finally identifying Chambers, Hiss stuck to his denial that he had been a Communist and challenged Chambers to repeat the accusation outside the committee chamber where he could be sued for libel. Chambers did repeat the charges August 27 on the radio program "Meet the Press." After a delay of three weeks, a delay which in itself tended to raise doubts about Hiss's candor, the suit against Chambers was filed.

In the end it was this lawsuit rather than the committee investigation as such that sent Hiss to jail. Hiss had assured his attorneys that there were no incriminating papers or documents that could possibly be produced against him. His attorneys therefore, in taking a deposition November 17 from Chambers, felt safe in asking the latter to produce any documentary evidence he might have to support his charge that he and Hiss had been Communists together.

Prior to that no one had known that Chambers in quitting the Communist party had taken the precaution to fashion a "life preserver." Counsel for Hiss, therefore, was thunderstruck when Chambers produced his life preserver—a thick envelope containing four pages in Hiss's handwriting and a number of typewritten documents which he said had been copied on Hiss's typewriter. He charged that Hiss had pilfered these confidential state documents and passed them on to him in the service of communism. Examination showed that they were in fact copies of authentic papers; and other testimony established that the transmission to the Russians of verbatim texts of these top-secret documents, or even one of them, would have enabled the Soviet government to break the secret State Department code.

Up to that point in the investigation there had been some skeptics willing to assert that Chambers was a psychopathic liar. The production of the envelope of papers put the whole case in a new light. Nevertheless there was an intimation from the Justice Department December 1 that the Hiss-Chambers case would be dropped unless additional evidence could be found. At that point Nixon performed his penultimate service in the Hiss case. In a private interview with Chambers, at the latter's farm at Westminster, Maryland, he was either told or was able to infer that Chambers had in his possession additional documentary evidence. Returning to Washington on the evening of December 1, Nixon made a forcing play.

"I ordered that a subpoena be served upon Mr. Chambers," he said later, "for any other documents that he might have."

Next evening, in a cloak-and-dagger scene that has few parallels in congressional history, an agent of the committee served the subpoena on the ex-Communist. Chambers led him in darkness to a pumpkin in his garden. From it he drew five rolls of microfilm containing photostatic copies of confidential and secret documents from the State Department and the Bureau of Standards.

To anyone familiar with Communist methods, Chambers' purpose in secreting the papers and microfilm must have been self-evident. In leaving the party he foresaw a possible need to defend himself some day against either the Communists or their enemies or both. Throughout the Hiss case his credibility as a witness was never successfully attacked, because he could always point to the documentation he had provided; it established his *bona fides;* it placed his renunciation of communism beyond challenge; first and last, it constituted the government's case against Hiss. Nixon drew a not too sophisticated inference that, after Chambers had put all his cards on the table, "he talked as if a great load had been lifted from his mind." No wonder. Once it became evident to Chambers that his life preserver had indeed saved him from the consequences of his flirtation with communism, he could afford to relax and romanticize.

The "pumpkin papers," for all their melodramatic qualities, gave the case an air of irrefragable substance and realism. In saving Chambers, they doomed Hiss. A New York grand jury that had been on the verge of indicting the ex-Communist for perjury reversed itself when Nixon rushed to New York and testified that it must have been Hiss who lied in saying he had not turned official documents over to Chambers. Simultaneously the FBI was able to establish that the pumpkin papers and letters from Mrs. Priscilla Hiss had been typed on the same Woodstock machine—a key factor in the case. On December 15 the grand jury climaxed the investigation by bringing an indictment for perjury against Hiss.

That ended Nixon's participation in the Hiss case. Two trials followed: the first ended in a hung jury voting 8 to 4 for conviction; the second, on January 21, 1950, brought in a verdict of guilty. All appeals were denied, and Hiss served a prison sentence.

In Nixon's mind there was never any doubt about the guilt of Alger Hiss. Chambers recalled later in his book *Witness* that he was sometimes amused by Nixon's "martial Quakerism" and by a "vivid picture of him in the blackest hour of the Hiss case . . . saying in his quietly savage way: 'If the American people understood the real character of Alger Hiss, they would boil him in oil.'"

Some others, however, have never ceased to regard the Hiss case as a miscarriage of justice. The distinguished British jurist Earl Jowitt concluded a book-length analysis of the strange and celebrated case with a series of questions which by their number and complexity tend to show that the inquiry and the verdict were not necessarily an unqualified victory for justice. Conceding that the association with Chambers was probably closer than Hiss admitted, and that at some time Hiss apparently had extremely left-wing or Communist sympathies and affiliations, Jowitt still found himself with reservations about the trial and its failure to provide convincing proof that only Hiss could have been guilty of the offense charged.

Nixon considered such questions not worthy of discussion. Waiting until Hiss had been convicted, he applied for the first time in three years for a special order to address the House of Representatives, and on January 26, 1950, reviewed at length not only his part in the original Hiss-Chambers investigation, but also the broader political implications of the case. By that time he was preparing to campaign for the Senate, and he couched his analysis of Communist infiltration of the federal government in terms of a far-reaching threat to the nation's security.

Pointing out, first, that the conspiracy of the 'thirties had been "amazingly effective," and, second, that Bentley and Chambers had named a "great number of people other than Hiss" as being implicated, Nixon cited the corroborative evidence of Julian Wadleigh and produced other hitherto unpublished papers said to be in the handwriting of a deceased Treasury expert, Harry Dexter White.

"The conspiracy was so effective, so well entrenched, and so well defended by apologists in high places," he said, "that it was not discovered and apprehended until it was too late to prosecute. . . . There were several occasions during the past ten years on which, if vigorous action had been taken, the conspiracy could have been exposed . . . [but] the three-year statute of limitations had lapsed and it is too late to do anything. . . ."

Nixon reviewed evidence indicating that the FBI, the White House, the State Department, the Atomic Energy Commission, and others were aware that charges had been made against Hiss and others; that "top officials were aware of the fact that the Russians were engaging in espionage activities against us even while they were our allies." He pointed scornfully to the fact that, whereas Canada had convicted nine atomic spies within a year after the Gouzenko revelations, the Truman administration had a record of "humiliating failure to take any action whatever in this country against the individuals involved in wartime espionage for the Soviet Union until it was too late to prosecute. . . ." He condemned the administration for "inexcusable inaction," ridiculed Truman for calling the Hiss case a "red herring," and marveled at Dean Acheson's refusal to "turn his back" on Alger Hiss.

Then Nixon went to the heart of his polemic against the administration, a theme that was to recur again and again in later campaigns.

"Why was it that administration officials persisted in their refusal to act through the years, even when substantial evidence of espionage activities was brought to their attention? . . . The reason for their failure to act was not that they were disloyal. . . . What was happening was that administration leaders were treating the reports of Communist espionage on a 'politics as usual' basis. . . . They treated Communist infiltration into our American institutions like any ordinary petty political scandal . . . rendered the greatest possible disservice to the people of the nation."

He concluded with two practical recommendations: the extension of the statute of limitations on espionage cases from three years to ten years, and a tightening of standards used in loyalty checks. Specifically he proposed that the "loyalty program" be abandoned in favor of a "security program" which would enable the government to resolve doubt in its own favor "without the necessity of proving disloyalty and thereby reflecting on the character of a possibly loyal but indiscreet government employee."

Nixon was but one of a number in Congress who favored "security" rather than "loyalty" as a yardstick. To legal hairsplitters, and in some cases as a practical administrative measure, disloyalty would have to border on treason, a charge that could be sustained under the Constitution only by an overt act and two witnesses. In the hysteria of the period the appealing simplicity of the Nixon proposal—as was later demonstrated when the McCarthy witch hunt began in earnest—was that individuals could be dismissed from government service arbitrarily, without knowing accuser or accusation or how even to frame an answer to so shapeless an anomaly. The cynicism of the procedure, which was adopted only gradually, lay in the fact that a government employee dismissed on the strength of anonymous charges as a security risk found himself no less brutally stigmatized than if the finding had questioned his loyalty.

In the peroration of his Hiss speech Nixon warned:

"The great lesson which should be learned from the Alger Hiss case is that we are not just dealing with espionage agents who get thirty pieces of silver to obtain the blueprint of a new weapon—the Communists do that, too—but this is a far more sinister type of activity, because it permits the enemy to guide and shape our policy; it disarms and dooms our diplomats to defeat in advance before they go to conferences; traitors in the high councils of our own government make sure that the deck is stacked on the Soviet side of the diplomatic table."

His objective as a skilled polemicist was to lay the groundwork for his later charge that the administration in power had shown gross defects of judgment in dealing with the issue and should therefore be summarily voted out of office. Disregarding others' doubts about Hiss's conviction, Nixon labeled him a "dedicated" Communist and "arch traitor of our generation," and billed him as the symbol of Democratic ineptitude or worse.

For his part in unmasking Hiss, Nixon's prestige was not only high but untarnished, this despite the fact that the procedures of the Un-American Activities Committee were subject to harsh criticism. While the Hiss case was still under investigation, October 5, 1948, Representative Jacob K. Javits, later senator from New York, launched a typical attack. In a signed article he asserted: "The un-American activities committee in the Hiss-Chambers controversy acted as a trial body, but the protections provided by a trial at law were entirely lacking." And Javits was one of those who at the time urged dissolution of the committee.

Nixon was not prepared to acknowledge shortcomings in the

Hiss-Chambers affair, but in talking with newsmen December 19 he was less reticent about other cases.

"I'll admit the committee has made mistakes and deserves criticism," he said. "Sure I'll name one. I believe the handling of the case involving Dr. Edward Condon was unfair. I firmly believe that Dr. Condon should have been heard by the committee before any statement about him was made public. I regret that he has not [yet] been heard by the committee—and I think he should be heard now."

Subsequent assessments of Nixon's conduct, based on a rereading of the record in the Hiss case, have been generally favorable. The California congressman was thorough but fair. Like an experienced detective, he undertook to make a case and he succeeded, but there is no evidence that he ever bullied a witness or subverted the truth. On one occasion Hiss bridled at Nixon's line of questioning, and went so far as to intimate that his answers could be leaked to Chambers and used to build a case against him, whereupon Nixon bluntly rebuked him for the imputation that "the committee's purpose in questioning you today is to get information with which we can coach Mr. Chambers so that he can more or less build a web around you."

Nevertheless, there was pressure for a revision of committee procedures to safeguard civil rights. Nixon himself, in an appearance before the *Herald Tribune* Forum in the fall of 1948 laid down his own personal set of rules for the protection of witnesses. His code provided that:

"Each witness should be allowed to present a statement in his own behalf where charges have been made against him before the committee. A witness should be allowed to submit the names of prospective witnesses who will testify in his behalf where charges have been made against him. A witness should be allowed to submit questions which he feels should be asked of individuals who have made charges against him. Televising of committee hearings should be prohibited because it places an unreasonable burden on the average witness."

Others, such as Representative Chet Holifield, joined Javits in demanding more far-reaching forms of committee self-discipline. Some were prepared to acknowledge that Nixon's personal code of investigation marked the first introduction of reasonable standards of fair play in the treatment of witnesses, but it took the strange and inglorious spy-chasing excesses of the McCarthy period to bring Congress as a whole back to a sane perspective. The irony of it was that, whereas Nixon as a campaigner seemed to gravitate naturally toward reckless overstatement, he left a largely blameless record in the House during his handling of some of the period's most explosive issues.

Politically the 1950 verdict against Hiss provided the impetus for a tortured struggle unique in American history. The issue in that struggle was essentially whether the guilt of an individual could by verbal legerdemain be transferred to a Democratic administration, to the Democratic party as a whole, and therefore to a majority of the American people, and whether that guilt could be defined as treason. The struggle was commonly thought to have begun a month after the January verdict, with Joe McCarthy's reckless speech at Wheeling, but it is a question whether the Wisconsin senator was the only or even the most culpable member of his party. Largely overlooked in the chorus of "treason" that erupted afterward was a message from Herbert Hoover congratulating Nixon on his role in the Hiss case.

"The conviction of Alger Hiss," the former President said, "was due to your patience and persistence alone. At last the stream of treason that existed in our government has been exposed in a fashion that all may believe."

When a respected former President could thus loosely assume the existence of a "stream" of treason, who need fear the consequences of echoing him? And how were men of lesser standing to get a hearing for their plea of caution? The hysteria latent in the word treason, used incautiously, was self-generating.

VI

One other major issue besides labor reform and spy hunting attracted Nixon's not wholly passive interest—foreign affairs and the consolidation of the free-world coalition against international communism.

An incident early in his Washington career was one of the forces that bent the twig. The House in the summer of 1947 created a select committee of nineteen to study the problem of overseas relief and rehabilitation: the available resources, qualified agencies, and measures to assess relative needs and correlate assistance. Nixon—the only freshman chosen—read about his appointment to the committee in the papers and in late August, under the chairmanship of Christian Herter, sailed with the group for Europe. It was on this trip that Nixon for the first time came in personal contact both with Communist activities and with the dreadful postwar poverty and suffering on which communism was nourishing itself. After setting up temporary headquarters in London, the committee toured the Ruhr and divided itself into regional teams for an intensive month-long survey of industry, agriculture, and administrative facilities. Returning to Washington in October, it compiled the first of a long series of congressional reports on foreign aid, a voluminous study that paved the way for the Marshall Plan and enlisted Nixon's lasting support for the doctrine of global interdependence.

Describing his views later, he classed himself basically as an internationalist because of his Quaker heritage, and told Alsop: "I'm not necessarily a respecter of the status quo in foreign affairs. I am a chance taker in foreign affairs. I would take chances for peace—the Quakers have a passion for peace, you know."

Whether it was Quakerism or the Herter committee that oriented his thinking, the record shows that from 1947 on he voted consistently and more or less generously for programs to support the free-world alliance. This was at a time when Old Guard Republicans and many Taftites were campaigning against the "giveaways" and "Globaloney" of the Truman administration and when bipartisanship was either frowned upon or flatly rejected in ultra-right-wing circles.

When it seemed politically expedient Nixon showed himself to be suspiciously partisan as well as aggressively bipartisan in his views on foreign policy. Even before the Herter committee episode, he rose in the House July 3 to utter the familiar protest of the party out of power.

"The matters which have come before us involving foreign policy," he said, "generally have come before us after the deed has been done. The Congress has come in after the decision has been made and the Congress has had to back up the decision that has been made by our State Department and by the Executive Branch.

"The question I should like to ask is this: Does the gentleman not feel that a true bipartisan foreign policy means that it must be bipartisan in its inception and creation as well as in its execution?"

Similarly, in December 1950, after he had entered the Senate, Nixon joined twenty-three other Republican senators in sponsoring a resolution which, however politically motivated, reflected faithfully his premise that the Executive Branch was not to be trusted. The resolution demanded that after the Truman-Attlee conference then in progress ". . . the President should forthwith make a full and complete report concerning the same to the Senate; and that the President should not enter into any understandings or agreements with the Prime Minister which might have the effect of committing the United States to any course of action, except by treaty entered into with the advice and consent of the Senate. . . ."

Later he had occasion to prove that he was ready to act on this concept of foreign policy. During the Middle Eastern crisis of July 1958 and the Berlin crisis six months later, it was Nixon who, arguing that Truman's omission should not be repeated, urged Eisenhower to call bipartisan leadership conferences where policy could be threshed out before rather than after implementation.

Nixon had little else to say about foreign affairs during his four years in the House. Some of his friendlier biographers have tried to suggest that he threw himself overtly into the fight for foreign aid, but the record indicates not. If he became a crusading internationalist, it was only after his experiences in Congress had been supplemented by a wealth of travel and high-level policy discussion as Vice-President.

In the House he was content to be a soldier in the rear ranks except where his own political life was at stake. On one occasion, when a poll showed his constituency was critical of his stand on the Marshall Plan, he flew to California and hurriedly made some fifty speeches to explain and justify his support of the program. Otherwise his chief contribution was in helping to overcome pockets of isolationism in the GOP. He did introduce two innocuous resolutions relating to the United Nations—one in 1948 calling for a revision of the Charter, and another in 1950 urging establishment of a UN police authority—but both vanished in committee pigeonholes.

All in all, the Hiss case remained the highlight of Nixon's two terms in the House. For a time he and his supporters nurtured a legend that in pushing the Hiss investigation he had incurred the implacable hatred of the Communist apparatus and its dupes in the ranks of "intellectuals" and "liberals." On the stump he enjoyed pointing to this as a formidable obstacle, and followed the line with some success during the evanescent revival of know-nothingism—the pre-sputnik revolt against the egghead.

After 1958, however, there were few references to this myth, partly because in retrospect Nixon's part in the Hiss case reflected no discredit on him and partly because he had added enough to his public stature not to require anything so shoddy in the way of a defense.

For the rest, his voting record on welfare and economic legislation showed him to be at once a skilled politician and a conservative party-liner. An analysis of his votes appears at the end of Chapter XVI, which covers his brief tenure in the Senate.

CHAPTER XVI

Senator

I

AFTER THE 1950 election, Nixon moved straight from the House to the Senate. To give him a leg up on the ladder of seniority, Sheridan Downey obligingly resigned on December 1, creating a vacancy in which Governor Warren could install Nixon a month early. The new junior senator took the oath and the seat December 4.

To a practical politician, 1951 was a time at which it paid to be a member of the opposition. The woods were full of issues, real and fancied. After three years of skirmishing with the Russians, the Cold War had still not fixed itself in the popular mind as a stony reality; the American public rejected what it preferred not to believe. Truman's conception of a free-world defensive coalition was by no means universally understood, and at every friction point there was room for bickering, on methods if not on aims.

Russia's brazen defection from the wartime alliance, its reversion to the dialectical rancor of prewar years, caused first dismay and then a massive revulsion against communism. From that came a mood of disillusionment that was to express itself by degrees in bouts of wordy masochism. For having misjudged the Russians, the country punished itself by imagining Red gremlins infiltrating and subverting every act of statecraft. No one was exempt, not even so great a patriot as General George Marshall. It was a period when off-the-cuff solutions in Congress were as facile and numerous as down-the-drain errors of judgment in the administration. This was all the more true because the Korean war had introduced a new and frustrating concept in international relations—the concept of "limited war" as something that had to be confined arbitrarily, and fought with less than the nation's best effort, lest it spill over into a nuclear doomsday.

While these concepts were sorting themselves out in people's minds, the pseudo-war was matched by a false boom, a euphoric state of well-being and high living that made the implications of both hot war and cold war distasteful. Finally, high in the catalogue of Republican serendipity, the Democratic party after twenty years in power found itself nourishing more than a fair quota of easy morals, and it would have been a flimsy opposition indeed that did not avail itself of such a windfall.

Nixon started his term in the Senate with a high degree of visibility, partly because of his top-heavy victory over Helen Douglas and partly because of his unremitting assault on administration foreign policy. A week after the election, with his usual perceptiveness, he recognized the public's anxiety over foreign affairs and the desirability of bridging the gulf created by his campaign attacks. In a San Francisco statement, he therefore took a reassuring line.

"It is erroneous to assume," he said, "that the new Senate will be made up of isolationists, or that we will oppose everything the State Department recommends. . . . The national security must be placed above partisan considerations in the development of our foreign policy.

"I will oppose and fight any attempt to return to an isolationist or obstructionist attitude on foreign affairs."

Then, in a quick genuflection toward the China Lobby and in what proved to be a faithful reflection of his intentions, he added, "I intend to work for a stronger policy in China, and I want to see that we get more for our money in Europe."

This haste to erase the scars inflicted in the campaign, a characteristic gesture, was narrowly political in the sense that it helped clarify his public posture without in any way foreshadowing an effective role for him as a member of the upper chamber.

Most accounts of Nixon's career in the Senate adopt an apologetic tone, as if it were hardly fair to count this interval against him. It is customary to brush lightly over the fact that he served only nineteen months, that freshman senators are more often seen than heard, that as a congenital lone wolf he failed to achieve any real personal standing in the "most exclusive club in the world."

His speeches were infrequent and when he spoke his language was temperate, disarmingly so in the light of his talents on the stump. The record is left all the thinner by reason of his 1951-52 blitzkrieg for the vice-presidential nomination, an effort that cut heavily into the time he could devote to senatorial duties. In the opinion of so informed an observer as William S. White, Nixon's record "was even more lacking in distinction" in the Senate than in the House.

It is fair to say that, although Nixon's background matched the temper of the times, the Senate offered him little chance to exploit it. He was too junior to win a place on the Foreign Relations Committee, and his interest in labor and subversion was bypassed, partly by circumstance and partly by his involvement in party machinations.

He profited from his experience in the House by drawing a berth on the Senate Labor and Public Welfare Committee, but the Eighty-second Congress let him down in that field. It wrote no labor legislation at all, and nothing noteworthy in such collateral fields under its jurisdiction as health, veterans' affairs, and fair employment practices.

A carryover of his reputation in the Hiss case won Nixon his other principal assignment, as a member of the Committee on Executive Expenditures. His presence there was seized upon by McCarthy, then the ranking Republican, to unseat Senator Margaret Chase Smith and summarily install Nixon in her place on the permanent investigations subcommittee. McCarthy was in some degree motivated by a desire to avenge himself on Mrs. Smith, whose courageous "Declaration of Conscience" was the only protest raised on the floor of the Senate in 1950 against McCarthy's excesses, but he had obvious reasons also for wanting to strengthen the Republican side by adding so experienced an investigator as the nemesis of Alger Hiss.

By acquiescing in this switch Nixon made himself a tacit ally of the Wisconsin senator, even though he never let himself be drawn into McCarthy's Red-hunting extremism. Surprisingly, however, it was not McCarthy's favorite security issue that made membership profitable for Nixon. In the months leading to the 1952 convention, corruption became the paramount issue and made the investigations subcommittee a provident outpost on the political firing line, notably so when Chairman Gabrielson and Chairman Boyle of the Republican and Democratic national committees were called on the carpet in the investigation of influence peddling.

As a freshman Nixon made no effort to take a leading role in sponsoring legislation. The record shows that he introduced thirty private relief bills, fourteen resolutions, and forty-three bills of general interest. The two latter figures, however, are subject to some qualification.

Of the fourteen resolutions to which his name was attached, he was a co-sponsor on thirteen—that is, one of a group of senators ranging in number from two to forty-four who lent their names to a colleague's favorite project. On his own account, Nixon bestirred himself on only one occasion, in April 1951, when he rushed to the defense of MacArthur with a resolution demanding the general's reinstatement as Far East commander.

Similarly, in the list of bills he introduced, he appears thirty times simply as a co-sponsor on a variety of measures that aroused his interest, such as statehood for Hawaii, famine relief in India, amendment of the Sugar Act, tidelands oil, medical scholarships, Marine Corps strength, ethical standards in government, and others. Strictly speaking, the bills introduced on his own behalf numbered only thirteen, none of major significance.

II

The dramatic highlight of the 1951 session of Congress was the MacArthur incident—Truman's peremptory order April 11 removing the general as supreme commander in the Far East and the Senate hearings that followed in May. For Nixon the MacArthur affair was a windfall that smacked of pure providence. He had campaigned against Truman-Acheson Far Eastern policies, and on his arrival in Washington in January his first word had been a rejection of appeals for unity.

"The fact that the policies of our State Department over the past five years have resulted in failure, at least in the Far East, makes it imperative," Nixon said, "that we develop a new policy which will have a better chance to succeed. . . . Unity on a policy which was wrong could bring even greater disaster. What we must have is unity on a policy which represents the best thinking of all our people."

To spell out such a policy, he called for military strength, a strong economy including price controls, rationing, and wage controls, and finally a policy of foreign alliances. In succeeding weeks he lost no opportunity to label the administration's foreign policy a failure and to criticize the conduct of the war in Korea. At the end of January, at the Women's National Republican Club in New York, he took an even bolder line, calling upon the United Nations to "get into Korea" or face the prospect that the United States would get out. He said our men were being asked to "fight a battle with their hands in effect tied behind their backs."

"In other words," he declared, "the time has come when either the United Nations should recognize the obvious fact of Chinese Communist aggression and take effective action to meet it, or the United States should withdraw its troops from Korea. Certainly we cannot ask our men to give their lives unless we back them to the hilt. . . ."

From the beginning, Nixon was one of those who failed to grasp the concept of a limited war as a combined politico-military struggle. His thinking, like that of General MacArthur, followed orthodox patterns. He took the familiar view that a war to be successful must end in the destruction of the enemy, or of his will to fight, and in the physical occupation of his territory.

When that enemy was nominally such a tiny patch of land as North Korea, Nixon and kindred formalists, whose adjustments to the strategic implications of communism were made slowly, considered anything short of victory a national humiliation. They had not perceived, or were not yet prepared to admit, that North Korea was not at all what it seemed, was not an independent sovereignty but rather the spearpoint of the Communist empire, and it was therefore unconquerable so long as the will to fight existed in the rest of that empire.

Hence, whether the United States was "backing to the hilt" its fighting men in Korea depended on what was expected of the war. Victory in the narrow military sense could be achieved only by an all-out struggle with the Soviet Union—in other words, the dread holocaust of a third world war. Victory in the larger political sense might and, as events proved, did consist of preventing the extinction of the Republic of Korea.

The logic of this analysis had failed Nixon and a good share of the American public in the early months of 1951. So had the corollary, that MacArthur, as the leading spokesman of the traditionalist view of war, was not only out of step with the times but was unwittingly endangering national security by his obduracy.

MacArthur's dismissal thus came as an unparalleled outrage to millions who had been led to accept his estimate of the war and its strategy. Nixon as an instinctive traditionalist found himself in their company. But, however faulty the senator's premises may have been in the light of history, he nevertheless judged aright in the immediate political context. Within hours after the announcement, he had taken up the cudgels in the general's defense.

"The happiest group in the country," he said in a statement, "will be the Communists and their stooges. . . . The President has given them what they have always wanted—MacArthur's scalp."

His next ploy, harking back to his success with it in the recent campaign against Helen Douglas, was to link the British with communism.

"The President has lined up with Dean Acheson and the British bloc of appeasers in the United Nations," he said angrily. ". . . The only possible explanation of the President's action is that he felt it was necessary to get rid of MacArthur so that Acheson would be free to make a deal with the Chinese Communists along the lines proposed by the British."

MacArthur, he said, "was fired simply because he had the good sense and patriotism to ask that the hands of our fighting men in Korea be untied." He pleaded for the avoidance of "tragic appeasement" and promised that the "policies of MacArthur will bring victory and peace in the Pacific. . . ."

On the same day he drafted and introduced Senate Resolution 126, in which he would have had his colleagues declare it to be the sense of the Senate "that the President of the United States has not acted in the best interests of the American people in relieving of his commands and depriving the United States of the services of General of the Army Douglas MacArthur and that the President should reconsider his action and should restore General MacArthur to the commands from which he was removed."

To climax that busy April 11 Nixon took the floor in the Senate to engage in a long colloquy setting forth his defense of MacArthur and his indictment of the administration's Asia policy. Following his time-tested debating technique, he deplored "emotional and personal considerations" and suggested "it would be wise for members of the Senate to consider objectively and factually what our differences are."

What followed was his usual skillful polemic; MacArthur was paraded across the stage from time to time as the martyred symbol of the other-than, but the spotlight focused hard and continuously on those in power, on "those who have failed so miserably."

"Let me say that I am not among those who believe that General MacArthur is infallible," he assured the Senate. "I am not among those who think that he has not made decisions which are subject to criticism. But I do say that in this particular instance he offers an alternative policy which the American people can and will support. He offers a change from the policies which have led us almost to the brink of disaster in Asia. . . .

"What has been the great error?" Nixon inquired. ". . . The policy has failed; and it has failed because of a basic error in the State Department, the error of taking the advice of men who whether knowingly or unknowingly came to the false conclusion that Chinese Communists were somehow different from other Communists. . . .

"When we speak of the responsibility for the war in Korea, let us remember that the Korean war would never have happened had not China gone Communist. . . . Now since we are confronted with the Korean war, the question is shall we persist in that mistake? . . .

"I believe that rather than follow the advice of those who would appease the Communists . . . we should do what we intended to do when we went into Korea, bring the war to a successful military conclusion. . . ."

To clinch his case, he wound up with a presentation of MacArthur's program: Stop all free world trade with Red China, bomb enemy bases on Chinese soil, impose a naval blockade, get assistance from every interested nation [a pitch for Chiang's forces on Formosa], and get assistance from others of the United Nations.

The *Congressional Record* notes "manifestations of applause in the galleries" as he sat down, but his presumptuous resolution and his prescription for victory were ignored except by doctrinaire right-wingers in and out of Congress, who welcomed MacArthur as a patsy, a convenient stalking-horse behind which the professionals could fashion an issue for 1952. Later that month Nixon ventured one more intrusion into the MacArthur affair. On April 26, a few days before Senator Richard Russell opened the full-dress hearings that led down a dignified blind alley, Nixon introduced a bill which, he explained to the Senate, would make it a "violation of law for any officer of the federal government to dismiss or otherwise discipline a government employe for testifying before a committee of Congress."

With the MacArthur hearings about to open, he said, it was "essential to the security of the nation" that every witness "have complete freedom from reprisal."

"Unless protection is given to witnesses who are members of the armed services or employes of the government," he asserted, "the scheduled hearings will amount to no more than a parade of yes-men for administration policies."

In the MacArthur hearings that followed, between May 3 and June 25, Nixon's bill served no practical purpose, but it fitted neatly into the evolving Republican political pattern. It was part of the over-all strategy of guilt-by-association and indictment-by-innuendo to suggest the existence of dire skeletons in the Truman closet, the existence of conspiratorial forces and secret plans undermining the nation's military and diplomatic defenses.

It was therefore good tactics to hint in advance of the hearings that powerful pressures would be used to cover up, and it was part of the masquerade to let voters know that the loyal opposition was on its toes, fighting the good fight. In the contemporary demonology, if the script called for a dragon against which St. George might pit his fearless sword, the simplest way to create the mythical ogre was to introduce a wholly matter-of-fact bill alleging or implying its existence. That way, at party rallies, the dragon could be made to look very real without the use of mirrors.

Nixon was on his feet in the Senate again April 27, pleading the cause of the Chinese Nationalists on Formosa, and ridiculing the administration's policy of fighting a land war "instead of using to the fullest extent our naval power and our air power."

"We are using our airplanes only for the purpose of tactical bombing," he said accusingly, disregarding the fact that we had no jet bombers capable of raiding China, and no long-range jet fighters capable of escorting our obsolete B-29's. "We are not using our navy for the purpose of a blockade. . . . We are unable to win a military victory in Korea. We are unable to do so because we are restricted in the use of both strategic bombing and naval power."

Repeatedly during this debate, Taft, as part of his relentless strategy of opposition, rose to his feet to echo Nixon and to spur him on. "The senator states the case very clearly," he said in his flat, passionless monotone. "I agree with the senator. It was a mistake originally to go into Korea. . . . That's correct. That is my view, anyway."

It was a question whether the junior senator from California, the youngest member on the Republican side, was his own spokesman or Taft's puppet. Certainly at no time during the Korean war did any responsible military staff member on the United Nations side endorse the Nixon-Taft-MacArthur thesis. Those charged with the grave responsibility of making decisions disagreed categorically with Nixon's assertion on May 1: "I believe the only way we can end this war is not by a ninety-day-long 'peace talk' but by military victories and economic blockades to shut out all foreign trade and smuggling such as now continues to aid Red China. There can be no 'political' settlement. . . ."

Nixon's judgment was wrong, of course, as the Eisenhower administration was eventually to demonstrate, not only in Korea but in Indochina as well, but this did not prevent him from using the discredited MacArthur thesis as a club with which to beat the Democrats in his 1951 and 1952 appearances at GOP rallies.

As early as May 12 he was assuring an audience of lawyers in Akron, without a shred of evidence, that MacArthur had won a personal victory in the great debate over Far Eastern policy. He listed what he called six "basic changes" in policy for which he contended MacArthur was responsible, culminating with the assertion that the administration had been "forced to agree" that the only way to end the Korean war was with victory on the battlefield.

Nixon's role in the MacArthur incident stands out with special clarity in any evaluation of his career. In it he took a categorical stand from the first moment. He carried on the fight aggressively, both on and off the Senate floor and over a period of months.

For political reasons, he committed himself impulsively to a military doctrine that lay outside the bounds of his training and experience. He staked his judgment, not on facts, but on a series of hypotheses, and he ignored facts that could have saved him. History will make the final assessment, but so deeply has his thesis been eroded in the interval that his basic capacity to judge and govern must seem to have been grievously impaired.

III

The MacArthur controversy had scarcely subsided when it was succeeded by a new sensation. On the initiative of the *St. Louis Post-Dispatch,* it was revealed that the Chairman of the Democratic National Committee, William M. Boyle, Jr., had intervened two and a half years earlier on behalf of a client to obtain a half-million-dollar loan from the Reconstruction Finance Corporation. At the end of September 1951 the case gravitated to Nixon's permanent investigations subcommittee, along with a parallel revelation that Chairman Guy G. Gabrielson of the Republican National Committee had also been a party to dealings with the RFC.

At senatorial hearings from September 31 to October 5, 1951, testimony showed Boyle had made an appointment February 28, 1949, for officials of the Lithofold Company to see Chairman Harley Hise of the RFC. What made that simple transaction suspect was that Lithofold had been three times turned down, that it got its loan three days after Boyle's intercession, and that Boyle, while using his position to arrange for the interview, was being paid a monthly retainer by the company. In addition it was learned that Boyle had built up a highly lucrative law practice while serving as acting chairman of the committee and had sold out to his partner, Max Siskind, for $150,000 on becoming permanent chairman. As for Gabrielson, it developed that, before he assumed the unpaid chairmanship of the Republican National Committee, he had once represented the Carthage-Hydrocol Company as president and general counsel in a successful loan-application proceeding before the RFC.

From this synopsis, manifestly, there was nothing resembling a genuine conflict of interest, but it was plain that both men had been playing politics according to rules that were ancient in Caesar's time. Nixon took an active part in the questioning, without developing any significant new facts, and when it became clear that no laws had been violated, he shifted quickly to the moral issue. It was easy to infer that there may have been influence peddling, as there always is, and the RFC, with its political administration and its millions in loans, was as likely a place as any to look for it.

"This inquiry has too many loose ends to call it closed," Nixon announced as the hearings recessed October 5, "and I think we'll have to resume hearings."

But no one wanted to flog a dead ox, except perhaps Nixon. Three days later, in what amounted to a farewell salute to the inquiry, he filed a political testament against corruption. In the appendix of the *Congressional Record* (weeks before a committee report could be filed) he inserted a careful summation and appraisal of the Boyle-Gabrielson circus.

"On the basis of their own testimony," he said, "both Mr. Boyle and Mr. Gabrielson should resign their positions as chairmen of the Democratic and Republican national committees.

"The basic issue is whether a high official of the national committee of either major political party should be in a position where he can profit financially from the influence which he may be able to exert with government agencies. . . .

"Mr. Boyle says that in making the appointment he was only doing what he would do for any person. . . . He sees no difference in the fact that the appointment in this instance was made for a client. The answer is that, when the national chairman of the party in power intervenes in behalf of a client, such action is influence in itself, regardless of whether he goes further and advocates the merits of the case.

"The Gabrielson case differs in many respects from the Boyle case but the same conclusion must eventually be reached. . . . There is no evidence of improper influence on behalf of his client during the time he has been chairman. On the other hand, Mr. Gabrielson's statement that he has no influence cannot be accepted. . . . He has the power of criticism and the potential power of recommending appointments and promotions. The opportunity for influence exists, and where the opportunity for influence exists, charges of impropriety are bound to follow. . . .

"I see no evidence of illegality or moral turpitude in the actions of either Mr. Boyle or Mr. Gabrielson [but] the paramount need today is to restore public confidence. . . . The top officials of both major parties should set an example of propriety and ethics which goes beyond the strict legal minimum required by the law."

From that time on, Nixon continued to capitalize on the issue. In November he accused Truman of defending "flagrant examples of misconduct" and proposed that Congress set up a special committee "or a group of special prosecutors similar to that set up in the Teapot Dome case to investigate charges of corruption in governmental bureaus." A month later when Truman repeated his determination to deal severely with dishonest government workers, Nixon demanded the dismissal of Attorney General McGrath and Treasury Secretary Snyder, and asserted the President's own actions "in defending and condoning unethical practices by members of his own official family have done more than anything else to encourage the decline of morality among government employes."

Nixon had subjected himself to some criticism inside the party for his boldness in censuring Gabrielson as well as Boyle, but in the end, in the climate of mink coats, deep freezes, and big and little scandals that pervaded the closing months of the Truman administration, he emerged as a champion of integrity in public life, a reputation that had no little bearing on his nomination for the vice-presidency.

A year later he was defending himself desperately on the same battleground, pleading his innocence against charges that, while he had indeed stayed within the "strict legal minimum required by law" in accepting $18,000 in gifts, he had blurred the same ethical lines as had the men he had stepped forward to condemn.

Again in 1956, Nixon came under attack when his campaign manager, Murray Chotiner, called on two presidential assistants at the White House and persuaded them to make telephone calls about Civil Aeronautics Board cases in which he was interested; on this occasion, Nixon kept silent and the defense took the pragmatic line that Chotiner did no wrong because his clients lost their cases. As for the ethical question—just what makes an influence peddler?—that question went begging.

IV

From time to time, as a senator, Nixon spoke without notable effect on a miscellany of other subjects: on the error of Truman's tidelands oil veto, on mineral leases and the administration of submerged lands, on the virtues of the Central Valley irrigation project in California; on veterans' legislation, housing, and the adoption of uniform codes for congressional investigations.

The last significant act of his Senate career, within a month of the 1952 nominating convention, found him involved with the national real-estate lobby in a move to kill public housing. In that year Congress had authorized construction of 35,000 units of public housing, and the Los Angeles Housing Authority, in its effort to relieve shortages and remove the Korean war's inflationary pressure on rents, had contracted to build 10,000 units. The real-estate lobby therefore picked Los Angeles as its first target in a heavily financed campaign to destroy the program through local action.

The first move was to subvert the Los Angeles City Council, which caved in under pressure and voted 8 to 7 to cancel the housing contract and submit the question to a referendum. The council's action led to a court ruling that the contract was binding, and that even a referendum would be powerless to abrogate it. However, since the housing proposition had already been printed on the ballot, it was allowed to remain; and the ensuing straw vote June 3 favored cancellation by a margin of about 8 to 5, with only a third of the electorate voting.

Since this vote was without legal effect, the pressure then shifted to Congress, where Knowland and Nixon agreed to carry the ball. In acquiescing, Nixon may have felt he had no real choice. Sponsor of the antihousing campaign was an organization calling itself the "Committee Against Socialist Housing" or CASH. One of the leaders of CASH was Joseph Crail, an attorney and president of the Coast Federal Savings and Loan Association. As it developed later, when Nixon's secret fund was made public, Crail was also one of the loyal contributors to the senator's fund, along with two other leading supporters of CASH.

The sequel was not without its ironic overtones. The initial Knowland-Nixon strategem June 12 was to fight for an amendment to the Defense Production Act that would have ordered a halt on any public housing project rescinded by local vote, provided the "community" refunded any money already advanced by federal agencies. The proposed language contained no definition at all of who in a "community" would be responsible for making such a refund or how the federal authorities could enforce repayment. The Senate killed that scheme on a technicality.

While the California senators were planning a second try, Representative Gordon L. McDonough solved their problem June 27 in the House by tacking a variation of the amendment onto a supplemental appropriation bill, during the rush toward adjournment. It might have slipped through the Senate also but for the watchfulness of Senator Joseph C. O'Mahoney, but at the latter's insistence the language of the rider was cleaned up to provide that, in any such contract cancellation, the local "governing body" must have "tendered the United States full reimbursement."

In that form the legislation achieved nothing, for neither CASH nor the Los Angeles City Council nor the Los Angeles Housing Authority was prepared to refund $13,000,000 in federal money already invested in the project! Hence the contract was fulfilled, not cancelled.

Nixon's part in the affair attracted relatively little attention at the time, except for the position he took on the Senate floor June 12 in advocating the proposal. Knowing that the referendum nine days earlier had been legally meaningless and had expressed the view of only a minority, he nevertheless said in the course of debate:

"The question before us . . . is whether or not Congress believes the federal government should force down the throats of people of a local community a public housing contract which they have voted to rescind and on which they are willing to reimburse the federal government. . . .

"It seems to me that the issue is clear; and under the circumstances members on both sides of the aisle, regardless of how they may feel about public housing or its merits—because that is not what is involved here—should vote to recognize the clearly expressed intent of the law and the will of the people."

V

Aside from the verdict of the 1952 Republican convention the only contemporary assessment of Nixon's contribution in the Senate came from a poll of political scientists conducted by Dr. B. L. Johnson of Denver and Dr. W. E. Butt of Pennsylvania. In the poll legislative specialists in the American Political Science Association rated senators on domestic and foreign attitudes, legislative ability, intellectual ability, and personal integrity.

The first ten on the list were Douglas, Kefauver, Morse, Lehman, Fulbright, Smith (Maine), Lodge, Aiken, Saltonstall, and McMahon. McCarthy beat out Jenner for last place.

Nixon was rated seventy-first among the ninety-six senators.

VI

In a sense Nixon's voting record has been all things to all people. If there was a discernible pattern, it escaped most of his contemporaries. Victor Lasky wrote, "He belongs to no party cliques, and his voting record defies classification." Scotty Reston said, "You can prove anything by Nixon's voting record." William Lee Miller put it down as "mixed and mildly conservative," something that "has to be carefully edited by the liberals who oppose him when they want to make it seem to be something fierce." William S. White observed that Knowland, the pillar of orthodoxy, nevertheless had "on domestic issues a much more liberal voting record than Nixon." And Richard Rovere rejected the effort of the Democratic National Committee to "establish him as a creature of the vested interests, an isolationist, a trifler with the national security, and a politician heedless of the plight of the exigent"; such a reading of the record is possible, he wrote, "only by omitting significant portions of it and carefully tailoring others."

The facts are less mystifying than generalizations of this kind. If he is not a stereotype, he is at least recognizable in terms of his basic commitments and of those pressures that become the monitors of every public servant. The meaningful measure of his voting record is in terms of those commitments, and four of them in particular: the Republican party, his California sponsors, political expediency, and his own private conscience.

During his six years in Congress he had 757 chances to express himself on roll-call votes, and his yeas and nays were counted 617 times. The record, as might be expected, shows his first commitment always to have been to the Republican party. During his first term in the House, according to *Congressional Quarterly,* his votes followed the GOP policy line 91 per cent of the time; in his second term, his acknowledgment of party discipline dropped to 74 per cent; and in the Senate, in a fractionally greater assertion of independence, he followed party leadership 70 per cent of the time. Summing him up in the light of these percentages, one observer said dryly, "There is nothing of the maverick about him." Even when on occasion he moved outside the frontiers of Republicanism, it was not to repudiate his spiritual home.

In the main his voting alignment with the Republican party expressed itself in a conservative view of economic policy. Typical of these roll calls were a series affecting agriculture; he was for killing the Brannan plan, for cutting farm tenant loans in 1947, for holding down Rural Electrification Administration loans in his first two years—but in favor of REA loans for rural telephones in 1949. In the field of housing, he voted to kill slum clearance and public housing (6/29/49), and the following year helped kill a provision for loans to housing cooperatives in the middle-income brackets (3/22/50), after which he voted yes on final passage of the mortgage insurance provision.

On legislation of more far-reaching significance, Nixon voted for the basing point bill of 1950, a system of price-fixing through the inclusion of fictitious freight charges; Truman killed the bill by veto, and the big industrial forces supporting it have since then been waiting to build up enough Republican strength in Congress to make another attempt.

In an allied field, Nixon lined up with a sizable majority of the Senate in July 1952 to restore the so-called "fair trade" laws that had been outlawed by the Supreme Court the previous year; while designed ostensibly to prevent chain stores from injuring small business by selling "loss leaders," the act proved basically restrictive and unworkable. In another case where the monopoly issue was raised, Nixon also voted the Republican big-business line; this was in June 1948, when Congress, over Truman's veto, passed an act permitting the railroads to make certain freight-rate agreements with full immunity from antitrust-law prosecution.

Nixon's votes on tax policy were strongly influenced by the Republican leadership. During his first year in the House he twice joined in straight party-line votes for income-tax reductions favoring the upper brackets, and when Truman vetoed both measures, he voted again the following year (4/2/48) for a tax cut which was passed over a third veto with the help of a divided Democratic party. In 1950 he was aligned with 94 per cent of his party in a move opposing higher corporation taxes (6/29/50). In the Senate he voted with his party to give corporations a ninety-day tax windfall of $500 million (9/26/51), and two days later he voted against any reduction in the oil-depletion allowance, the biggest unplugged loophole in the federal tax structure.

In the field of social welfare, he opposed (7/18/47) an increase in school-lunch appropriations to $75 million after the Republican-dominated appropriations committee had recommended only $45 million. He voted not to add 750,000 workers to the social-security system (2/27/48), and the following year opposed a plan for the inclusion of eleven million more until it became clear that passage was certain, when he climbed on the bandwagon (10/5/49). He voted in June 1947 to pass the Taft-Hartley bill over the President's veto and worked for the Wood amendments two years later. He helped pass a bill (8/10/49) that withheld the benefits of the 75-cent minimum-wage law from an additional million workers. He showed no conspicuous interest in education, absenting himself from the 1948 roll call on federal aid for school districts in defense areas, voting against a public-library demonstration bill (3/9/50), and voting for a 9-million-dollar reduction in funds for defense-area schools on June 13, 1951.

Although Nixon's record in foreign affairs fell largely in the liberal category, at least in matters affecting national security, it shows him following a consistently Republican voting pattern where matters of economic concern were paramount. In 1947 he voted to permit higher import duties on wool (6/16/47). The next year he joined others of his party in the Eightieth Congress in imposing a gag rule on the Democratic minority when the reciprocal-trade program was up for extension; he refused a three-year extension (5/26/48) and joined in the enactment of the reciprocal-trade bill containing the escape clause and "peril point" provisions. In the new Democratic Congress of 1949 he continued to vote for weakening or crippling provisions supported by the Republicans, but when these efforts failed he voted (2/9/49) in favor of a three-year extension of the trade program without such provisions. In July 1950 he was against the bill to guarantee American investments abroad under Point Four, and in 1952, after having voted favorably the previous year for another extension to the Reciprocal Trade Act, he again aligned himself

(6/11/52) with Republican conservatives in opposing United States participation in an international materials conference.

VII

Nixon's second major commitment can be traced logically to those who sponsored his advent in politics—the Committee of One Hundred in the Twelfth California District and the informal Dana Smith clique that elected to finance his political activities in the Senate. Nixon and his friends have repeatedly denied suggestions that members of either group were in a position to derive any personal advantage, but analysis has left a fair inference that their economic interests largely coincided with his. Basically they were people with property, interested in real estate, in oil, in public utilities, and in banking. There had to be a tacit understanding when they supported Nixon that he was not hostile to these interests.

Thus it was simply a matter of course that in the tidelands oil dispute Nixon should vote to hand over the submerged offshore oil properties to the states. It went without saying that the oil companies would find it easier to work their will on pliable state legislatures than on federal authorities, and it was implicit in Nixon's original recruitment that he would see the issue in this practical light. Hence in both 1948 and 1952 he threw his votes unquestioningly on the side of cession. Similarly in August 1949 he allied himself with the oil industry in voting to exempt from regulation by the Federal Power Commission the independent producers of natural gas.

On a variety of roll calls dealing with public utilities, his position uniformly favored private over public ownership, operation, or financing. In both 1948 and 1952 he voted against authorizing the Tennessee Valley Authority to construct supplementary steam plants for the production of electric power. In various votes dealing with the Rural Electrification Administration he tended to restrict rather than to encourage its growth. He was for cutting funds in 1947 and 1948; for limiting the extension of the Southwest Power Administration (7/10/51), and against an authorization to permit REA construction of power lines in Minnesota and Iowa (7/12/51). Previously he had voted against funds for power development and transmission lines in the

Missouri Valley and at Bonneville (4/25/47), and in January 1948 embraced an amendment to the reclamation laws making it difficult to authorize new projects and obtain reduced power rates.

His hostility toward public ownership of utilities carried over into matters affecting industry. Thus, in considering the Defense Production Act of 1951, Nixon cast his vote against proposals for federal construction of standby defense plants that private industry could not build and operate economically in peacetime (6/28/51). The following June, during the steel wage dispute, he voted consistently against federal seizure of the steel plants and in favor of invoking a Taft-Hartley injunction to halt the strike.

He was conscientious in safeguarding the real-estate interests that were an implicit part of this commitment. In that respect his votes in the fields of housing and rent control were perhaps as consistent and affirmative as any part of his congressional career.

In the House he opposed the liberal Taft-Ellender-Wagner public housing bill (6/17/48) and voted instead for the Wolcott "millionaire's housing bill." The following year, still opposing a federal program of housing for low-income groups, he voted down the line (6/29/49) against an omnibus public-housing, slum-clearance, and farm-housing program—a measure pushed through by the Democrats which is still the basic act in the field. In the Senate, he voted to cripple the public-housing program by cutting new starts from 50,000 to 5000 units (6/20/51) and the next year (6/3/52) he held the line by voting against a bill that eventually did authorize 45,000 instead of 5000 new low-cost housing units for 1953. It was during this same month that Nixon made his most overt move to assist the real-estate lobby, by urging cancellation of the $13,000,000 Los Angeles public-housing contract.

In dealing with rent-control problems of the postwar and Korean war periods—a time when shortages of housing and construction materials as well as powerful inflationary pressures were threatening to push rents through the roof—Nixon's voting record showed some vacillation. Out of sixteen opportunities to vote, he was absent five times, on four of which occasions the roll call was of major significance. During his four years in the House, he tended more and more toward decontrol, voting in March 1949 for local option, and for a three-month extension of control; and in 1950 opposing a six-month or even a three-month extension. However, when the full effect of the Korean war made itself felt, he voted as a senator (6/28/51) to continue rent controls; a year later, reverting to his basic position as the economic pressures of the war were on the wane, he voted (6/4/52) for the earliest discontinuance of the whole rent-control program.

VIII

The most ticklish and indeterminate commitment in a politician's life is that of conciliating the home constituency, whose interests tend toward the self-serving and parochial. Now and then in practice there are sensitive issues which must be neutralized for fear of alienating one or another sector of the electorate. These votes tend to be measured in terms not of principle or national interest, but of their impact on the next election.

To the problem of expediency thus posed, Nixon addressed himself nimbly. The way out of the dilemma is to appear on both sides of the issue. This double image is achieved as a rule by voting first for or against amendments calculated to reflect one point of view, so that, after their defeat or adoption as the case may be, it then becomes possible on final passage of the bill to reflect the contrary view by voting against or for the measure as a whole. The art of devising such amendments is a shell game in which political wizards of both parties join, and for many members the greatest professional satisfaction of serving in Congress is this exercise in sanctimony.

Out of many votes of this kind, Nixon's role in the India wheat bill of 1951 is an uncomplicated illustration of the technique. When the measure was introduced, calling for a free gift to India of $190,000,000 worth of wheat to prevent mass starvation, he added his name as a co-sponsor. He was one of those who emphasized that the gift must be free of political strings. Before the final vote was taken, he had first favored a proposal that the wheat should go to India, half loan and half free; and when that move failed, he wound up joining the ranks of those voting to change the transaction from a free gift to a long-term loan, with a stipulation that India should supply strategic materials in return for aid.

On other international issues where public opinion was skittish, he followed the same tactic. The reciprocal-trade bill was always a tricky one to field. Republican Old Guardists opposed tariff reduction in any guise, but Nixon's one-worldism (he had campaigned for Willkie in 1940) inclined him toward the program. His strategy was therefore to favor all enfeebling amendments—to add peril points, and escape hatches and limit extensions, and on one occasion (2/9/49) to favor recommittal, as proof of his loyalty to the conservatives—but in the showdowns to keep the act alive.

Similarly, in August 1951, in the fight over adoption of the Battle Act and of the Cannon amendment of the previous year, refusing aid to countries trading with the Communist bloc, he unsuccessfully opposed consideration of the measure, voted unsuccessfully for recommittal, voted unsuccessfully again for the more rigid and less workable Kem substitute (8/28/51), but after all this maneuvering joined finally with the majority in passing the bill.

The onset of the Cold War found Nixon voting for the Truman Doctrine (Greek-Turkish aid, 5/9/47), and for the Marshall Plan and successive economic aid appropriations in 1948; but the first major military assistance measure (8/18/49) had him once more straddling the issue. When the administration proposed funds to rehabilitate the armies of the North Atlantic Treaty Organization, he voted with 94 per cent of the Republicans in the House for a pinchpenny slash (from $1.1 billion to $580 million), then went along on passage of the bill, only to end up voting for a Senate-House conference report authorizing $1.3 billion for Europe and Asia together (9/28/49).

His votes in the highly sensitive field of social security and minimum wages showed the same ambivalence. He invariably voted for this legislation on final passage—after all, it had a direct impact on individual voters and pocketbooks—but he showed himself to be acquiescent whenever the Republicans fought to tighten coverage or reduce benefits in the interest of economy, notably so in 1949 when he voted three times (10/5/49) for crippling amendments to the social-security bill.

On internal security—where a good share of Nixon's reputation as a fearless anti-Communist was built—the record also has equivocal overtones. In July 1947, when the House considered a loyalty program for federal employees, Nixon joined a minority which voted for the right of judicial review, but when this safeguard was defeated, he nevertheless cast an affirmative vote for the bill. Similarly in 1950 on a motion to give the Civil Service Commission power to review summary dismissals by the heads of eleven sensitive agencies and departments, Nixon favored the procedure (7/12/50), but not enough to vote against passage of a bill that eventually became law without it.

In general, on these measures and on such related legislation as the McCarran Act of 1950 and the McCarran-Walter Immigration Act of 1952, Nixon's position was that protection of individual liberties was desirable but that in any question involving national security the rights of individuals were second to those of the state and it was his duty to resolve his doubts in that direction. This doctrine of state supremacy has not found universal acceptance in the courts, and the plea of those like Nixon that they were guarding a higher national interest is answered from time to time with judicial findings that such statutes tend in fact to undermine liberties of the citizenry which are paramount.

It would be incautious to conclude that Nixon's doctrinaire votes in these limited instances show him to be wholly at fault in defense of constitutional liberties, but there are critics who feel that he made unprincipled concessions.

To a practical politician such arguments are captious. He pitches his answer on the general proposition that he must make difficult choices if his whole constituency is to be represented and if he is to remain in office. If there is antiforeignism—and it does flare up at intervals—it has to be reckoned with, as in Nixon's switch on aid to India, preferably by a compromise that finally lands the wheat in India. Politicians affirm there is nothing hypocritical in voting to cut social security or to scruple over the costs of military aid, if in the end the programs are kept in being. They contend that idealists who carry the fight for their scruples to the last extremity too often end as victims of the public's fickle whims—as ex-officeholders. Nixon took this part of his public life for granted and seldom alludes to the apparent contradictions in his record.

IX

The ultimate commitment in public life is to the individual's private conscience, and in the light of history, it is a question whether or when it can be wholly excluded as a governing factor. Among Nixon's hundreds of votes, no one would dare say that one or another had been wholly influenced or uninfluenced by the innate character bias that sets one man's moral values apart from others'. What can be said, without inquiring too closely into motives, is that he took a relatively more independent line on social and international issues than on economic, and that he was nowhere more consistent than on issues appealing powerfully to his sense of patriotism.

Typical of these latter votes were those on national defense. He approved selective service, 1948; voted first for a 58-group and later for a 70-group Air Force in 1949; favored confirmation of General Marshall as Secretary of Defense in September 1950, and voted for the doctors' draft; opposed cuts in the defense budget for 1951 and 1952. He accepted the doctrine of the anti-Communist coalition uncritically on Truman's Greek-Turkish aid bill in 1947, and went on to support in most respects the burgeoning European Recovery Plan, the NATO alliance, and the military and economic implications of the mutual-assistance program. When he quibbled, it was in general over how to proceed, not whether.

His strict family background expressed itself in his support of such bills as the FEPC, but his feeling for racial equality was tempered by his insistence that such a bill, in order to work, must have compliance on a voluntary, not a compulsory basis. The same attitude expressed itself in his 1949 votes against the imposition of poll taxes as a requirement for voting in federal elections. It expressed itself further in his co-sponsorship of the amendment to grant women equal legal rights with men, and in his consistent support for Alaskan and Hawaiian statehood. Notwithstanding hatcheting tactics on the stump, he revealed a strong affinity for the Christian doctrines of brotherhood, even going so far in 1951 as to co-sponsor a so-called "Atlantic Union" resolution proposed by Kefauver, a request that the President invite representatives of the NATO powers to send delegates to a federal convention that would explore the feasibility of a free federal union within the framework of the United Nations.

Now and then his universalism faltered, as when he co-sponsored the Bricker resolution during his Senate term, only to find subsequently as a member of the Eisenhower administration that Bricker's attempt to undermine the presidential treaty-making powers would be anathema to any administration. Whether his original support of Bricker was a genuine expression of conscience may therefore be a subject of some doubt; as may also his vote in February 1947 for the Twenty-second Amendment limiting Presidents to two terms, and his April 1951 vote as a senator for the resolution calling on the President to consult Congress before stationing more than four divisions in Europe.

x

On issues of a bipartisan character, chiefly those dealing with foreign affairs, *Congressional Quarterly*'s analysis of Nixon's voting record reveals a baffling contradiction. At a period when his interest in global affairs and international cooperation was said to be expanding and maturing, he voted less and less often with the majorities of the two parties when they lined up together. The percentages take this tabular form:

Congress	Dates	Percentage
80th	1947–48	96
81st	1949–50	95
82nd	1951	90
82nd	1952	80

In statistical profile, Nixon's voting record looked about the same as the average congressman's. He was on hand for roll-call votes almost 90 per cent of the time in both the House and Senate, with two notable exceptions which pulled his average down substantially. In 1950, when he was campaigning against Helen Douglas, he missed one out of every three roll-call votes, including ten in February, fourteen in May, and eleven in August and September. In the Senate, his record of attendance dropped sharply in the summer of 1952 when he missed twenty roll calls in June and July; his score for the session was twenty-nine absences on 129 record votes, which meant he missed more than one-fifth of his opportunities. In tabular form his scorecard looks like the table on page 228.

Year	House HOUSE	No. of roll calls	No. of absences	Percentage of absences
1947		84	11	13.1
1948		79	9	11.4
1949		120	14	11.7
1950		143	48	33.6
	House totals	426	82	19.2
	SENATE			
1951		202	29	14.4
1952		129	29	22.5
	Senate totals	331	58	17.5

Apart from anything Nixon himself may have said about his views, the record is enough to show that his conservatism was no airy nothing palmed off on the credulous by his detractors, and that his internationalism was by no means unqualified.

He voted loyally for his friends and their philosophy and their interests. If his impulses toward farmers, workers, pensioners, and the downtrodden were magnanimous, his manner toward them was one of remarkably tight-fisted illiberality. If he was not entirely a skinflint, neither was he a do-gooder.

As a congressman he worked at his job conscientiously, but his votes fail to show him as endowed with a sense of mission. If he suggests a capacity for dedication, it is not so much to ideals or principles in the abstract as it is to expediency and the tools of the pragmatist.

CHAPTER XVII

———◆———

Vice-President

For Nixon, by a combination of tact, hard work, and good fortune, the vice-presidency became not the blind alley of tradition, but an avenue to influence and preferment.

Primarily, it was President Eisenhower who made it so. As an experienced staff officer, he considered it wasteful as well as dangerous to exclude from the executive process the man who might at any time assume its direction. His first order, during the preinaugural consultations at the Commodore Hotel in New York, was that Nixon was to be fully informed and included in all activities at Cabinet level. The Chief Executive rationalized his action on two grounds.

"The Vice-President of the United States should never be a nonentity," he said. "I believe he should have a very useful job." And at a sternly pragmatic level, both before and after his illnesses, Eisenhower had no hesitancy in saying that Nixon must be trained for the job "so that if the Grim Reaper would . . . remove me from this scene, he is ready to step in. . . ."

In this fashion, Eisenhower and Nixon established an unprecedented intimacy. They saw each other three times a week while Congress was in session. The President from the first unloaded on Nixon a variety of ceremonial duties and appearances, and it was he who launched Nixon as a traveling goodwill ambassador.

After Eisenhower's coronary, when he virtually abdicated his responsibility as Republican party leader, he was wholly content to let Nixon fill the vacuum.

In this official relationship, however, there was no suggestion of personal intimacy. The two had disparate backgrounds, and neither interests nor friends in common. They were separated by twenty-two years in age; and in Nixon's arduous self-made career there had been little leisure for hunting, fishing, golf, bridge, or any of the activities that might have linked him to Eisenhower socially. Nixon did take up golf after 1952, but without visible enthusiasm, and it was only infrequently that he was invited to join the President in a foursome at Burning Tree. The Vice-President made his appearance socially at the White House when protocol required, but sporadically otherwise, except for an informal breakfast now and then with the President.

This lack of intimacy and the psychology underlying it were tacitly acknowledged in September 1956, at the Gettysburg picnic for Republican party workers. In the course of a chat with Nixon, the President turned to another in the company and blurted out cheerily, "Did you hear that? Dick says he's never seen the inside of the house here!"

On that note he seemed fully prepared to let the subject drop, and would have, save for Mrs. Eisenhower, who had simultaneously been reminded of the oversight by Mrs. Nixon. There was a whispered colloquy between the First Lady and her husband, after which the Eisenhowers whisked the Nixons into a jeep and whirled them away to the house for a quick circle of the first-floor living quarters.

What struck observers was not merely that the Nixons had not previously been invited to Gettysburg but that the President saw no significance in the omission. And it was not until two years later, at the 1958 Christmas holiday season, that the Eisenhowers were entertained for the first time at the Nixon home in Washington.

It is a question which of the two discouraged a closer relationship. It may have been the Vice-President. At various times he found himself not wholly in sympathy with Eisenhower policy, and on occasion he put his reservations on record. Too intimate an association might have inhibited his freedom in such situations; a cordial but correct relationship left him tactical elbowroom the better to protect his future. As an added factor of indeterminate bearing, some loyal Nixonites neither forgot nor forgave Eisenhower's having subjected the Vice-President to the seven-day ordeal over the 1952 secret fund. To the degree that resentment persisted also in Nixon's subconscious, real friendship was foreclosed.

Certainly the President did not stint any public effort to make the vice-presidency rewarding for Nixon, and in a gesture emphasizing the cordiality of his official feeling he wrote occasional short appreciative letters, thanking him for this or that recent service. Eisenhower's attitude was simply that he preferred to keep his public and his private life separate, and his treatment of Adams, Dulles, and others in his official family was characterized by much the same reserve that he showed toward Nixon.

As Vice-President, Nixon kept the same arduous schedule he had maintained as a legislator. Workdays he reached his office by nine o'clock and seldom left till after six. With a fairly small staff he handled a heavy volume of mail, and at some seasons delivered as many as three speeches a week, all of which he drafted himself. Early in the administration, he conducted a series of seminars for newly elected Republicans in the House, and his door was always open to state and national committeemen and party workers visiting the capital.

He dined out industriously, presided over the Senate infrequently, and sat in on White House meetings of the Cabinet, the National Security Council, and the Republican legislative leaders. As part of a move to gain quasi-executive experience, he supervised the work of the President's committee on government contracts, and later headed a Cabinet committee on price stability for economic growth. Normally he read eight or ten daily newspapers —*The New York Times, New York Herald Tribune, New York Journal-American, Chicago Daily News, St. Louis Post-Dispatch, Los Angeles Times, Dallas Morning News, Atlanta Constitution,* and the Washington newspapers. On weekends he looked over the weekly news magazines and other periodicals.

During Nixon's incumbency the office of the Vice-President underwent a physical as well as political transformation. Truman and his two predecessors ran the office on an allowance of $11,460 a year. In Alben Barkley's term the appropriation was increased to $47,970 to give him a small staff, and Nixon started at about

that level. By 1957 he still had only one male administrative assistant and seven women secretaries, about half what he had been
allowed as a senator. To handle the increasing volume of work
he relied heavily on a group of fellow Californians in and out of
Congress who became known on Capitol Hill as his "errand boys,"
taking soundings at the grass roots, lobbying for administration
bills, negotiating patronage deals, running political interference,
and managing campaigns.

Beginning in 1957, however, there was a concerted drive to
rescue the office of the vice-presidency from its official desuetude.
Admiral Arthur Radford, chairman of the Joint Chiefs of Staff,
who was indebted to Nixon for strong support of his geopolitical
thinking, decided that the Vice-President as well as the Commander-in-Chief ought to have military aides, so he assigned two
junior officers to serve as appointments secretary (Major J. D.
Hughes) and assistant for national security matters (Marine Col-
onel Robert E. Cushman). These two were paid by the Pentagon,
but Congress at the same time raised the office budget to $102,000
a year, besides the Vice-President's $35,000 salary and $10,000
allowance for personal expenses. Under this arrangement Nixon
found himself early in 1959 with five male assistants and a secre-
tarial staff of more than a dozen.

Like any political phenomenon, Nixon has attracted a circle of
admirers, advisers, assistants, and hangers-on, who comprise his
staff, his base of political support, his reservoir of future power.
The men around Nixon have been drawn mainly from three sub-
urbs of his experience—from California, from the loyalties forged
in the Chowder and Marching Club, and from the Eisenhower administration and its close allies. In preparation for the 1960 campaign, Nixon's personal staff was rounded out with the appointments of Robert H. Finch, a Los Angeles lawyer and chairman of
the Los Angeles County Republican committee, as his chief political lieutenant; Charles McWhorter, a New York lawyer and
former chairman of the Young Republican National Federation,
as his versatile and efficient legislative assistant; and Herbert G.
Klein, editor of the *San Diego Union,* a warmhearted, extroverted
professional newsman, as his press secretary. Finch was thirty-
three, McWhorter thirty-seven, and Klein forty-one.

Besides the room off the Senate floor which has traditionally
been assigned to the presiding officer, Nixon's staff had working

quarters in Suite 361 of the Old Senate Office building; the space was crowded with files that overflowed into storage areas in other parts of the building, for he kept an extraordinarily complete record of his public life. In the office a magazine rack held an assortment of periodicals and bound mementos of his travels. A feature of one wall was a picturesque display, framed and mounted on green felt, of a dozen keys to cities or countries that he had visited, with a matching display of fourteen gavels which had been bestowed on him. Near the entrance was a handscript copy of Eisenhower's 1952 inaugural prayer, and opposite it a large photograph of the President inscribed affectionately to the Vice-President.

In Nixon's own words, the training process he underwent in his new office was a "liberal education in what goes on in the world." Talking informally to a small circle of Washington correspondents on the morning of his second inauguration, he was relaxed and self-assured in making that acknowledgment.

"Four years ago I didn't even know what the drill was," he said, comparing this day with the first inaugural. "Four years ago I was really as green as I could be regarding the responsibilities of the vice-presidency. I didn't have the slightest idea of other than the ceremonial responsibilities. Now, through these four years have evolved rather definite lines of responsibility."

And that evolution, he explained reflectively, without aggressiveness, gave him a foreknowledge that in his second term he would be "doing something more substantial than acting as a figurehead," and would enable him to "make a policy-making contribution to the administration."

There was no one to challenge that estimate. Eisenhower himself had said the previous September that "no one in the history of America has had such careful preparation" as Nixon, for whatever might befall. The Vice-President for his part had taken full advantage of his opportunities. He kept himself in the background, worked indefatigably, and fitted himself into a unique niche as legislative errand boy, political fixer, presidential stand-in, party broker, and globe-trotting celebrity.

In playing this complex part, he recognized that his was an office with limited influence and responsibility but without power, and he was therefore careful not to overstep the bounds of propriety in his relations with the White House. He was first called upon to explain that relationship after the coronary crisis in 1955; and he was pressed to discuss the subject again in November 1957, after the President's stroke, when he held a news conference at the White House.

"I would not say that this is an instance in which the Vice-President has stepped in for the President," he said, facing up to a suspicion that he was ready to encroach on presidential prerogative. "What actually happens is that the President has directed the Vice-President to assume certain duties and responsibilities . . . when the President is unavoidably absent. . . .

"My role . . . I think, is best described by my title. I am the Vice-President. . . . In a situation of this type, it is true that the Vice-President does assume some additional duties. Most of these duties are ceremonial, as, for example, my attendance at the dinner for the King of Morocco this evening. . . . Some of those duties involve consultation with the Cabinet officers and others in clearing away nonessentials and in preparing subjects for presentation to the President, which he must decide. . . .

"I do not, in the normal course of events, have press conferences," he explained with labored precision, ". . . because I think it is not helpful to have a press conference held by a Vice-President on the same subjects that a President may be holding a press conference on. . . . Getting down to this meeting today . . . there were a number of inquiries . . . and it was the view of all of us . . . in the White House offices here that it would be well to meet the press. . . . It would not be my intention to have general press conferences on the area of government which would be generally covered by the President."

As he spoke his manner was composed. If he felt strain, it was not visible. Only once in such a situation did he let his feelings show; that was in Minneapolis during the 1958 campaign when his nerves were raw with fatigue and foreboding and he strode from a news conference trembling with rage after an innocuous question on civil rights.

Curiously, though, even when his outward bearing was thoroughly urbane and circumspect, he seemed on the defensive as often as not. His movements were dogged by a latent suspicion that at the first opportunity he would be offside in scrimmage. The press in its dealings with other Washington notables was content to inquire into plans, opinions, activities, behavior, but with Nixon it showed a morbid tendency to toy with motives. On both sides, as they probed and he responded, there was a hint of shame, as if what had to be said were better left unsaid, but the compulsions could not be hidden.

II

In some quarters much has been made of the fact that Nixon was a regular attendant at Cabinet and Security Council meetings and that he presided over them in the President's absence. Some enthusiasts have magnified this fact to suggest that the Vice-President was thereby enabled to play a major policy role, but such inferences can be treated with reserve.

Nixon's role as a Cabinet-level counselor and stand-in for the President has been nowhere more clearly set forth than in Robert J. Donovan's *Eisenhower: The Inside Story*. That work was based primarily on the minutes of Cabinet meetings in the first three years of the administration; and according to Donovan, it included every significant allusion to Nixon shown in the minutes.

If this was indeed the case, merely to catalogue the excerpts would be to assign Nixon a minor role on policy. They indicate that in only twenty-odd instances did he enter the Cabinet discussions significantly enough to be quoted. Four observations attributed to him deal with substantive matters, seven with public-relations advice, and a dozen or so with political aspects of pending problems.

The portrait is of a diffident young man, holding his tongue on matters outside his province and trading on his capacity as a vote-getter to speak out when political judgments were appropriate. Donovan, while attempting no quantitative assessment, was nevertheless able to conclude: "It is in the political field, particularly in the area of political maneuver involving Congress, that Nixon's help has been most sought by the President and his associates."

"The President," Donovan explained, "welcomes Nixon's judgment on how certain proposals will be received in Congress. Occasionally someone at the White House will telephone Nixon at the Capitol and say that the President would like to know what he thinks about a measure under consideration. In the Cabinet and N.S.C. the President looks to Nixon to reflect the Congressional viewpoint and raise a red flag whenever he thinks something will breed political trouble. Nixon's role has been described as that of political broker between the conflicting wings of the Republican Party."

At various times in that early period, Nixon is recorded as observing at Cabinet meetings that: the importance of local issues in congressional elections is exaggerated; the time might be approaching when patronage should be used to help force the President's legislative program through; it was the policy of the administration to give positions to pro-Eisenhower Democrats; the ultimate success of the Eisenhower administration might depend on the outcome of the 1954 election; appearances of the President before joint sessions of Congress should be limited; a good public-relations program was the key to success; he thought it important that Eisenhower be identified with a school building program; the administration could not support the Bricker amendment as it stood; the administration should fight McCarthy only when his facts were quite wrong; if the minimum wage was to be raised and if the effect on the economy would not be harmful, a $1 level would be preferable from a political point of view.

So far as Donovan's research was able to show, the Vice-President carefully avoided entangling himself in substantive matters of policy falling within the jurisdiction of the various Cabinet departments. When he did interject a comment, it was on a subject well within his competence.

No comparable record of his part in National Security Council discussions has been made public, nor have the minutes of Cabinet meetings during the second term. If Nixon after 1957 contributed more than he had previously to shaping policy, the evidence is not known, except for the solemn and unwearying assurance of the press that he sat "in the high councils." But the impression created by this facet of his career is in no wise unlike that created by his public utterances.

Essentially he revealed himself as a man whose interest focused on the how of things rather than the what or why. He possessed a talent for judging the impact that issues would have on the ballot boxes, and he had a way of putting them in lucid juxtaposition, but he applied himself only with conscious effort to the rationale of the issues themselves. When he opposed the Bricker amendment, it was not on principle (indeed he had been one of its co-sponsors in the Senate), and he was neither for nor against higher wages or school aid or McCarthyism on any ground that lent itself to ethical evaluation. Where his cosmos crystallized was in the field of strategy, not policy.

III

As presiding officer of the Senate, Nixon captured the spotlight on two occasions—in January 1957 and two years later at the opening of the Eighty-sixth Congress when he defied and outraged conservatives of both parties by ruling against that most jealously guarded of all senatorial prerogatives, the right of extended debate.

For the most part the duties of the Senate's presiding officer are routine; disputed points of order are settled by the staff parliamentarian or, rarely, by a vote of the chamber. Nixon normally spent less than ten per cent of his time in the chair, although this is the one specific duty assigned to the Vice-President by the Constitution. His custom was to call the session to order, sit through the opening prayer and the Majority Leader's announcements, then turn the tedium over to freshman members. He worked a good deal in his private office just off the Senate floor, where he could be on hand to break tie votes.

Over the years the struggle to limit debate and outlaw filibusters has been fought as a series of guerrilla actions, with the Northern and Western liberals assailing the Senate's Rule XXII whenever the question of civil-rights legislation assumed urgency, and with a mixed coalition of conservative Republicans joining hard-core Democrats of the Deep South to preserve the status quo.

To many "filibuster" is a word of ill repute, a fighting word, the tactic by which a willful minority is able to frustrate the will of the majority, especially on civil-rights legislation. The connotations and emotional overtones on the civil-rights issue have had the effect of damning all filibusters, no matter what their purpose. Among politicians, however, there is another and more tolerant view, one which was acknowledged in the 1959 debate by Senator Wayne Morse of Oregon, one of the great lawyers of the modern Senate and an ardent liberal.

"I am the only liberal Senator who has publicly confessed that he filibusters," Morse said with tongue in cheek; and he promised that he would probably filibuster again "on the same principle on which I have filibustered in the past; never for the purpose of preventing the final majority opinion of the Senate from prevailing, but filibustering only long enough so, first of all, that the Senate may be apprised of what is involved in the issues."

Morse on that occasion went on to recall that in 1954 he joined with Senator Clinton Anderson in a filibuster against the atomic-energy bill which "succeeded in adding certain amendments to that bill which would not have been added had we not engaged in prolonged debate."

"As a result of that filibuster," he declared triumphantly, "we stopped a steamroller in the Senate."

In the filibuster controversy Nixon concentrated on the first, the political, aspect, ignoring or rejecting the prospect that an unwise change in the rules of debate might pave the way for a procession of legislative steamrollers, liberal, conservative, or demagogic.

The issue in 1957 was posed as usual by a motion to liberalize Rule XXII. For years Nixon had been looking forward to this moment. As a senator in 1951-52, he had been denied a chance to vote on the filibuster issue because no move was made to amend the rule. A motion to liberalize cloture was made in January 1953, but Nixon had then resigned from the Senate in preparation for his inauguration as Vice-President. During the two years of the Eighty-fourth Congress the issue did not arise. Thus it was not until 1957 that circumstances made it possible for Nixon formally to register his opposition to the filibuster.

What he did on that occasion had been foreshadowed in his campaign for the vice-presidency five years earlier. In a speech at the Commodore Hotel in New York, October 19, 1952, he dwelt on the need for civil-rights legislation and charged scornfully that "we have had promises but no performance" because "bills cannot pass the Senate of the United States as long as the filibuster exists in the Senate."

"I think," he said in an obvious salute to the big Negro vote in Harlem, "that we can recognize that Dwight Eisenhower can keep his promises, because he is going to have a Vice-President who opposes the filibuster, and you can be sure that once Dwight Eisenhower becomes President of the United States we are going to have performance on civil rights, not just promises."

What Nixon thought he could do as Vice-President to sway the august assembly over which he presided is unclear. On this first test, January 3, 1957, Anderson moved for the adoption of new rules. The Vice-President in an advisory opinion held that the motion was in order. The Senate's answer next day, by a peremptory 55-38, was to table the proposal and spurn Nixon's interpretation.

What made Nixon's ruling historic was that it rejected the very heart of traditionalist dogma, the plea that the Senate was a continuing body with enduring rules. The effect of his opinion was therefore, at least theoretically, to open the way for the adoption of new rules at the beginning of any session, not by a two-thirds but by a majority vote. In the event the ruling was sustained, the South lost its veto power over civil-rights legislation, and the conservative coalition as a whole lost its dominant voice in economic policies.

What threw a more lurid cast over Nixon's role in the anti-filibuster fight was the subsequent revelation that he took his stand in defiance of the entire Republican high command in the Senate. The day before his challenge, he met with Styles Bridges of New Hampshire, Leverett Saltonstall of Massachusetts, and William Knowland of California, the GOP hierarchy. According to one of those present, each of the three was bitterly angry with Nixon, all pleaded with him to withhold his ruling, and, as Joseph Alsop learned the story, they "came as close to blows as men can without actually using their fists." When Nixon asked the President's advice, he was told to make his own choice.

The impact of this short, sharp struggle—which was to become a legend of the Senate's inner history—was not easy to assess. In this crucial situation, why should Nixon have risked alienating his strongest supporters, the Senate conservatives, who had already begun to embrace him in their hopes for 1960? It is not enough to suggest that his basic convictions left him no choice, for the political implications were patent.

Earl Mazo, in his book, went so far as to suggest that an "implied threat" on Nixon's part "was a major factor in the passage that year of the first civil-rights legislation enacted since Reconstruction." Senate historians scoff at this insinuation. The South, they concede, had begun to recognize by 1957 that the power of the filibuster was on the wane. Nixon's determination to set down his opinion as a matter of legislative history and precedent, coming as it did on the heels of the 1956 election trends, could be interpreted, not as a threat, but at most as another straw in the wind, a cue to enact a bill the South could live with before extremism got the upper hand. Nixon's stand did nothing either to help or hurt the 1957 civil-rights bill; his foresight lay in the fact that, as a vote-hunter, he could see the ramparts of the filibuster crumbling and put the change to work for him in the Negro voting community.

In 1959 the ritual was repeated but with significant variations. This time Nixon was pale and tense, plainly ill at ease in the chair, as he jockeyed for position between the contending liberal and conservative factions.

Under Lyndon Johnson's leadership a bipartisan conservative coalition took the initiative January 7 by offering an amendment to Rule XXII that would: (1) permit cloture by two-thirds of the senators present and voting and (2) make cloture apply to rule changes as well as legislation. Moreover, in a direct slap at Nixon's earlier ruling that the Senate was not a continuing body, the proposal included a new section asserting categorically that "the rules of the Senate shall continue from one Congress to the next Congress unless they are changed as provided in these rules."

The previous day Nixon had conferred with the Republican leadership. Once again, as in the painful interview two years earlier, he had been warned against too drastic a change in Rule XXII. Under this pressure, Nixon temporized, agreed that any proposal for change would be considered under the old rules.

This concession led him into a fatal box. In a series of parliamentary inquiries that followed on January 8, he was first led to rule that proposals for changes in the rules must be handled in accordance with Rule XL, requiring one day's delay or unanimous consent for amendment or suspension of the rules. He then ruled that the majority had the right to cut off debate notwithstanding any existing rule to the contrary. A question was raised: by what right did he feel free to select some rules as applicable while holding others not applicable? His answer was that certain rules involved constitutional issues, after which he conceded that only the Senate itself was a judge of what constituted a constitutional impediment. The legal wizards on the floor then led the Vice-President to express the view that "a constitutional right which exists at the beginning of a new Congress . . . will no longer exist once the Senate has proceeded to the consideration of substantive matters. . . ."

At that stage, Senator Lyndon Johnson exploded. "The majority of the members of the Senate can rewrite the rules," he cried, "each one of them, all forty of them . . . in any respect it may desire, at any time. . . ."

Senator O'Mahoney said scornfully, "When he [Nixon] attempted to answer my inquiry as to where in the Constitution there is any line to indicate that a failure of the Senate to adopt all its rules at the beginning of the session would cut off the right of the Senate to act, he could not answer." O'Mahoney called it a "perfect absurdity" to suggest that the Senate by majority vote could deny itself the right to amend its rules, and thus by indirection amend the Constitution!

Senator Monroney called it "perfectly ridiculous for anyone to assume the Senate ever loses its right to change its rules," and pointed out that the Legislative Reorganization Act of 1946 was adopted in the summer of that year, not at the beginning of a session. Said Monroney, "The Constitution . . . necessarily permits the Senate to change its rules whenever the Senate wishes."

In a matter of minutes the master parliamentarians on the floor thus proceeded to demolish the Vice-President's carefully prepared position. Nixon abandoned the attempt to defend his ruling and withdrew from the chamber. His purpose had been to facilitate efforts of a minority group to bring in a more liberal modification of Rule XXII, but it was a futile exercise. Lyndon Johnson threw open the doors to a series of counterproposals, voted them down in quick succession, and capped the performance by a top-heavy 72 to 22 alignment in favor of his own compromise amendment.

Somewhere along the way, the filibuster as a political issue got lost in a backwater, for it became evident that the paramount consideration, after all, was the Senate's tradition of extended debate. The Senate's answer to Nixon, overwhelmingly, was that the rights of minorities both in and out of the Senate could best be preserved in the long run by calm deliberation, not by the power of sectional steamrollers. To an indeterminate degree that fact blurred Nixon's success in establishing a leftward position on civil rights, but no one could point to a bolder commitment.

IV

Because Nixon had no experience whatever in the administration of important executive policy, sporadic efforts were made after 1953 to give him scope of a quasi-executive nature. The first such move was made in August 1953 when Eisenhower created the President's committee on government contracts and made Nixon its chairman. The committee's function is to eliminate discrimination against minorities on work done under government contracts. With a membership of sixteen it holds monthly meetings to review the work of twenty-five staff members in Washington, Chicago, and Los Angeles. The committee's activities take two forms: it surveys government contracts for evidences of discrimination, usually analyzing about five hundred contracts a year; and it processes complaints charging contractors on government jobs with specific acts of discrimination.

Nixon has taken an active interest in this committee's work, and its impact is attested by the fact that, as the work of the committee becomes better known, it has received a mounting volume of complaints. Since the committee has no enforcement powers and works entirely by persuasion, it has carried on an active educational program. Within the limited framework of the committee's powers and resources, the Vice-President has been credited with having done a most effective job.

A somewhat more ambitious undertaking was placed in the Vice-President's hands January 31, 1959, when Eisenhower announced his appointment as chairman of the Cabinet committee on price stability for economic growth. The purpose of the appointment was twofold: to make budgetary retrenchment respectable and, as Edwin L. Dale, Jr., reported in *The New York Times,* to give Nixon a "precise and publicly known administrative role that would help his chances for the presidency in 1960." Serving with the Vice-President were the Secretaries of the Treasury, Agriculture, Commerce, and Labor, together with the Postmaster General and the chairman of the President's Council of Economic Advisers.

Nixon's appointment was hailed as a welcome move if it meant "an attempt to ventilate the process of economic policymaking a bit," and the study group was urged to re-examine "the narrow premises of the 1960 budget, which exalts a dubious 'stability' at the expense of urgent domestic defense and economic assistance needs." In assembling a staff, Nixon's first act was to appoint as his executive vice-chairman Dr. W. Allen Wallis, a statistician and economic standpatter of the old school. Thus, although Nixon was expected to exercise a liberalizing influence, his first act reflected the same pattern of economic orthodoxy that had characterized his voting record in Congress.

Barely five months had passed, with a number of staff study projects under way, when the price-stability committee published its first interim report, a 3000-word manifesto which was released by Eisenhower with a statement that he had himself submitted to Congress each of the three recommendations contained in the report.

The story behind this "me too" approach to the politics of economics was that, when the Vice-President saw months of study producing nothing, he ordered some raw data forwarded to his desk and then himself dictated what purported to be an economic report but what sounded remarkably like some of his better stump speeches. In keeping with the GOP policy line, he warned against "strong pressures for irresponsible spending," noted an "alarming tendency in the Congress to work toward only an illusory balance in the budget," rejected "government control of prices and wages" (which no one had suggested), and concluded that "we are confronted with overwhelming evidence that we have arrived at a time of decision. . . ."

No part of the report contained the type of statistical or supporting data that might have been expected in a serious economic study. So patently political were the overtones that the *Washington Post* was led to call the report "one of the most redundant, uninspired, and generally useless documents lately to come off the Government's mimeographing machines."

Following publication of the interim report June 29, the Vice-President's committee produced on August 17, as the first of a series, an eight-page statement on the "aims of economic policy." The key passage asserted the economic aims of the American people should be "economic growth, maximum employment opportunities, and reasonable stability of the price level." This was promptly interpreted as an attempt on Nixon's part to pre-empt for his own use in 1960 the economic growth issue, which had long been a favorite of the Democratic party. The statement, however, while explaining why such aims were desirable, made no attempt at all to suggest how economic growth was to be achieved. Hence the Vice-President's effort to reinforce his standing as an executive and as a knowledgeable economist got off to a sluggish and not perceptibly impressive start.

Nixon's most provocative attempt to win a foothold in the executive branch not only backfired but helped to explain why he made such scanty progress. After the 1956 election, when Herbert Hoover, Jr., was preparing to resign as Undersecretary of State, Nixon's friends in the administration came up with a proposal to transfer one of Hoover's ex-officio jobs to the Vice-President. That job was the chairmanship of the Operations Coordinating Board (OCB), a little-known offshoot of the National Security Council, whose function it is to make sure that government agencies carry out NSC policy recommendations approved by the President.

The first chairman of the OCB had been Undersecretary of State Walter Bedell Smith and upon his retirement the assignment had automatically passed to Hoover as his successor. Hoover had been one of the contributors to the Nixon expense fund and was therefore predisposed in the latter's favor, but he chose to interpret the move for Nixon's appointment to the chairmanship as an affront to the State Department and a reflection on his own handling of the job. Christian Herter, who was scheduled to succeed Hoover, professed a willingness to waive his rights to the OCB assignment, and Nixon, who saw the post as an avenue to power in virtually every agency in the government, was on fire with eagerness to get it.

In the infighting that followed, Hoover took the case to Secretary of State Dulles, and, as Arthur Krock of *The New York Times* unraveled the story, it was Dulles's direct intervention with the White House that carried the day against Nixon. Months later, when Eisenhower was asked to explain the background of his rejection of Nixon, he dismissed it as a "very simple" matter.

"The Vice-President has statutory constitutional duties," he said. "It would be impossible as a matter of practice to give, within the executive department, the Vice-President specified duties because if you happen to have a Vice-President that disagrees with you, then you would have . . . an impossible situation. . . . I don't know of any Vice-President that has ever been given the great opportunities to participate in difficult decisions, conferences, and every kind of informative meeting that we have than Mr. Nixon. But I decided as a matter of good governmental organization that it would not be correct to give him a governmental position in the executive department."

RONALD SPANANY
great opportunities to participate in difficult decisions, conferences, and every
Mr. Nixon. But I decided as a matter of good governmental organization that it would not be correct to give him a governmental
position in the executive department.

CHAPTER XVIII

Globe-trotter

I

NOT THE LEAST difficult of Nixon's many roles as Vice-President
was that of overseas goodwill ambassador. The trips, nine in all,
began late in 1953 on Eisenhower's personal initiative, and the
White House each time was at pains to emphasize Nixon's status
as the President's representative and to lend him the full weight
of the President's prestige. From Eisenhower's point of view the
reasons for the excursions varied, in some cases being merely to
satisfy protocol, in others to conciliate the restless heads of friendly
governments, and in still others to add a new facet to Nixon's education, to wriggle out of a pressing invitation to himself, or to
focus public attention on a significant but neglected aspect of
American foreign policy.

In undertaking the assignment to visit the Far East in the fall
of 1953, the Vice-President made a circumspect effort to define
his status and narrow the trip's political horizons.

"It is not my purpose," he explained, "to act as an unofficial
secretary of state. It will be a fact-finding trip, to listen and to
learn rather than to tell any people what we think they should do.
I do not propose to go into policy matters or discussions as such.
That is the province of the Secretary of State."

To this modest frame of reference—which was to undergo an

OVERSEAS TRAVELS

Year	Itinerary		Mileage
1953	FAR EAST, *October 6-December 14*	Air	42,881
	New Zealand, Australia, Indonesia, Singa-pore-Malaya, Thailand, Cambodia, Vietnam, Laos, Hong Kong, Formosa, Korea, Japan, Okinawa, Philippines, Burma, Ceylon, India, Afghanistan, Pakistan, Iran, Libia	Auto	2,550
			45,431
1955	CENTRAL AMERICA: *February 6-March 5*	Air	8,550
	Cuba, Mexico, Guatemala, El Salvador, Honduras, Nicaragua, Costa Rica, Panama, Canal Zone, Virgin Islands, Puerto Rico, Dominican Republic, Haiti	Auto	1,029
			9,579
1956	BRAZIL: *January 29-February 4*	Air	10,263
	Presidential Inauguration	Auto	122
			10,385
	ASIA: *June 30-July 12*	Air	27,477
	Honolulu, Wake Island, Guam, Manila, Vietnam, Formosa, Thailand, Pakistan, Turkey, Spain	Auto	407
			27,884
	HUNGARIAN REFUGEE INSPECTION: *December 18-24*	Air	10,500
		Auto	503
	Austria, Germany, Iceland		11,003
1957	AFRICA AND ITALY: *February 28-March 21*	Air	19,210
		Auto	1,102
	Morocco, Ghana, Liberia, Uganda, Ethiopia, Sudan, Libia, Italy, Tunisia		20,312
1958	SOUTH AMERICA: *April 27-May 18*	Air	12,528
	Uruguay, Argentina, Paraguay, Bolivia, Peru, Ecuador, Colombia, Venezuela, Puerto Rico	Auto	642
			13,170
	ENGLAND: *November 24-29*	Air	6,765
	American Chapel Dedication at St. Paul's	Auto	140
			6,905
1959	SOVIET UNION AND POLAND: *July 22-August 5*	Air	13,750
		Auto	746
	Opening American exhibition in Moscow		14,563[1]
		Total Air	151,924
		Total Auto	7,241
		Total Miles	159,232[1]

[1] Includes 67 miles by ship.

intermittent and sometimes disturbing transformation on later trips—Nixon added another misconception whose influence he never quite outgrew.

Relying for guidance on the folkways of a small-town Quaker background, Nixon set out to find the grass roots of the world. He adopted uncritically the premise that by an energetic show of friendliness he could be accepted anywhere as a working symbol of the brotherhood of man. In a poetic mood of one-upmanship he undertook to walk with commoners nor lose the kingly touch.

His method of testing his thesis—to the consternation of statesmen and peasants alike—was put into practice on his very first tour of Asia and continued without interruption until he came within minutes of losing his life at the hands of a mob in Caracas. His favorite gesture was to stop motorcades, sometimes comprising as many as a hundred cars, in order to shake the hands, pat the heads, and kiss the babies of astonished onlookers. To the dismay of security officers he strolled in crowded markets, invaded hostile demonstrations, engaged in street-corner debates with students.

In all this there was nothing haphazard. The effects were calculated. He knew what he wanted. He wanted to radiate democracy.

It was a generous, well-meaning gesture but not the most sophisticated. If he was right in assuming we are all brothers under the skin, he was not necessarily right in believing that local tradition is everywhere prepared to acknowledge it. With the characteristic egocentricity of the Western man, and with a somewhat missionary fervor, he persisted despite all protests in practicing his private brand of egalitarianism. In his own picture of himself he was the iconoclast, the innovator, projecting a new and necessarily better set of values.

Where Nixon was probably more nearly right was in believing that his political image with minority groups at home could hardly suffer at the sight of him mingling unselfconsciously with all creeds and colors and classes, putting into practice his faith in equal rights and the century of the common man. The pains he took to see that his trips were well staffed by news-media representatives testified to his awareness of these connotations.

Nixon's mistake on these voyages of discovery, as Lippmann

pointed out, was in acting "as if he could build up the influence of the United States abroad by behaving as if he were running for office at home." In most of the world there is no tradition of back-slapping, baby-kissing politics. Japanese or Indonesians or Burmese might laugh with what appeared to be exuberant good humor to hide their embarrassment, and teen-agers might flock hilariously to witness the spectacle of a frock-coated American official hobnobbing with his inferiors, but it was not easy for any of them in the light of their own history to take such capers seriously.

He was no more successful in adopting a nonpolitical pose in his dealings at the official level. Since he was traveling as himself, and not incognito, governments had no choice but to receive him in state and treat him as Eisenhower's personal deputy. Although he excluded himself from policy discussions or substantive negotiations that might tread on Dulles's prerogatives, his position was enough to give even oblique remarks a meaningful coloration.

As a state visitor he could not have refused to discuss real problems without being callously offensive or without failing in his obligation to Eisenhower; yet once he had embarked on or been drawn into political discussions with his ministerial host of the moment, Nixon the politician found himself in a dangerously exposed and compromising position.

Once he had consented to listen to appeals, proposals, or complaints, whatever their nature, there was no escaping the consequences. He could hardly take refuge in the stultifying plea that the Vice-President is a constitutional figurehead, for he presented himself as the President's personal representative. Moreover, with an eye to his own future at home, he could not place himself in the ridiculous position of conferring at length, or of going through the motions, only to confess himself finally nothing but a play-boy Throttlebottom.

II

Nixon's invariable practice before starting a trip was to call on the State Department for at least a two-hour briefing on each country scheduled for a visit, and to have supplementary embassy briefings en route. By all accounts he was an apt and avid pupil. Despite this attempt to present a knowledgeable façade, he was described during his first Asian tour as "eager and juvenile," as "an emissary who may influence further favors," as "a young assistant to the President," and (by Prime Minister Nehru later) as "an unprincipled cad." His commitment to the China Lobby made itself visible, as well as his tendency to think, at least at that stage, in terms of military alignments.

In ten weeks of travel in the late autumn of 1953 he was quoted on nearly a dozen major policy issues. In Tokyo he was the first American in the postwar period to say that the United States made a mistake in disarming Japan. On Formosa he emphasized heavily the policy of nonrecognition of Red China, and when Secretary Dulles at a Washington news conference hinted at a two-Chinas policy, an angry Nixon issued a special statement rejecting Dulles's thesis. At the same time, when Generalissimo Chiang Kai-shek implied he was preparing for the reinvasion of the mainland the following year, Nixon lent himself to the impression that American policy endorsed Chiang's hopes. After that it was five years before Secretary Dulles was able to renounce the reinvasion thesis and suggest a new lease on life for the two-Chinas policy.

In Burma, the Vice-President urged more speedy evacuation of 10,000 Kuomintang guerrillas. In Vietnam he urged that the war be fought to victory, although, as the premier in Paris was quick to point out, France felt no more obligation than the Americans in Korea to "make war for war's sake"; Nixon also acknowledged that he would confer with General Cogny, commander-in-chief in Vietnam, on the latter's request for military supplies and would make recommendations to President Eisenhower; at a formal dinner he told top officials, "Under no circumstances could negotiations take place which in effect would place people who want freedom and independence in perpetual bondage."

At various points along the way he expressed himself critically of neutralism, entirely ignoring the distinction between political and moral neutralism which he himself was to make three years later; and to the degree that his dogmatism seemed to contradict Eisenhower's generous views on the subject, he won no new friends for the United States in southern Asia. In Pakistan, the day after he had bade his hosts in India farewell, he intimated that he was prepared to support proposals for military aid to Pakistan, a revelation whose timing caused blistering resentment in New Delhi. At Benghazi, visiting King Idriss of Libia, Nixon frankly undertook to speed up the dilatory negotiations for an American air base. On his return to the United States, the Vice-President added his voice to those urging the creation of a "military crescent" extending from Turkey to Japan, a part of the Radford thesis of closing a ring around the Communist heartland which eventually took form in the South East Asia Treaty Organization and Northern Tier alliances.

At no time afterward did Nixon express himself quite so freely on foreign policy during his travels, but in 1955 on a quick swing through Central America and the Caribbean he was still the ever-ready activist. When he discovered that the Inter-American Highway between Texas and Panama had become a gigantic boondoggle, he made strong and effective recommendations that the project be completed in three years. As a result of his visit in Guatemala, where Castillo Armas had dislodged the Communist Arbenz regime, Nixon successfully urged that red tape be cut and money funneled in quickly to support the new administration. In Nicaragua and Costa Rica, where animosity between President Anastasio Somoza and President José Figueres had led to border disturbances and dangerous tension, the Vice-President intervened actively with his good offices and exacted "solemn assurances" from both that they would preserve the peace.

During his visit to Haiti he urged the countries of Central America and the Caribbean—to their outspoken distaste—to form a strong regional coalition, adding he would repeat this recommendation to President Eisenhower, the NSC, and the State Department. As part of an extensive report he said he would also urge that the Export-Import Bank take a "fresh new look" at its lending policies in Latin America. On his return he went further, proposing that the whole policy of economic assistance grants to the southern republics be abandoned and that necessary aid be made available in the form of loans, a plan which was still fighting for a foothold in the White House budget four years later.

Fortuitously, 1956 saw him going abroad three times, besides carrying a heavy burden of campaigning. First came a seven-day pilgrimage to Brazil to attend the inauguration of President Juscelino Kubitschek, a wholly ceremonial occasion on which Nixon had only to announce another 35-million-dollar loan and warn Brazilian unionists against Red infiltration.

His second trip that year was also his second trip to Asia. This time he moved rapidly and took a more cautious line. As a guest of Chiang Kai-shek in Formosa he again nailed the American flag to the Nationalist masthead, reiterated American policy toward Red China, and spiked Peking's bid for a Dulles–Chou En-lai meeting with the offhand judgment that there was no such possibility "at the present time" in view of the line taken by the Chinese Communists. On an itinerary which pointedly omitted the neutrals, he warned in Karachi that "Soviet aid is given not with strings but with a rope."

"Any country taking assistance from the Soviet runs almost certain risks of having that rope tied around its neck," he said bluntly.

And in reply to Nehru's remark that Nixon's views on neutralism as he had expounded them a few days earlier in Manila were opposed to democracy, Nixon observed acidly, "Anyone who suggests Communist assistance is not inconsistent with freedom has not been reading history correctly." On a somewhat more cautious note he refused to say whether the United States would "ever" recognize Communist China, but foresaw no "situation" that would cause the United States to change its mind.

His final trip of the year came as an aftermath of the Hungarian revolt, when President Eisenhower acquiesced in his suggestion that an investigation of the refugee problem would be in order. With Christmas only a week away, the Alsops observed dryly that "an adroit and intelligent man wishing to build himself up to the stature of a future Presidential candidate could hardly ask for a better chance than Dick Nixon has now secured. . . ."

While the administration floundered irresolutely, wondering whether it dared take a larger quota of refugees, Nixon dramatized the problem by playing Santa to some four hundred children in a refugee camp and spent an hour and a half at the Andau camp within sight of the Hungarian secret-police watchtowers. He saw no refugees actually make the crossing, but as he stood in the pre-dawn darkness looking eastward toward the reedy marsh over which 145,000 had struggled toward freedom since October 28, he told a reporter it was "the most thrilling experience of my life."

Meanwhile a cynical editor in Madison, Wisconsin, observed there was no need for Nixon to go all the way to Austria to help the refugees. He alluded to the McCarran-Walter Immigration Act as the biggest barrier against refugees and recalled that when that bill was passed over President Truman's veto by a margin of two votes, Nixon's was one of those two votes.

It was only a few weeks later, at the end of February 1957, that Nixon set forth on the most colorful of all his safaris—a 20,000-mile invasion of darkest Africa. The trip had its origin in his appointment to represent the United States at Ghana's independence ceremonies. By a process of accretion, it was enlarged to include Morocco, Liberia, Uganda, Ethiopia, Sudan, Libia, and Tunisia, as well as a brief stopover in Rome and an audience with Pope Pius at Vatican City. The African trip was exceedingly well reported, for it included thirty newsmen, half of them representing the American Negro press.

He flew to Morocco February 28. Perched on the roll-down top of a blue convertible, he toured Casablanca like a candidate for office, shaking hands, passing out ballpoint pens left over from the 1956 campaign, and answering cheers with a shout of "Long live his majesty, the Sultan." In Liberia he sweltered in a top hat and crowned a tribal chieftain. In Ghana he praised British colonialism and passed out autographed cards to villagers dressed in colorful togas and sandals. In Ethiopia, wearing a top hat and striped pants, he reviewed an honor guard in the rain.

But in a less eccentric vein—no longer shrinking from an interest in the Secretary of State's province—he talked high policy with high officialdom. With the Sultan of Morocco he covered four major subjects: United States air bases, U. S. economic aid, the Algerian problem, and the Eisenhower Doctrine. In Ghana, where Prime Minister Kwame Nkrumah received him first of the seventy foreign representatives, he was authorized to offer American technical aid but to refuse financing for the giant Volta River project. On the shores of Lake Victoria, on the veranda of Government House, he announced he would welcome a chance for a broad discussion of proposals to develop the Nile in Ethiopia and Sudan. That offer met with a silent rebuff, at least on the record, but in Ethiopia the Vice-President did negotiate with Emperor Haile Selassie for anchorage facilities and the right to operate a military communications center at the Red Sea port of Massawa; the Emperor's price was more military aid.

By the time Nixon landed back in Washington to receive a gala welcome from diplomats and administration officials, the verdict was that his soundings had been none too successful. The

Eisenhower Middle Eastern Doctrine aroused suspicion and resistance; and, in an effort to make it palatable, the Vice-President had found himself virtually begging officials in the area it embraced to accept America's no-strings-attached assistance.

"If Nixon has sounded at times as a Secretary of State," observed Peter Lisagor of the *Chicago Daily News*, "or even as the President, he can perhaps be excused."

His recommendations to the President—those made public—favored establishment of four more consulates and creation of a bureau of African affairs in the State Department (something the Senate Foreign Relations Committee had approved before he left), urged an expanded program of technical Point Four aid, and after alluding to information failures on the continent, recommended a larger and better-qualified staff and a more energetic USIA program.

Later in 1957, after Congress had adjourned, Nixon quietly launched plans for his most ambitious junket, a grand tour of Europe. He asked the State Department for an itinerary and a program which would not only command the presence of the most influential people and groups in Europe, but would also put him down photogenically in the midst of the ethnic and other minority groups whose votes were important in the big pivotal states. As columnist Doris Fleeson reconstructed the story, the State Department shied away, pleading a lack of time, partly to keep the aggressive Vice-President out of Dulles's province, partly because the Nixons had already shown themselves in their passion for detail to possess a "whim of iron."

And foreshadowing the disaster that befell Nixon the following year in Latin America, there was also an awareness that Nixon would be asking for trouble by making himself too conspicuous a target.

"Experienced eyes," Doris Fleeson reported, with her talent for the significant detail, "discerned pitfalls in the wide scope of Mr. Nixon's travel ideas. It would be one thing if *he* fell into them, but nobody, of course, wanted to fall in with him."

III

In May the following year, visiting eight Latin-American countries, Nixon not only found the pits and fought desperately to keep from falling into them, but finally at Lima and Caracas managed to bring the whole U.S.A. tumbling in after him when he did fall. Cursory efforts were made to turn what Lippmann called a "diplomatic Pearl Harbor" into a propaganda victory, but the record shows the timing for the trip was not propitious, and the Vice-President found himself compelled to assume personal responsibility for as shameful a humiliation as the United States ever endured.

Ostensibly the Vice-President's reason for going to South America was to represent the United States at the inauguration of President Arturo Frondizi of Argentina. Intelligence sources had warned in advance there would be serious trouble if he carried out his plan to tour the continent. In his National Press Club speech afterward, Nixon admitted receipt of the warnings, and his only defense was: "I have never taken a trip yet in which I have not been warned that there would be demonstrations." And he added as an oblique commentary on the lengths to which "goodwill" can be carried that ". . . if we allowed what I would call a bunch of blackmailing bullies to keep the officials of the government of the United States from doing what we think needs to be done to carry out our foreign policy, then we better get off the face of the earth."

Historically the moment was ripe for violence. Throughout Latin America the self-serving autarchies of the privileged classes— those of Carias, Odria, Perón, Rojas Pinella, Perez Jimenez, Batista—were being uprooted, sometimes peacefully, sometimes in a passion of bloodletting, and the rudiments of popular democracy were asserting themselves. Under the dictators the Communists had been ruthlessly suppressed, but in the transitional period that followed their overthrow the Reds seized their opportunity to agitate, proselytize, and martyrize their dupes and puppets to build a broader base of support.

It was Nixon's ill fortune that 1958 was such a year of transition, when the reins of government lay slack, and his trip was made to order for the activist cadres emerging from the Communist underground. They were ready for him at his first stop in Montevideo, Uruguay, with handbills and catcalls and insults. That was where the Vice-President made his first mistake. He ignored the fact that Montevideo had replaced Mexico City as the main Communist headquarters in Latin America. Instead of shrugging off the handbills that had been tossed at his motorcade by the Communist-dominated Student Union, he insisted on making an unscheduled visit to the university the next day, despite strong advice not to go near the campus. There, with his superior skill in debate, he easily bested the twenty-six-year-old Communist leader of the Union before a packed hall of excited and astonished youngsters, but it was a costly victory. It served notice at that nerve center of the Red conspiracy that they had a formidable antagonist and would have to take formidable measures against him.

He was relatively safe in Argentina because of the festivities surrounding the inauguration of Frondizi, but before he left Buenos Aires, the Vice-President debated with another hostile university group, and his tour of the continent was denounced at a mass meeting of 10,000 Argentine Communists. In Paraguay, under Stroessner's iron dictatorship, he was isolated from the populace. In Bolivia there were no more than a few mimeographed Communist leaflets and the usual university debate, but nine days after the incident at Montevideo, the Peruvian outpost of the Communist International was organized for a tough greeting in Lima.

A warning went to the American embassy and to Nixon that violence was "likely in ancient San Marco university," which the Vice-President was scheduled to visit May 8. He promised to study the situation, and at the appointed day and hour he gave orders to drive by the university gates to reconnoiter the chanting throng of 2000 massed in the gateway and armed with insulting signs and stones.

"I watched them closely," the Vice-President reported later. "They were pretty old for students. They were the real pros."

Knowing this but following his basic combative instinct, he jumped from his open car and strode directly into the mob, calling on the students to "Come on over. . . . What's the matter? . . . You afraid of the truth?" As he hustled through the swirling sea of humanity, a stone struck one of his Secret Service guards, breaking a tooth. That was more ominous. The crowd spat on him. Nixon backed away, made his way slowly to the motorcade.

Then came the extraordinary spectacle of a Vice-President of the United States standing in his car, facing his tormentors, and shouting, "All right, you cowards!"

After that he spoke without hindrance at Catholic University, where there were no Reds, and the police and the armed forces firmly headed off other Communist efforts at violence. It was much the same in Ecuador and Colombia: more handbills, more abortive efforts to stir up trouble, but good police work on the part of the government. One new element, however, was added. Word came from Venezuela, the last stop on the itinerary, that the Communists there were planning an all-out effort to discredit Nixon, an effort that was said positively to include plans for his assassination. Simultaneously news dispatches revealed for the first time that Venezuela was the most dangerous spot on the itinerary and had been so labeled in intelligence reports even before Nixon left Washington a fortnight earlier.

Nixon had a short answer for the death warning. Talking by radiophone with his brother, Donald, in Whittier, during the flight from Quito to Bogotá, he said, "Pat and I are fine and are going to try and continue to meet people from all walks of life despite any danger that may be involved."

At Caracas, almost complete anarchy prevailed from the moment of Nixon's landing. He walked off the plane in a roar of boos and Bronx cheers and cries of *"Fuera, fuera, fuera"* that drowned out "The Star-Spangled Banner." The hooting continued as he reviewed an honor guard. In a ghastly parody of goodwill, he and Pat ran a gantlet of frenzied youngsters, who coated them with a sustained shower of spit when they stood at attention outside the terminal for the playing of the Venezuelan national anthem.

The party made its escape from this first ambush when they pushed through the surging crowd to the cars, but eighteen miles beyond, where the superhighway runs into Avenida Sucre, another angry mob waited, on the edge of the toughest working-class district in Caracas. They ran this blockade, but half a mile farther the motorcade encountered a massive traffic jam, with all three inbound lanes blocked by cars, trucks, and busses. As Nixon's car slowed down, youngsters hurled themselves in front of the wheels, and a crowd of Venezuelans rushed it. After a tense two minutes of inching through the traffic jam, the motorcade picked up speed again, but the worst of four ambushes was still ahead. Another traffic jam had been organized by the Communists, with all three lanes solidly packed. This time the motorcade came to a dead stop. Then out of a side street flowed the mob that had been lying in wait for this moment.

The next twelve minutes witnessed a scene as fantastic as any in American history. Six Secret Service agents leaped to the side of the Vice-President's car, while he crouched inside with the Venezuelan foreign minister and three guards. Around them milled a hate-filled mob that screamed imprecations, smashed against the window glass with rocks, pipe metal, jagged cans, and their naked fists. They kicked and hammered at doors and fenders. Shattered glass flew in showers. All the while, seven Venezuelan motorcycle policemen, forming a V in front of the car, sat with one foot balanced on the pavement, motionless. At one point two of them drew their revolvers nervously, only to be warned by shouts from the Secret Service men to put the weapons out of sight. It was only the skill of these six agents, using nothing but open hands, body blocks, and iron nerve, that kept an international incident from leading to a bloody denouement.

In the tumult, Mrs. Nixon's car was largely ignored. The American correspondents riding an open truck ahead of the Vice-President were unmolested. The Communist objective, quite simply, was to wrench open the car doors and trample Nixon to death. Somehow, then, as the mob grew more frenzied and the situation grew desperate, a path opened up through the traffic jam, Nixon's car zoomed through, and what was left of the crisis was a post-mortem.

So great was Washington's mortification that for the first and only time in his administration Eisenhower panicked; in a reflex the enormity of which was not realized until later he dispatched four companies of airborne Marines and paratroopers to Caribbean bases, an act that was recognized as a stultifying exercise in gunboat diplomacy the moment it became necessary to claim the riots as a propaganda victory for Nixon.

Nixon had once confided: "There are tricks in dealing with crowds, and if they begin to push too hard, I look around for a thin spot and move back through it toward a car. . . ."

In Caracas his thoughts inside the car were not of tricks or tactics. "My thoughts," he acknowledged later, "were, What are you going to do in the next minutes—the next five minutes?"

In the circumstances the Latin-American trip of 1958 was almost devoid of vice-presidential pronouncements on policy issues. The Reds took the spotlight. Afterward Nixon defended his errors of judgment by suggesting that, if his misfortunes moved the story of Latin America and its problems from page 8 to page 1 of the newspapers, "the trip will have been worthwhile." This, after putting his life, his prestige, and the nation's pride in jeopardy.

"It would be a great mistake just to attribute what happened in Venezuela to communism," he said in an oblique reproof for the failures of American policy in the southern republics. "It is true that the Communists spearheaded the attack. But you have to remember that they had a lot of willing spear-carriers along with them."

A more perceptive historian, even without benefit of hindsight, might have acknowledged that statesmanship does not consist of *kami-kaze* charges like the Vice-President's, but of shadowboxing with time. Nixon in his Latin-American vendetta with communism let himself be drawn out of position and booby-trapped. It was another case of the wrong war at the wrong time in the wrong place.

IV

Two subsequent trips went off without a hitch. The first, to London late in 1958, was wholly ceremonial. The Vice-President appeared with quiet dignity at the Chapel dedication at St. Paul's, spoke at the Pilgrims Society and at Guildhall, and, in something of a tour de force, submitted to an unrehearsed television press conference over BBC. All observers agreed he "did not make a misstep." Representative Britons who had regarded him as an uncouth adventurer came round to the view that he was, after all, an "earnest, vocal young man trying hard to win friends and influence people." What this added up to, in the opinion of one British M.P., was that Nixon accomplished nothing substantive for Anglo-American relations, but that as a celebrity he was "correct," which is to say, he did and said certain things which obviously ought to be said and done in the situation, and he got the applause any celebrity would be entitled to as the curtain rang down.

The Vice-President's fifteen-day trip behind the Iron Curtain in mid-1959 proved no less disappointing than his tour of South America. Nixon spent weeks preparing every detail of the sortie.

His mission, nominally, was to open the American exhibition in Moscow July 24, but on the eve of his departure the Geneva conference of Big Four foreign ministers was deadlocked, and Nixon's supporters reflected a zealous hope that his meetings with Premier Nikita Khrushchev might somehow find a formula to surmount the crisis. The *New York Herald Tribune* went so far as to say editorially, "A ceremonial visit has now become a diplomatic mission of the first importance."

Khrushchev threw cold water on this talk by confessing publicly that he didn't understand what Nixon's aim was in coming, and Eisenhower in the same vein reminded his news conference of the constitutional limitations of the vice-presidency.

"We should be careful," he said, "to understand one thing about the vice-presidential position in this government of ours. He has a position of his own. He is not a subordinate of the President, and he is not a part of the diplomatic processes and machinery of this country. . . .

"Now, he is going here this time on goodwill, on a goodwill gesture. . . . He knows all about government, he knows about the attitudes, he can impart information, but he is not negotiating anything."

What Nixon did not know until the President told him a few hours before takeoff was that serious negotiations had been in progress since early July for an Eisenhower-Khrushchev exchange of state visits. Hence, although the Vice-President handled himself with poise and dignity in Russia, even when the Soviet premier subjected him to a rough-and-tumble public debate, the ground had actually been cut from under him politically. He had nothing to talk about. The Geneva deadlock had been resolved by the President's prior decision to inaugurate the bilateral process of diplomacy. Eisenhower admitted August 3 in announcing the agreement with Khrushchev that, in taking Nixon into his confidence, he wanted no interference.

"I told him, and I said, 'So that you will not be astonished or surprised and feel let down by your government, should they [references to the negotiations] be opened up by the other side, you are not, yourself, and of course will not open this subject.' "

The disaster for Nixon from a 1960 public-relations point of view was that the Soviet-American agreement was formally announced two days before the Vice-President's return, before he could so much as go through the motions of offering the White House his views on the subject. Thus Nixon's landing August 5 —after weeks of exciting conjecture—became an anticlimax to what had been billed as a major effort to pre-empt the peace issue for his 1960 campaign.

The popular assessment of the Moscow trip was inconclusive. Nixon's rating in the polls showed the quick upsurge normal in such situations. There was applause for his tough reaction to Khrushchev's verbal assault at Sokolniki Park, but there remained the underlying constraint toward all dealings and dealers with communism. Neither at that time nor in September, when Khrushchev visited the United States, did anyone charge that Nixon or the Eisenhower administration had gone "soft on communism," but the public mood was one of reserve, as if poised for retreat from the administration's embrace at the first sign of disillusionment.

For those who ask what kind of President Nixon might make, his behavior and opinions as a globe-trotting inquisitor repay careful study.

PART FOUR

POLITICIAN

CHAPTER XIX

———◆———

Operator

I

POLITICS is perhaps an art, perhaps a scale of values or a conjunction of possibilities, but never a science.

It is here, in the realm of artifice and intuition, that Nixon is most at home. He is credited with having set the political style of the Eisenhower regime, has been called the ranking politician in an administration "headed by a soldier and staffed by merchants." If this is so, it is because, working, scheming, talking, fighting, manning the ramparts and battlements of his enclave, he radiates conflict, holds himself poised always for attack or defense. His operational code makes him half witch doctor, half soldier of fortune, a mixture of superstition and the latest Madison Avenue gimmickry.

The umbrella incident is a case in point. It was August 1955, the day of Eisenhower's return from the Geneva summit meeting, a chill, rainy afternoon at Washington National Airport as the Vice-President and leading officials gathered to welcome the President home. Many carried umbrellas, but what gave the scene a bizarre aspect was that none of the umbrellas was raised. The dignitaries huddled in the open, wet and bedraggled, because the Vice-President had given the order—no umbrellas!

In Nixon's mind, this order was necessary for propaganda reasons. At that moment it was still not clear whether Geneva had been a triumph or a setback for the West; and for lack of a better estimate of the situation, there were uncomfortable reminders of Neville Chamberlain and Munich. The umbrella had been Chamberlain's trademark and the emblem of his appeasement policy. Nixon wanted no such untoward symbol. His intuition on this occasion, as on many others, played him false, yet it revealed the lengths to which he might go and would expect his enemies to go in the give-and-take of the political arena.

II

Nixon built his reputation as a politician and his position of leadership in the Republican party by using his conspicuous talents on the platform and by the sheer drudgery of cultivating the keepers of the Republican vineyard. One year he spoke in twenty-five states, another in thirty-one, another in twenty-three, and from 1950 on, there was hardly a sizable city in the United States where he did not oblige with an appearance, speaking at election rallies, supporting fund-raising activities, struggling with patronage problems, finding personable candidates, and interceding at subordinate levels to keep party machinery in friendly hands.[1]

His position of leadership, aside from his own unflagging effort, owed itself partly to circumstance and partly to a specious process of deduction. Primarily, the events that thrust him forward were Taft's death, Eisenhower's illnesses, and Dewey's virtual retirement from active politics. The President remained the head of the party in name but not in fact; and since no other authoritative voice was raised, either in Congress or in the states, the party organization was leaderless. Nixon had only to let himself be pushed into the vacuum.

Nixon's strength in professional circles has been primarily among the Old Guard that keeps its hand on the party machinery year in and year out, in good times and bad. He has worked assiduously with the national committee, with state and district committees, with women's groups, and with the Young Republicans. In all this he has operated without an overt assertion of

---

[1] In four national campaigns he ran up these mileages:

| 1952 | 48,381 | 1956 | 34,453 |
| 1954 | 28,072 | 1958 | 24,042 |

leadership, in fact with a studied effort to stay out of the lime-light nationally in party affairs.

A hundred politicians and writers will testify to Nixon's stand-ing with the Republican hierarchy, and they have drawn the in-ference that *ipso facto* he is a masterly politician and an acknowl-edged leader of men. The inference does not necessarily follow, for the relationship is shadowy at best. Some of his support is presumptive and vaguely anonymous, and some not unqualified; and his position has to be deduced in part from data which are ephemeral and by means of logic which is intuitive.

What is factual is simply a personal pledge of support from half a hundred or half a thousand individuals who undertake to reflect or manipulate public opinion. Under the pounding rhythms of change, no one, not even Nixon, would dare say precisely how much substance there might be in that relationship from day to day or from week to week.

Now and then these phantoms make themselves visible. An instance in the spring of 1959 was the appointment of Senator Thruston B. Morton as caretaker chairman of the Republican National Committee after Alcorn's resignation. Morton had been a charter member of Nixon's 1946 Chowder and Marching Club; and his presence at committee headquarters in the preconvention period was one means of insuring that the committee would be neutral for Nixon.

Another instance was the fight for chairmanship of the Young Republican Federation at the organization's June 1959 convention. The contest was between Nixon's candidate and Nelson Rocke-feller's, and the ease with which the latter was defeated showed the months that had been spent on the selection of solidly pro-Nixon delegations.

There have been other instances. The 1956 national conven-tion and its antecedent intrigues dramatized Nixon's strength, and in fact may have overdramatized it, because the issue of party unity was at least as significant as the identity of the candidate. Nevertheless, Nixon in that case had nailed down more than 800 delegates months beforehand, and the refusal of this bloc to waver in the face of Stassen's attack had a significant impact on the party.

At the practical operating level, Nixon knows how to move decisively and shows no hesitancy in taking risks. In 1958, as

Alaska prepared for statehood, he visited the territory to take soundings and offer Republican candidates and leaders his advice. What he found appalled his professional instincts. He thereupon ordered Victor Johnson, director of the Senate Republican campaign committee, to provide $5000 for expenses, and promised to send a young congressman to introduce some know-how in the campaign. The congressman he chose was his most reliable errand boy and trouble shooter, Representative Bob Wilson of San Diego; but, as it turned out, neither know-how nor risk-taking could save that situation for the Republicans. They lost everything.

Among political pros, such reverses at the local level are considered incidental. They think, or like to think they think, in larger terms. In reality, they are under a compulsion to interpret results with a high degree of egocentricity. A case in point was the 1957 contest for the New Jersey governorship. Nixon campaigned for Malcolm Forbes against the Democratic incumbent, Robert Meyner. After Meyner's easy victory, a friend commiserating with a Nixon staff member observed casually, "The outcome must have been rough on the Vice-President."

"Oh, not at all," was the cheerful response. "He made a lot of friends in New Jersey."

That estimate had to be paired off against the fact that, in five of the seven counties in which Nixon campaigned, the Republican vote for governor was less in 1957 than it had been four years earlier.

Many party workers make Nixon an odds-on favorite for 1960 because they have been coming to him with their problems for years. After the 1958 election, twenty state chairmen out of thirty-five who were queried by the Associated Press named Nixon as the leading candidate for the nomination. At the Des Moines meeting of the national committee a few weeks later, 85 per cent of the high command was estimated to be for him. In mid-1959 columnist Roscoe Drummond reported that Republican leaders outside New York were ready at that moment to pledge Nixon a minimum of 800 convention votes, 137 more than the necessary majority.

Nixon's position of leadership is neither real nor wholly false. It is not false because he does clearly have a following of genuine power and magnitude, a clutch of partisan creditors who want to repay him and who see no likelier candidate. Whether they follow him only because he is available to fill the vacuum or because he is the only possible person to fill it is a wholly iffy proposition.

At the same time, the unreality of Nixon's position is indicated by Meade Alcorn's statistical analysis of the relative party standings at the polls. This analysis pointed out bluntly, on the eve of Alcorn's resignation, that from 1950 to 1958, the exact period of Nixon's activity on the national scene, the Republican vote remained stationary at 20 million while the Democratic vote climbed to nearly 26 million.

During this interval Nixon made three extravagant efforts to put a Republican majority in Congress and three times he failed. Thus the weakness of his position is that, while party regulars exert a dominant influence in the long intervals between elections, and while they might be eager to nominate him in 1960, they have not controlled a national convention since 1936, and neither they nor Nixon have a strong base of popular support.

In his ascent toward party leadership, Nixon's guiding principle has been to hold rival blocs in line by a process of conciliation, and to make winning elections his transcendent concern. His activities have been so conspicuously oriented toward the party, rather than its program, that cynics no longer call him unprincipled; his one indubitable principle, they say, is the unity and survival of the Republican party.

His concept of his role has therefore been tactical. He has treated politics not as a process of accommodation under a body of fixed principles, but as a series of guerrilla actions based largely on improvisation. In this way he is credited with having interested Eisenhower in politics by showing him the similarities between a political and a military campaign.

At various times he has tried to defend himself against charges that he concentrates narrowly on scoring debating points instead of going to the heart of issues. He argues that "your instinct is to strike back" when attacked. He has told of advising young politicians to take a "positive line" and ignore attacks, but with him a positive line always seems to come back to a definition of the party line. This tendency to confuse tactics and principles betrayed itself in the advice he gave Los Angeles GOP workers in calling on them to rebuild the party after it was overwhelmed in 1958.

"You hear a lot these days," he told them, "about how we should change our image. . . . Well, I think we've heard too much such talk and not enough about our principles. I don't think we could make a greater mistake than to say that, because some people don't like being called conservative, the Republican party should stop being conservative."

Then he explained, as a matter of making the party's philosophy palatable, that the traditional conservatism of the GOP should be interpreted with connotations of "progress" rather than "standpattism." The accent as always was on how conservatism should be made to appear, not on what it should be and do.

What he has done to enunciate party principles and to create an image of progressivism has been less manifest than what he has said on the subject. Nixon has gravitated naturally to men of power whose conservatism is unadulterated. He recognizes these men as his own kind; and on matters of principle he alienates himself instinctively and dangerously from the more liberal wing of the party.

Not infrequently he makes meaningful gestures of sympathy toward the left. He backed the social-welfare provisions of the earlier Eisenhower budgets. His position on civil rights is unequivocal. He puts a liberal stamp on his defense of foreign aid. His major concession to the popularist wing of the party was to urge the nomination of Republican candidates of the Eisenhower stripe as differentiated from the Eisenhower coattail-riders—a frank move to dump the dinosaurs of the old courthouse gangs and compete with the Democrats for the type of "glamorous" candidate who had something to say and the knack of saying it.

In taking this line, Nixon ignored the sporadic revolts of right-wingers and wealthy contributors, arguing they would have no choice but to return to the GOP "because it's that or something worse." In defiance of the Taft thesis, he brushed off the protests of reactionary congressmen, on the theory that they come mostly from rockribbed Republican districts where they would win as a matter of course. If by this tactic he drove ultra-conservatives away from the polls, he considered that part of the price he had to pay to broaden the popularist image of the party.

In these exercises, Nixon was not unaware of the risks to which he subjected the party and his own future. There were predictions in both 1954 and 1958 that defeat would fatally undermine his ambitions, but he survived both defeat and his inability to define the issues. His leverage derived, at least in part, from the fact that, with a sick man in the White House, he might become President any day. This contingency made it dangerous for professionals to oppose him openly, even when his strategy and his policies seemed injudicious.

So reckless were his tactics that by 1959 members of the Republican National Committee admitted in effect that the party's position had reverted to what it was eight years before. The 1960 nomination, they told Edward T. Folliard of the *Washington Post,* would be worth "very little unless the nominee is stronger than the party."

Nixon himself had no illusions. He told Mazo that his primary desire was to rebuild the party organization everywhere so that the nomination would be "worth something to somebody." He professed a desire to cut out the "deadwood" at all levels and introduce "vitality and fresh ideas." The implication, manifestly, was that, despite Eisenhower's personal popularity, the party organization, with Nixon generally acknowledged as its effective operating head, had fallen to pieces as a result of the tactics that had been pursued.

Nowhere was the disorganization of the Republican party more apparent than in Nixon's home state. While the strength of the GOP in California began slipping in the thirties, there was still plenty of room for optimism as late as 1952, when four political giants—Warren, Knowland, Knight, Nixon—bestrode the state. Internecine strife broke out after that, and by November 1958 the party lay in ruins. With Warren, Knowland, and Knight gone, Nixon was an undisputed leader of California Republicanism, standing like King Pyrrhus amid the wreckage of his victory.

Inevitably, as W. H. Lawrence pointed out in *The New York Times,* politicians raised the question every presidential nominee has to answer: Could Nixon carry his home state? The Vice-President himself was asked whether it was possible to rehabilitate the party in time to carry California in 1960 for the Republican ticket.

"It is definitely possible," he said. "I agree it is a big job, but the difference of a million votes last November was not an indication of the relative strength of the two parties."

Actually, the point at issue was more complicated than a difference of a million votes. The question Nixon had to face was whether it was possible to reunite the California Republican factions while he himself remained in public life.

For nine years he had been at the center of a disastrous series of internal party squabbles. The trouble began in 1949, when Los Angeles Supervisor Raymond V. Darby had been sidetracked to make room for Nixon in the Senate race. Professionals could regard that as a neat piece of hijacking, but it left ill feeling.

The events of 1952 created new and deeper cleavages that spread statewide. Nixon offended Governor Warren and his supporters, first by his private presidential poll, then by the convention train episode, then by his "fair play" resolution speech, and finally by his order not to cheer General MacArthur's keynote address.[2] He then proceeded to administer a number of slights to Goodwin Knight, starting right after the convention when Knight was brusquely shoved into the background at the welcome-home rally for Nixon. Thus, in quick succession, the Vice-President made enemies among followers of Warren, Knowland, and Knight, and even allowing for the impermanence of political alliances, there were enough charges of bad faith in some of these encounters to cause lasting factional scars.

In 1954, there was the Howard Ahmanson affair. This was a deal that did not come unstitched. As part of an agreement to share control of the California state central committee with Knowland and Knight, Nixon's representatives had agreed on Knight's man, Ahmanson, as vice-chairman. However, after Knight had put to sea on a honeymoon trip, a telephone campaign was launched to dump Ahmanson and elect a Nixon man. Word was flashed to both Knowland and Knight; the former flew back from Washington while the latter brought his yacht to wharfside and got busy with a telephone counterattack. The Nixon forces were crushed, and the Vice-President's apology, totally unconvincing among the pros, was that his boys had been a little overeager and he himself had known nothing about their plans. Eventually the intrigue cost Nixon heavily, when Ahmanson, whose fortune in insurance and banking is estimated at $150 million, transferred his political support to Governor Pat Brown and the Democrats.

After the Ahmanson episode, Teddy White reported, there were

---

[2] See Chapter VIII for the full story of these incidents.

flat statements in California Republican circles that no deal with Nixon would stick unless it could be policed.

Finally, in 1958, there was the fratricidal split when Senator Knowland insisted on pushing Knight out of the gubernatorial contest. The senator's aim was clear enough—to put himself in position to fight Nixon for the 1960 presidential nomination. When Knight threatened to oppose Knowland in the primary, it was Nixon who intervened in his familiar role as fixer and broker. He told Knight he could support him only for the Senate race, and Knight let himself be convinced. To Nixon it was a purely tactical situation; the question of whether Knight, having made a good record, had established an ethical claim to a second term was subordinated to a specious appearance of party harmony. Close students of California politics were led to conclude that Nixon was satisfied to see his two rivals kill each other off, since the battle was guaranteed to leave him the only Republican of stature in the state organization.

It would be incautious to suggest that Nixon has been responsible for the decline of Republican fortunes in his home state, but it is none the less anomalous that, coincident with his rise in the hierarchy, the over-all position of his party has steadily deteriorated.

III

The Vice-President's reputation as a factional middleman was a product of his own ingenuity. At the second meeting of the Eisenhower Cabinet in January 1953 the minutes show that Nixon volunteered his services to try to overcome difficulties between the White House and the Republicans in Congress arising out of "investigations."

The investigations uppermost in all minds at that moment were McCarthy's. With the opening of the Republican Eighty-third Congress, he had taken over the chairmanship of the Senate investigations subcommittee and had left no doubt that he intended to cut a wide swath. Nixon, having served with McCarthy on that same committee in the previous Congress, knew what to expect. Moreover, the Vice-President had confidence in his ability to make McCarthy a useful member of the administration team. On the strength of his reputation in the Hiss case, Nixon had lectured the Wisconsin senator in 1950 when the latter was accusing the

State Department of keeping eighty known Communists on its payroll.

"Your mistake," Nixon had argued, "is in calling these people Communists. You'd have been on sounder ground to say they are sympathetic toward Communist points of view, are fellow travelers, or have Communist-front ties. Never make a charge unless you can back it up. Always understate your case."

In 1952 their relations were cordial enough for McCarthy to give Nixon his blessing for the vice-presidency, and for Nixon to call for the re-election of "my good friend, Joe McCarthy" when his campaign special crossed Wisconsin, October 25.

For Nixon, McCarthyism was not so much a form of demagoguery as it was an operational code that differed only in degree from the southern California strategy on which he had been reared. The Chotiner school proceeded on the theory that Democrats could be conned into voting with the Republican minority, not by plausibility and persuasion, but with evangelical hellfire and brimstone. Adlai Stevenson put his finger on that aspect of McCarthyism in a speech December 13, 1951, calling it the "trademark of a new breed of political demagogue who frightens people with epithets, carelessly impugns the loyalty of patriotic men, and shouts dire forebodings of a treacherous doom for America and for all her cherished institutions."

Nixon, having been brought up as a political pulpit-pounder, naturally felt at home with McCarthy's epithets, and he regarded the Wisconsinite as he would any other phenomenon susceptible of manipulation in the partisan struggle. He made that clear in March 1953, after he had undertaken his role as middleman. In a conference with the USIA Director, Dr. Robert Johnson, and Martin Merson, Nixon tried to reassure them about McCarthy's attacks on the Information Agency. Joe wasn't a bad guy, he told them; you simply had to understand him. When Johnson expressed a desire to talk personally with the senator, Nixon made it clear that he would decide when the time was appropriate and advised Johnson to keep in touch with him.

The Vice-President's relationship with McCarthy during the crucial months of 1953 was not easy to define. He was credited with having worked hard behind the scenes to bring moderation and judgment to McCarthy's investigations. He intervened several times to prevent direct, open warfare with the Executive Department.

When Harold Stassen denounced McCarthy in the spring of '53 for negotiating a deal with Greek shipowners on China trade, Nixon got Dulles together with the senator, and the upshot was a statement praising McCarthy and humiliating Stassen. At the same time Nixon persuaded McCarthy to call off his threat to investigate the Central Intelligence Agency, the most sensitive counterespionage branch of the government. He talked McCarthy out of keeping J. B. Matthews as chief investigator after the latter had outraged the administration and even GOP party stalwarts with a threat against the Protestant clergy; and when McCarthy sent the President a letter demanding to know his position on trade with Iron Curtain countries, Nixon persuaded the senator to let him intercept the letter at the White House before the President was placed in the embarrassing position of having to answer it.

In June, after Eisenhower's speech against book-burning at Dartmouth, Nixon again had a heart-to-heart talk with McCarthy and extracted a promise that he would wind up his book investigation in USIA and turn to less fought-over fields. Earlier, the Vice-President had made his own files available to McCarthy for his attack on communism, but when the Eisenhower administration itself began to suffer from the senator's inquisitions, Nixon shifted his strategy. He tried to guide McCarthy away from the whole Communist issue, telling him that he would benefit by broadening his field of activity.

"You should not be known," he told McCarthy, "as a one-shot Senator."

In November the Vice-President urged President Eisenhower not to attack McCarthy directly, notwithstanding a flood of contrary advice from Republican circles. At the end of the year, Nixon and McCarthy had another chat in Florida, after which Nixon went out on a limb, telling reporters they could quote a "high administration source" (himself) to the effect that McCarthy would definitely turn his attention in the new year to Democratic corruption and away from "Communists" in the present administration. McCarthy rewarded him for his pains by branding the story a lie, but not even that affront alienated the administration's tenacious middleman. He came back to Washington and resumed the pattern of conciliation.

Nixon was able to take this latitudinarian view because, according to the Republican party's official line, Senator McCarthy was a "great asset"; and in the Lincoln Day celebrations of February 1954, the Republican National Committee sponsored the Wisconsin demagogue on a ten-day coast-to-coast speaking tour, the theme of which was "twenty years of treason" under Democratic rule. At the end of the month, Nixon was still in McCarthy's corner, arranging the celebrated chicken luncheon for the humiliation of Secretary of the Army Robert T. Stevens.

On the eve of the even more celebrated Army-McCarthy hearings, Nixon was still striving unsuccessfully for a negotiated peace, but with the broadcast of March 13 answering Stevenson's charge that the Republican party was "divided against itself, half McCarthy, half Eisenhower," the Vice-President finally warned against "reckless talk and questionable methods." Even then he did not challenge the essential ethics of the Wisconsin witch hunter. His complaint was tactical: the McCarthyites had made "themselves the issue rather than the cause they believe in so deeply."

"McCarthy's intentions were right," he said later in defense of his course, "but his tactics were, frankly, so inept at times that he probably did our cause more harm than good."

Thus in a unique party crisis Nixon's final evaluation was in terms of ineptitude, not of the anguish McCarthy had engendered in the nation's body politic.

IV

Although Nixon's original undertaking as a middleman applied primarily to the McCarthy investigations, and although Eisenhower refrained from giving him any formal status as a deputy administration leader, his talents as a legislative broker were invoked from time to time on a variety of problems.

In the first weeks of the administration, the President ran into trouble on the confirmation of two key ambassadorial appointees —Bohlen to go to Moscow and Conant to Bonn. In both cases, it was Nixon who reassured the edgy right-wingers and who engineered the scrutiny of the FBI reports which settled the security issue. Again, it was Nixon who during that Congress got

Senator Pat McCarran to call off a filibuster on the immigration bill, and persuaded Chairman Dan Reed of the House Ways and Means Committee to swallow the President's tax program after giving vent to violent rumbles of dissent.

At that period, the Vice-President was described as "somersaulting in and out of opposing Republican factions," as "a kind of double agent, now the left's ambassador to the right, now the right's ambassador to the left," whose office "was like the truce tent at Panmunjom."

The Korean truce was one of his problems in those early days —it took some persuading to get Republicans to accept a political settlement after both they and Nixon had long clamored for a military victory. The Bricker amendment, in turn, called for Nixon's best talents. The White House set itself adamantly against the amendment's proposed limitation on the President's treaty-making powers, and it was Nixon who brought the report that sentiment both in and out of Congress was more sympathetic to Bricker than the President had supposed. The Vice-President, after first proposing compromise, found himself in loyalty to the White House stalling, placating, instructing, and negotiating, and finally joining Eisenhower in opposition to Bricker's demand.

Nixon was no less helpful in lesser matters such as the pique of Senators Russell and George at not having been consulted on the formulation as well as the implementation of foreign policy. Through Nixon's efforts as intermediary, Eisenhower invited the distinguished Georgians to lunch, and politeness was restored. When the Vice-President learned that most freshman Republican congressmen were against foreign aid, he assembled a group and in two hours of explanation and argument converted most of them to the administration's position.

Nixon repeatedly came to the rescue of the foreign-aid program. Nothing he has done in official life is more forthright. In 1956 and 1957 he spoke at every opportunity in defense of all aspects of the mutual-security program, economic as well as military. At a time when right-wingers in the party still clung to the "giveaway" slogan they had coined as a weapon against Truman, Nixon did his best to undo the mischief.

"We hear today a chorus of opposition to the so-called 'giveaway foreign-aid programs,'" he told the Poor Richard Club in Philadelphia, January 17, 1956, "while at the same time we find virtually no opposition to programs which build up our armed strength. . . ."

In succeeding months, he attacked the "giveaway" theme before the Lions International in Miami, before the U.S. Chamber of Commerce in Milwaukee, before the Committee for Economic Development in Washington, and before the National Association of Manufacturers in New York. He even defended aid to Communist Poland; and when his political philosophy was challenged at a Baltimore news conference just before the 1958 elections, his first thought was of these foreign-aid battles.

"I challenge anybody," he said, "who has a more consistent record in the field of foreign aid, starting with the Greek-Turkish loan, going through the Marshall Plan, and making speech after speech for foreign aid two years ago during the budget fight when very few people were speaking for it."

What he said on these occasions was being echoed privately in party councils, with generally favorable effect on the President's program. There is no clear public record of his participation in these secret struggles—at least none so well documented as the McCarthy affair—and there is some doubt whether Nixon's efforts as a legislative go-between were as effective as those of his predecessor, Alben Barkley, but no doubt at all that he did what he could on Eisenhower's behalf.

If the Vice-President's office was not the crossroads it had been in Barkley's time, this may have been partly because Nixon was not so gregarious, but the conspicuous limiting factor was Sherman Adams, assistant to the President. By and large, the "word" that caused GOP congressmen to spring into action came direct from Adams in the White House. Adams had won his political spurs in the House and the New Hampshire governorship. By temperament he was a crusty, self-reliant introvert. He had a jealous regard for the prerogatives of the Chief Executive, and as his own power grew, there was less and less need in his scheme of things for an intermediary, especially one whose constitutional position placed him outside the administration.

The full story of Nixon's relationship with Governor Adams remains for the latter's telling, but from 1955 on there were recurrent rumors of a quiet struggle for power; gossips called it the biggest backstage story in Washington. Whether Adams ever deliberately prevented the Vice-President from moving to the center of the stage, within the administration as well as the Republican party, is obscure because neither side could afford the appearance of discord.

At any rate, some eyebrows were lifted quizzically when a House investigating subcommittee in the summer of 1958 stumbled on the fact that Adams had been indiscreet—that the keeper of the administration's moral code had accepted a vicuña coat and other gifts from Bernard Goldfine, a wealthy fringe operator in New England textiles and real estate. When it also appeared that Adams had telephoned federal agencies about Goldfine cases which were under administrative review, the President's assistant became an obvious political liability. It was a case of a vicuña for a mink, and the symbol of Trumanite corruption vanished like smoke.

Eisenhower made a desperate effort to save Adams. In June, Nixon became involved when he rebuked Republican leaders publicly for "acting like a bunch of cannibals" as soon as one of their number got in trouble, but he took a less forthright tone when the President called on him three times in July and August for advice. Adams thanked Nixon for his public support (Knowland was demanding his resignation), but two Adams-Nixon conferences failed to hit on a formula for rescuing the governor. When it became apparent that in the fall election Republican candidates would be compelled almost universally to repudiate Adams, and that the latter's relationship with the incoming Congress would thereby be fatally impaired, his resignation followed quickly in September.

If Nixon was powerless in the situation, Adams's fall nevertheless cost him nothing in prestige; and, for all anyone knew, it may have given him access to new power. No one suggested the Vice-President had cause to grieve over the President's loss of a trusted aide.

On one other occasion, Nixon's hand showed clearly in the GOP's factional in-fighting and in the struggle for control in the 1960 preconvention period. That occasion was in January 1959, in the revolt against House minority leader Joe Martin. After nearly twenty years in the leadership, the Massachusetts veteran was taken unawares when a cabal of insurgents, meeting between

Thursday and Tuesday, hammered out a bare majority of 74 to 70 and elected Charles Halleck as a more aggressive captain for the shrunken GOP opposition.

Martin absolved the President from personal responsibility for his overthrow, but with the rueful bitterness of an old man he laid the blame squarely at the door of White House staffers, Vice-President Nixon, and "the Dewey crowd."

Martin specifically named Representative Bob Wilson, the same Wilson who handled Nixon's campaign in 1956 and who was rushed to Alaska to handle that campaign in 1958, as the "Nixon man" who had helped organize his downfall.

"If you'd done everything Ike ever asked you," he said sadly, "wouldn't you think he'd stand by you?"

The answer of course was that Ike had left the political preparations for 1960 in other hands, self-serving hands, the hands of men in a hurry whose loyalties were in pawn to the future, not the past.

CHAPTER XX

Moralizer

I

THE PARADOX of Nixon is that, while few politicians have expressed themselves more volubly on issues, the core of his beliefs escapes identification; and although he displays a shopkeeper's punctilio in matters of personal honesty, few men in public life have been more harshly challenged on the moral plane.

Nixon himself is nettled at the intimation that any part of his philosophy should seem infirm or mysterious. Both his public and his private life has been lived in a goldfish bowl; he has answered questions indefatigably about his insights and opinions. But there persists a feeling that, as in his high-school debating days, he "kind of slides round the argument instead of meeting it head on." Somehow, to his as well as others' bafflement, something is missing.

When he talks about his philosophy, he tends to talk not about abstractions, not about what is remote and impersonal and timeless, but about what he knows. His thoughts are cast most naturally in terms of contemporary political doctrine. He is, for example, eloquent on the need to protect the private sector of the economy against government encroachment, a piece of dogma which to him is of central importance. When he is accused of putting tactics ahead of a spacious personal credo, he argues impatiently that he advocates such controversial programs as civil rights, foreign aid, and labor reform as socially desirable without regard to the question of profit or loss at the polls.

When he talks about the Republican party, he shows no disposition to make it over in a new image, or to make it conform to his fundamental concept of the good. He takes it as he finds it, and, like a competent lawyer, using the evidence at hand, makes the best case he can for his client.

He tries to reflect a seasoned breadth of view, but just as in the Checkers speech he answered the ethical challenge with an analogous discourse on his household budget, so in the case of first principles he talks about them in parochial rather than universal terms.

His philosophy has a myopic quality. He magnifies what is close at hand at the expense of remoter meanings. He is farsighted in the tactical sense of being able to make book on the ratio between social and political change, but his choice is for a tight frame of reference, and when he projects his thoughts on a roomier plane he has a taste for the colloquial. As a sports enthusiast he finds, in the jargon of sports, a natural parallel with the Great Game of Politics.

"You can't just play safe," he reflected on one occasion in the company of tennis stars Alex Olmedo and Althea Gibson. "You've got to play to win. That's the world today."

The dynamism, the fighting instinct implicit in that view of life, does not glorify team play or the pride of losing gamely but it is authentic Nixonism. In dedicating the Los Angeles sports arena, he echoed the thought publicly.

"Don't play merely not to lose. Play to win!"

The more elusive Nixon's beliefs, the greater the temptation to judge him superficially; his personality gets in the way of his philosophy. He becomes fair game for the epigrammatists.

"When his public and private personalities meet," said one, "they shake hands."

If he did wrestle with his conscience, said another, "the match was fixed."

"It is not paradoxical," said a third, "that Nixon, who leads a blameless personal life, who does not smoke or play cards, drinks sparingly, and is a devoted family man, is known to his opponents in politics as 'Dirty Dick.' "

In some minds what engenders doubt is that Nixon's relations with people tend to burn themselves out. He holds himself aloof. Of his reticence he says, "It doesn't come natural for me to be a buddy-buddy boy," but others have charged more expansively that "nobody really gets through to him" because he "climbs on people and then discards them." He is indestructible in the sense of being proof against slights that would destroy a thin-skinned man. He is afraid to be challenged, is therefore afraid to have men around who would challenge him. He has no real sense of inner security, has not had since the secret-fund incident which so shattered his surety that he has never since been able to take people at face value.

He himself takes a cynical view of political friendships. Writing for *Life* magazine June 8, 1959, in tribute to John Foster Dulles, he shrugged off Washington as "a city where a political leader learns that the number of his friends goes up and down with his standing in the public-opinion polls. . . ." No room there for sentimentality; in his measure of his trade, loyalty has turned out to be a commodity, a caprice.

What further frightens some politicians about the Nixon operational code is that he understands the use of power but not the unwritten restraints on its use. The essence of the Anglo-American system is that a majority is sometimes too intangible for counting, that the rights of a minority are irrevocable when they are profoundly felt. In this concept there is a time when might does not make right, when superior numbers find it imperative to exercise self-restraint and seek an accommodation that all can live with.

Whether Nixon's intuition recognizes the subtle frontier separating what can be done from what cannot be done is an unresolved question. At times he shows a rigid, puritanical streak. When he is for civil rights, he talks of gradualism, but there is a high coefficient of tension in the pace and temper of his gradualism. When he is against corruption, he is hard and inflexible, with few of the saving graces of tenderness, humor, generosity toward the fallen. Even when he is right, he sometimes gives himself an air of smugness and self-righteousness. When he condemned Boyle and Gabrielson, no one rose to challenge his indictment but no one cheered. It was the same for Harold E. Talbott, whose careless relationships between his business enterprises and his position as Secretary of the Air Force made him, in Nixon's view, expendable. Similarly in the case of Murray

Chotiner, questionable though his dealings might have been, there were some who shook their heads doubtfully at the haste with which Nixon dropped an old and trusted associate. Politicians find it unpleasant and sometimes costly to defend old friends who have strayed from the path of rectitude, but some feel there is no option if one is to live with his conscience.

Not infrequently, attempts to analyze Nixon's moral values end with an excursion into his methods. It has been said his platform appearances are "more central to his public personality than any clear political commitment."

His skill with audiences relies less on the power of persuasion than on the power of suggestion. His method in campaigns is to skim the surface of a dozen subjects, ticking off an epithet here, an epigram there, skillfully blending warnings, assurances, invocations, and defiance. His voice trembles with indignation, purrs with sincerity, or throbs with hope. He carries audiences swiftly from thesis to thesis—national survival is worth whatever it costs; "the mushroom cloud that hangs over our heads spells a solemn warning"; inflation must be dealt with; "the remedy . . . is self-discipline at the bargaining table"; "mountainous farm surpluses lead to molehill prices"; "there is no room for complacency."

With a dash of the obvious, a tincture of faith, an infusion of canting solemnity, he lets it be assumed that his reasons are self-evident; his very didacticism is reassuring. He is the epitome of the high-pressure pitchman whose product may be shoddy but whose semantic skills make him irresistibly attractive to the crowd.

His unique talent is in the use of language to arouse inferences going beyond anything he has actually said. He plants ideas by a calculated process of association. In two campaigns, Adlai Stevenson got the full treatment.

"Who is Mr. Stevenson," Nixon asked in 1956, "to be talking about the low road when he is the man who puts his arm around Harry Truman?"

In this he did not say Harry Truman was on the low road, but what other inference was possible? On another occasion Nixon linked the Democratic candidate with the worst elements in labor by the same sort of meretricious juxtaposition: "Stevenson's is a slave-labor program hammered together by a union clique that wants to continue holding workingmen captive to their selfish whim."

In one short sentence, by suggesting evil connotations, Nixon planted a series of invidious ideas on Stevenson: that he was associated with "slave labor," with a "clique," with "captives," and not just ordinary whims but "selfish" whims. In another passage which has become a classic in the use of innuendo, Nixon managed to indict Stevenson, not just for what he had said or done, but for what he might have done!

"I have just been thinking what would have happened if Mr. Stevenson had been President for the last three years," he said. "We, of course, do not know the answer to that question, but of these principles I am sure: Indecision, weakness, retreat, and surrender do not bring peace in dealing with dictatorial, aggressive communism."

In so saying, Nixon did not charge that Stevenson had been in a position to make mistakes in the handling of foreign policy; he did not say that Stevenson had shown the weaknesses of character he enumerated. He did not even say that peace had been achieved. What he did, by an odious association of ideas, was to invite his audience to assume that Stevenson's unfitness had been fully demonstrated.

II

For want of a philosophy in the broad sense, Nixon has shown an affinity for geopolitical thinking. Yet even this interest as it relates to the process of political manipulation provides an uncertain ground for judgments. In the Korean war he misjudged MacArthur's strategic concept and failed to see the struggle in true global perspective. In 1951, he was so obsessed with the doctrine of federal intrusion in economic affairs that he could not foresee the rising costs of government which were implicit in an inflationary world economy. In 1953, he failed to see the essential immorality of McCarthyism and its possible threat to the two-party system. In 1956, he failed again to grasp the scientific implications of nuclear testing and the inevitability of suspending the tests.

In deducing general principles from the events of the day, Nixon has a tendency to make headlines rather than history. Consider the pat formula he laid down in the summer of 1957 before the Young Republican Federation.

"There are only three sure-fire issues against an administration in power," he pontificated. "Failure in foreign policy leading to war; failures in domestic policy leading to depression; failure in administration resulting in corruption."

The Eisenhower administration was proof against all such adversity; of that he was confident. Yet twelve months later all these issues were on the front pages—recession, the Adams-Goldfine scandals, the landing of American troops in the Middle East— and the GOP went down to its worst defeat in twenty-two years.

After the outbreak of the Korean war in June 1950, Nixon took a tortuous path in his treatment of war as a partisan issue. He began in his Senate campaign by advocating all-out support of the national effort in Korea, but from time to time he took an ambivalent line in assessing responsibility for the conflict.

In the Senate, August 24, 1951, in one of several similar comments on the subject, he attributed the success of the Communist revolution, in China as elsewhere, to "native Communist groups" who were "won to the cause" of communism by effective propaganda. His analysis of the problem was by no means profound, but his acknowledgment clearly was that communism is a self-starting, inner-directed movement.

The 1952 campaign found him on both sides of the issue. At the outset, in the August 29 issue of *U.S. News and World Report,* he refused to subscribe to the views of "my good friends on the Republican side who refer to the Korean war as Truman's war in the sense that we should not have gone into Korea." Having thus established himself as a fair-minded patriot, he added this caveat: "By the same token, I believe that the administration must assume the responsibility for the course of events which made it necessary to go into Korea." This after having said "native groups" were the motive power in Communist successes. On the stump he did not hesitate to go further, calling the Korea war "fruitless and unnecessary" and a result of the "Truman-Acheson stumblebum program."

A year later, before the American Legion convention in St. Louis, he was again saying, "Let's recognize right now that the decision to go into Korea was right. . . ." And in his 1956 tenth-anniversary speech in Manila he boasted, "What would have happened if the free nations had not joined in defending Korea?" Meanwhile, in January 1951, he had uttered the threat to pull American forces out of Korea unless other United Nations members matched the American man-power commitment.

In all this he contrived to have it both ways without seeming aware of any contradiction. At the supra-partisan level, he recognized the power and cunning of the Communist conspiracy, but at the partisan level he chose to put full blame for the East-West conflict on his political opponents. By 1955 he was ready to say "there is no war party," but on October 24, 1952, and countless times thereafter, he declared that Truman's administration "cannot be trusted to get us out of war in Korea or keep us out of future wars." He was at various times for containing communism or for pushing it back behind the Russian frontiers. Suppose he had been President in January 1951 when he was threatening in a mood of petulance to pull American forces out of Korea on the flimsy pretext that our sacrifice was disproportionately heavy?

His values tend to veer and flex with the headlines. His record on the Yalta Pact can be taken as a fair sample because it is articulate and categorical.

One of the least savory postwar charges against the Democrats —a byproduct of bitter GOP resentment toward Roosevelt—was the cry that "secret" agreements in 1945 at Yalta had constituted a sellout to communism. In this running feud, Nixon used the venom undiluted as part of his attack, and showed again the lengths to which he was ready to go in support of narrowly partisan ends. There is no evidence that his moral sense or his adherence to the gentle precepts of Quakerism warned him to study the facts.

In a round-table discussion of American foreign policy with Senator Knowland, October 26, 1950, Nixon was quoted by the *Los Angeles Times* as saying:

"It is my belief that before we can assume a position of moral leadership among the free nations of the world, we should denounce the Yalta Agreement and should make it clear that while communism may have destroyed in Poland and in China human liberty with its freedoms of religion and the press, it will not be done with our blessing. On this question, I sharply differ with the views of Mrs. Douglas, who still endorses the Yalta Agreement."

Two years later, in his campaign for the vice-presidency, Nixon was no better informed. He issued a statement (10/5/52) in connection with New York's Pulaski Day parade asserting that Poland was "shackled by its Communist masters" because of "the shameful Yalta Agreement." The only hope for Poland, he said, was "our repudiation of Yalta commitments that abet Communist slavery of free nations and by working unremittingly, in peaceful fashion, for Poland's liberation."

The Eisenhower administration had hardly taken office, however, when it became apparent that there were no "secret" agreements. The President had promised Congress a resolution repudiating such agreements, but when none was found, the draft resolution he sent Congress February 20 proved vastly disappointing to the Republicans. When they protested, Dulles warned against any program of repudiation which might in turn give the Russians grounds for unilateral repudiation, and the President specifically warned at a news conference that the West could be put in a very awkward position in places like Berlin and Vienna if the United States undertook to renounce wartime agreements.

The legal value of the Yalta agreement was in fact so warmly defended by the administration that Taft and the GOP leadership simply dropped the proposed resolution as meaningless. Two years later, in a speech before the Executives Club in Chicago, however, Nixon still hesitated to acknowledge his error. While conceding that Roosevelt at Yalta had not made "a deliberate attempt to sell out to the Communists," he insisted that it would take more weeks and months of study to enable him to comment intelligibly on the agreement.

History had the last word, however, during the winter of 1958-59 after Soviet Premier Nikita Khrushchev threatened unilateral abrogation of the Berlin occupation statute. Dulles authorized a State Department white paper putting the Yalta Agreement and our Berlin rights in perspective. What it revealed was that, pursuant to agreement at the Moscow Conference of 1943, a three-power allied commission drafted plans in 1944 for the occupation of Germany and Berlin, and as the final act of the 1945 Yalta meeting the conferees said in a joint statement:

"We have agreed on common policies and plans for enforcing the unconditional surrender terms which we shall impose together on Nazi Germany after German armed resistance has been finally crushed. . . . Under the agreed plan, the forces of the three powers will each occupy a separate zone of Germany. . . ."

This statement, with the accompanying protocols, had the effect of ratifying the Berlin occupation statute and became the legal means of saving two million West Berliners fourteen years later.

If Nixon had had his way, and if Yalta had been repudiated in a fit of partisan pique, only armed force could have saved the city. There is an unspoken hint now and then that Nixon should be forgiven the Yalta episode as one of the faults of youth and overeagerness. He may indeed regret it, but as a politician who puts a high premium on the myth of infallibility, he has never stepped forward to make that acknowledgment.

Over the years, painfully at times, Nixon learned the danger of impugning people's motives, but a minor incident in 1958 raised again the question whether his moral values had changed for the better or changed at all. During the Quemoy-Matsu crisis in September of that year, when the administration had determined to resist Chinese Communist pressure for concessions, *The New York Times* reported one Saturday that the State Department had received 5000 letters on the Formosan situation, 80 per cent of them criticizing administration policy.

On more than one previous occasion, when the mail count was favorable, government agencies had not hesitated to embrace the results as a public mandate, but Nixon was in no mood to tolerate an adverse proceeding. With an election looming, and with all the polls and issues running against him, he could not afford to shoulder another burden. Hence, after two hasty conferences with Undersecretary Herter, Nixon took it upon himself to issue a statement which not only challenged the significance of the mail count but contained a brutal threat to State Department personnel.

"What concerns me primarily," he said, "is not the patent and deliberate effort of a State Department subordinate to undercut the Secretary of State and sabotage his policy. What is of far greater concern is the apparent assumption on the part of those who put out the story that the weight of the mail rather than the weight of the evidence should be the controlling factor in determining American foreign policy."

It was the charge of sabotage and the oblique imputation of disloyalty that caught the eye of observers who had been watching the image of the new, mature, high-level Nixon. The mail-count story had, in fact, been written casually on a dull Friday afternoon. The denial could have knocked it down merely by a matter-of-fact evaluation of the messages; another official probably would have taken this straightforward line, but Nixon gave it the authentic stamp of his controversial personality.

Convinced there was a group in the State Department which was trying to undercut Dulles's Far Eastern policies, and contending (despite evidence to the contrary) that the story had been "leaked" with sinister intent, the Vice-President's reflex was instinctive. He struck back with a harsh *ad hominem*. It was a deliberate attempt to intimidate federal workers; he admitted as much by saying later that the warning implicit in his statement "had the effect I intended." By his veiled threat he exposed himself again to a charge of "fascist tendencies," for no one could escape the inference that, if it were his administration, anyone running afoul of policy, even inadvertently, could expect only the swiftest and most merciless reprisals.

III

The irony of Nixon's career is that he has made the least admirable impression when, in seeming most effective, he overreached himself; and conversely, he has been truest to his best self when he acted with the greatest restraint. He made history, when he did, not in the headlines for which he strove so hard, but by the application of a trained legal mind to problems that could be solved by careful adherence to facts.

The tragedy of Nixon is that he made a fetish of understatement, but unhappily, the kind of understatement that said too much by indirection. He placed in jeopardy his reputation as a moral man, not in the sense of cheating at cards but in the school of one-up-manship, of how to win without actually cheating.

In his lexicon, despite every effort at candor, the dark threat is always implicit. The unspoken warning lingers, a shadowy source of anxiety and fear. The hint of omnipotence carries with it an insinuation that Big Brother is watching.

Is there any real warrant for such inferences, such apprehensions? Nixon's admirers would say that the question is disingenuous. His critics have no ready answer. Their portrait of him is diffuse, negative, lacking in warmth. Their favorite refuge, for want of a final characterization, is an old English rhyme:

> I do not like thee, Dr. Fell,
> The reason why I cannot tell;
> But this I know, and know full well,
> I do not like thee, Dr. Fell.

RICHARD NIXON: A CHRONOLOGY

1913   January 9: Born, Yorba Linda, California.

1934   June: Graduated from Whittier College, A.B., second in class.

1937   June: Law degree from Duke University, third in class.

November 9: Sworn in as member San Francisco bar; returned to Whittier to join law firm of Wingert & Bewley.

1938   June 5: Registered as Republican in Los Angeles County.

1940   June 21: Married Thelma Catherine "Pat" Ryan at Mission Inn, Riverside.

Campaigned for Willkie.

1942   January 9: Began work at OPA.

March: Applied for Navy commission.

September 2: Commissioned Navy Lt., j.g., sent to Quonset, R. I., for training.

1945   September 29: Appeared before Committee of One Hundred at William Penn Hotel, Whittier.

1946   February 12: Announced candidacy for House of Representatives.

February 21: Daughter, Patricia, born.

March 19: Filed in Democratic and Republican California primaries.

November 5: Elected to Eightieth Congress, defeating Voorhis by 15,592 votes.

1947   January 3: Sworn in as member of Eightieth Congress.

February 18: Maiden speech in House—Eisler case.

August: With Herter committee to Europe, to study foreign-aid problems.

1948   May 14: Floor manager Mundt-Nixon bill.

July 5: Daughter, Julie, born.

August 3: Whittaker Chambers' testimony against Alger Hiss.

August 5: Hiss's rebuttal.

November 2: Re-elected to Congress (Eighty-first).

1949   November 3: Announced Senate candidacy in Los Angeles.

1950   February 12: Lincoln Day address—Administration would "impose British socialist system upon people of U.S."

September 29: Appellation "Tricky Dick Nixon" appeared in *Independent Review*.

October 26: Los Angeles round table—called for repudiation of Yalta Pact.

November 7: Elected to Senate over Helen G. Douglas.

1951   May: Attended World Health Organization conference at Geneva; visited Eisenhower in Paris.

June: Los Angeles housing authority incident.

June 15: Retail Grocers Convention address.

June 28: Young Republican National Federation speech, Boston.

September 31–October 5: Boyle, Gabrielson "influence" hearings.

1952   February 26: Pennsylvania Manufacturers Association speech.

March 20: House Ways and Means subcommittee, Brewster–Grunewald hearings.

May 8: Speech before New York Republican party.

June 11: Mail poll of California precinct workers.

July 11: Received vice-presidential nomination.

September 14: Questioned about fund by Edson, after "Meet the Press" session.

September 18: Secret Nixon fund story published in *New York Post*.

September 23: Broadcast "Checkers" speech from Los Angeles.

October 25: Endorsed "my good friend McCarthy" in Wisconsin.

October 27: Texarkana: Stated that President Truman and Adlai Stevenson were "traitors to the high principles of the Democratic party."

November 4: Elected Vice-President.

1953   January 20: Inaugurated, at forty, second youngest Vice-President in history.

August 13: Appointed chairman of President's committee on government contracts.

August 31: American Legion speech, St. Louis.

October 7–December 11: First goodwill tour, Asia and Africa.

1954   March 13: Speech answering Adlai Stevenson and breaking with McCarthy.

April 16: American Society of Newspaper Editors off-the-record remarks—trial balloon re troops to Indochina.

June 26: Milwaukee speech—"Acheson policy was directly responsible for the loss of China. . . ."

October 13: Speech at Van Nuys, California—"When the Eisenhower administration came to Washington on January 20, 1953, we found in the files a blueprint for socializing America."

October 18: Beverly Hills speech—criticized Adlai Stevenson for saying, "While the American system has been shrinking, the Soviet economy has been growing fast."

1955 January–February: Goodwill trip to Caribbean.

March 14: Republican party meeting—"The Republican party is not strong enough to elect a President."

September 24: Eisenhower's heart attack.

1956 January 29–February 4: Trip to Brazil for presidential inauguration.

February 12: Lincoln Day address, New York, attributing school integration ruling to "a great Republican Chief Justice, Earl Warren."

April 26: Announced candidacy for second term as Vice-President.

June 8: Eisenhower's ileitis attack.

June 30 –July 11: Second goodwill trip to Asia.

August 22: Renominated for second term as Vice-President.

September 13: Nixons' first visit to Eisenhowers' Gettysburg home.

November 2: Hershey, Pa., address—"declaration of independence of Anglo-French policies toward Asia and Africa . . . colonial tradition."

November 6: Elected Vice-President for second term.

December 6: Automobile Manufacturers Association, New York—"Strong bipartisan support in Congress" for Britain.

December: Hungarian refugee inspection trip, Austria.

1957 January 3: First antifilibuster ruling.

January: Told David Astor, British publisher, re Douglas campaign: "I'm sorry about that episode. I was a very young man."

April 27–May 18: Trip to Africa and Italy.

November 25: Eisenhower's cerebral occlusion.

1958 February 27: National Conference of Christians and Jews, Cleveland—"The U.S. cannot afford a prolonged recession."

April 24: American Newspaper Publishers Association—"The Soviet economy is growing faster than ours. . . ."

May 8: Lima, Peru—San Marco University demonstration.

May 13: Caracas, Venezuela: Communist anti-Nixon riots.

September 6: Harvard Business School Association—tax reform speech.

October: Campaign trip to Alaska.

November 26: Guildhall, London—"Colonialism . . . brought the great ideas which provided the basis for progress."

Christmas holidays: Nixons entertained Eisenhowers at home for first time.

1959   January 7: Second antifilibuster ruling.

January 31: Appointed chairman of Cabinet committee on price stability for economic growth.

June 28: Issued first interim report of price stability committee.

July 22–August 5: Trip to Soviet Union and Poland.

BIBLIOGRAPHY

Alsop, Stewart. "Nixon on Nixon." *Saturday Evening Post,* July 12, 1958.
Andrews, Phillip. *This Man Nixon.* Philadelphia: John C. Winston Company, 1952.
Begeman, Jean. "Nixon: How the Press Suppressed the News." *New Republic,* October 6, 1952.
Bell, Raymond Martin. "The Nixon Chart," 1954; "A Story of the Forebears of Richard Milhous Nixon," 1954; "From James to Richard—The Nixon Line," 1957; Washington and Jefferson College.
Bendiner, Robert. "All Things to All Republicans." *The Reporter,* November 4, 1954.
———. "The Chotiner Academy of Scientific Vote-Catching." *The Reporter,* September 20, 1956.
Bohn, William E. "Washington's Era of Ill Feeling." *The New Leader,* January 24, 1955.
Bowers, Lynn, and Blair, Dorothy. "How to Pick a Congressman." *Saturday Evening Post,* March 19, 1949.
Brashear, Ernest, "Who is Richard Nixon?" *New Republic,* September 1, 1952, September 8, 1952.
Business Week, October 8, 1955; December 7, 1957.
Carleton, William G. "A Grass-Roots Guide to '58 and '60." *Harper's Magazine,* July 1958.
Cater, Douglass. "Nixon for Nixon." *The Reporter,* November 13, 1958.
———. "Who is Nixon, What is He?" *The Reporter,* November 27, 1958.
———. "Government by Publicity." *The Reporter,* March 19, 1959.
Chamber of Commerce of the United States. "Communists Within the Government." January 1947.
Champion, Hale. "California's Governor Knight: Balance of Republican Power?" *The Reporter,* February 23, 1956.
Commonweal, The. "Mr. Nixon Again" (editorial). March 9, 1956.
Congressional Quarterly. "Office of the Vice President Gains Stature." March 27, 1957.
Cooke, Alastair. *A Generation on Trial.* New York: Knopf, 1950.
Corbin, Phil. "Why Senator Nixon?" *Frontier,* September 1952.
Coughlan, Robert. "A Debate, Pro and Con—Subject: Richard M. Nixon." *Life,* July 16, 1956.
———. "Success Story of a Vice President." *Life,* December 14, 1953.
de Toledano, Ralph. *Nixon.* New York: Holt, 1956.
Democratic Digest. "They're Nervous over Nixon." July 1956.
Donovan, Richard. "Birth of a Salesman." *The Reporter,* October 14, 1952.
Donovan, Robert J. *Eisenhower: The Inside Story.* New York: Harper, 1956.
Flynn, William; Dinneen, Joseph F., Jr.; Harris, John; McCaffrey, Edward J. "Life Story of Vice President Nixon." *Boston Globe,* October 16 to November 5, 1955.

295

Gehman, Richard. *Cavalier Magazine*, August 1956.
Harris, Eleanor. "The Nixons." *American Weekly*, August 24, 1952.
————. "The Dark Hours of the Richard Nixons." *American Weekly*, March 4, 1956.
————. "The Richard Nixons: The Intimate Story of Their Early Struggles." *American Weekly*, March 11, 1956.
Harrison, Selig S. "Nixon: The Old Guard's Young Pretender." *New Republic*, August 20, 1956.
Heckscher, August. "The Future of 'the Party of the Future': The Nixon problem is not yet settled." *The Reporter*, September 20, 1956.
Hiss, Alger. *In the Court of Public Opinion*. New York: Knopf, 1957.
Horton, Philip. "The China Lobby," Part II. *The Reporter*, April 29, 1952.
Jerger, Wilbur. "High Level Smiles, Low Level Smears." *Los Angeles Free Press Home News Magazine*, June 7, 1956.
————. "The Real Nixon Story." *Los Angeles Press*, October 4, 1956.
Jowitt, Earl. *The Strange Case of Alger Hiss*. Garden City, N.Y.: Doubleday, 1953.
Keogh, James. *This is Nixon*. New York: Putnam, 1956.
Kerby, Phil, "Richard Nixon Charts his Course." *Frontier*, June 1956.
Knebel, Fletcher. "Did Ike Really Want Nixon?" *Look*, October 30, 1956.
Lasky, Victor. "Why Nixon Was Nominated." *Look*, September 23, 1952.
Life. "Nixon Fights, Wins and Weeps." October 6, 1952.
————. "Time of Trial for the Republic." December 2, 1957.
Marine, Gene. "What's Wrong with Nixon?" *The Nation*, August 18, 1956.
Mazo, Earl. *Richard Nixon: A Political and Personal Portrait*. New York: Harper, 1959.
McGill, Ralph. "Why the GOP Bites Its Nails Over Nixon." *Opinion Digest* (condensed from *Atlanta Constitution*), April 1956.
Merson, Martin. *The Private Diary of a Public Servant*. New York: Macmillan, 1955.
Miller, William Lee. "Religion, Politics, and the 'Great Crusade.'" *The Reporter*, July 7, 1953.
————. "Piety Along the Potomac." *The Reporter*, August 17, 1954.
————. "The Debating Career of Richard M. Nixon." *The Reporter*, April 19, 1956.
New Republic. "Nixon: Hero and Heavy" (editorial). November 3, 1958.
Newsweek, March 12, 1956.
Nixon, Patricia Ryan (as told to Joe Alex Morris). "I Say He's a Wonderful Guy." *Saturday Evening Post*, September 6, 1952.
O'Donovan, Patrick. "No Flaws on the Plastic Politician." *The Observer*, November 23, 1958.
Opinion Digest (condensed from *Washington Daily News*). "How Richard Nixon Unmasked Himself." April 1956.
Phillips, Cabell. "One-Man Task Force of the G.O.P." *New York Times Magazine*, October 24, 1954.
Reuben, William A. *The Honorable Mr. Nixon*. New York: Action Books, 1958.
Riggs, Robert L. "Flexible Dick Nixon." *The Progressive*, November 1955.
Roper, William L. "The Man Who Might Be President." *Frontier*, September 1955.
————. "Can Nixon Make It?" *Frontier*, November 1955.
Rovere, Richard H. "Nixon: Most Likely to Succeed." *Harper's Magazine*, September 1955.

————. "A Reporter at Large: The Campaign: Nixon." *The New Yorker*, October 13, 1956.

————. *The Eisenhower Years*. New York: Farrar, Straus and Cudahy, 1956.

Rubin, Morris H. "The Trouble with Nixon, A Documented Report." *The Progressive*, October 1956.

Schlesinger, Arthur, Jr. *The Age of Jackson*. Boston: Little, Brown, 1945.

Shannon, William V. "The Nixon Story" (series of six articles). *New York Post*, October 17–22, 1955.

———— and Katcher, Leo. "The Story of 'Poor Richard' Nixon" (series of four articles). *New York Post*, September 30–October 3, 1952.

Time. "Fighting Quaker" (cover story). August 25, 1952.

————. "Picking the Veep." June 13, 1955.

————. "The Realized Asset." November 5, 1956.

————. July 21, 1952; September 29, 1952; October 6, 1952; January 18, 1954; April 26, 1954.

U.S. Bureau of the Budget. *The Federal Budget in Brief, Fiscal Year, 1960*. January 19, 1959.

U.S. News and World Report. "Quizzing Nixon." August 29, 1952.

————. "Nixon: The Real No. 2 Man." October 2, 1953.

————. "Vice-President Nixon's Own Story of Campaign." November 12, 1954.

————. "The Nixon Story." May 11, 1956.

————. "Nixon's New Role." December 6, 1957.

Voorhis, Jerry. *Confessions of a Congressman*. Garden City, N.Y.: Doubleday, 1947.

Wertenbaker, Charles. "China Lobby." *The Reporter*, April 15, 1952.

White, Theodore. "The Gentlemen from California." *Collier's*, February 3, 1956.

White, William S. "What Bill Knowland Stands For." *New Republic*, February 27, 1956.

————. "Nixon: What Kind of President?" *Harper's Magazine*, September 1957.

Wilson, Richard. "Is Nixon Fit to be President?" *Look*, February 24, 1953.

————. "The Case for Nixon." *Look*, November 29, 1955.

————. "The Big Change in Richard Nixon." *Look*, September 3, 1957.

————. "Can Rockefeller Knock Off Nixon?" *Look*, April 28, 1959.

Woods, Rose Mary (as told to Don Murray). "Nixon's My Boss." *Saturday Evening Post*, December 28, 1957.

———. "A Reporter at Large: The Hawaiian Nixon." *The New Yorker,* October 22, 1955.

———. *The Kennedy Years* (New York: Simon and Schuster), 1938.

Rubin, Morris H. "The Trouble with Nixon, A Documented Report." *The Progressive,* October 1956.

Saltonstall, William G. *In The Age of Jackson.* Boston: Little, Brown, 1945.

Shannon, William V. "The Nixon Show" (review of six articles). *New York Post,* October 13, 1955.

———. and Martin Agronsky. *The Story of Their Majesty Nixon.* Review in *New Republic,* New York Post, September 20, October 1, 1957.

Time. "Technical Knock" (cover story), August 25, 1952.

———. "Nixon the Vice," June 15, 1953.

———. "The Richard Nixon," November 1, 1955.

Today. "The Trials Tomorrow for 1972," October 6, 1972, January 26, 1956, April 16, 1956.

U.S. News & World Report. "Opinion of the Judges, Yet Reason Report of Brush Fires?" Text, 1968, August 25, 1952.

———. "Nixon: The Next No., 2 Man," October 2, 1953.

———. "Vice-President Nixon's Own Story of Campaign," November 12, 1956.

———. "The Nixon Story," May 31, 1955.

———. "Nixon's New Look," December 6, 1956.

Vassilis Gerry. Companions of a Congressman. Capitol City, 1954, 1961.

———, July 1951.

Weisberger, Charles. "Dean Rusk," *The Reporter,* April 16, 1951.

Wills, Theodore. "The Gentleman from California," *Collier's,* February 9, 1946.

Wolfe, William S. "What Bill Knowland Stands For." *New Republic,* February 22, 1956.

———. "Nixon: What Kind of President?" *Harper's Magazine,* September 1957.

Wilson, Richard. "Is Nixon Fit to be President?" *Look,* February 24, 1958.

———. "The Case for Nixon," *Look,* November 15, 1955.

———. "The Big Change in Richard Nixon," *Look,* September 1, 1951.

———. "Can Eisenhower Knock Off Nixon?" *Look,* April 27, 1956.

Woods, Rose Mary. "As Life in Dick Nixon's Intimate Say Book," *Saturday Evening Post,* December 26, 1958.

Index